Wedding Sanity Savers

Wedding Sanity Savers

How to Handle the Stickiest Dilemmas, Scrapes, and Questions That Arise on the Road to Your Perfect Day

Dr. Dale Atkins

AND

Annie Gilbar

BROADWAY BOOKS

New York

PRINTED IN THE UNITED STATES OF AMERICA

BROADWAY BOOKS and its logo, a letter B bisected on the diagonal, are trademarks of Random House, Inc.

Visit our website at www.broadwaybooks.com

First edition published 2005.

BOOK DESIGN BY AMANDA DEWEY

Library of Congress Cataloging-in-Publication Data
Atkins, Dale V.
Wedding sanity savers : how to handle the stickiest dilemmas, scrapes, and questions that arise on the road to your perfect day / Dale Atkins and Annie Gilbar.
p. cm.
ISBN 0-7679-1874-6
1. Weddings—Planning. 2. Wedding etiquette. I. Gilbar, Annie.
II. Title.

HQ745.A85 2005
395.2'2—dc22
2004054637

1   3   5   7   9   10   8   6   4   2

Contents

Wedding Sanity Savers

Introduction

S O W E H E A R you're getting married! Super! and Congrats! Now what?

What *really* lies ahead?

Lots. Starting with gowns, diamonds, flowers, invitations, gifts, and moving on to guest lists, bridesmaids, budgets, decisions . . . Ooops. Is that what those jitters are about? Is that why there is a knot in your stomach?

Yup.

Because the image in your mind of what your life is going to be like in the next several months may be nothing like the reality.

You, your fiancé, your family, your fiancé's family, and your friends are all going through major changes. And sometimes these people you love so dearly may be unrecognizable to you (and perhaps you to them as well!). You may be surprised to find that rational friends and family you have known all of your life can begin to behave *very* strangely when a wedding is in the air.

So throughout the wedding planning process, you may find yourself asking, more than once: *Who are these people?* And why are they pressuring me? Why does everyone around you seem to have an opinion about your wedding—and whose wedding is it anyway? You've been waiting for this day your whole life. And suddenly what should be a joyous, heartwarming, unforgettable experience begins to turn into a frightening, foreboding, intimidating, anxiety-provoking hell of a mess. It's overwhelming. And, with so much to do and plan before the big day actually arrives, all the conflicting opinions and emotions may start to make you feel like catching the next plane to Vegas. At least when you elope, you don't have to worry about what to do if your dress doesn't fit, or where to seat Dad's new wife whom Mom despises!

Fortunately, you don't have to pack your bags for the Elvis Chapel just yet. That's what we are here for. *Wedding Sanity Savers* is the ultimate troubleshooting guide, an emotional survival kit that will see you smoothly through it all, based on the answers to hundreds of questions from real brides just like you.

The truth is that even though the wedding industry is built upon offering options and solutions—with choices of themes, styles, fabrics, colors, venues, music, flowers—it offers very little help with regard to the questions you really want to ask. We wanted to provide a forum for brides to seek answers to questions not covered in the hundreds of other wedding planning guides. Questions that are often the most hair raising and baffling of them all!

Maybe you, like the brides who e-mail us every day, are feeling confused, frustrated, or just unsure about how your engagement and your wedding are unfolding. Surely, with all that a wedding involves, you are stressed. So join the club. We all were. Just know that whatever the reason, whatever you are feeling or experiencing, it has been felt or experienced by someone else (actually by many people!). And we have received thousands of letters that ask the same questions you are asking, from brides of all different circumstances and backgrounds.

So, as they say—and they are right when they say it—first of all, take a deep breath. It's going to be OK. We have the answers—and it's going to be fine. Honest. The questions in this book will help clarify the issues at stake and help you understand the different forces at work, think through your situation, mull over the options, be honest with yourself, tackle the difficult choices, and emerge confident, clearheaded, self-assured, full of love for your fiancé, and ready to smile as you walk down the aisle. We will guide you through the process, holding your hand every step of the way.

So if you find yourself wondering:

- Is my family really behind me?

- How will I manage to get through this with everyone around me being so needy and thinking it's all about them?

- Why can't I make up my mind about a china pattern?

- How can my fiancé and I ever agree on anything when we have such different tastes (and I hate his!)?

- Is it a realistic goal to get my parents to be civil to each other if they have not talked to each other in the five years since their divorce?

- How can I honor the people in my life who have been very important to me but who are not my relatives?

- Is it too much to ask that my future husband be respectful to my parents when he does not like them?

- What can I do about Uncle Norm, who always gets drunk and embarrasses himself at family events?

- Why am I fantasizing about my old boyfriend? And, should I tell my fiancé about this? Does it mean I don't want to marry him?

- How can I be sure I will be faithful to one man for the rest of my life?

- Should I tell him that I hate his old furniture and don't want it in our home?

- How can I ask my parents to throw a small, intimate wedding when they have always wanted to have a big, gala event?

- Why am I waking up at night with fears that I've never had before and pains in my stomach?

- How will I ever get his kids to love me since I am not their biological mother?

- How can I stop thinking about the high divorce rate?

- Why am I having dreams about being hemmed in and restricted?

- How will I know that our marriage will be different from my parents' marriage and, more important, from *his* parents' marriage?

Relax. Now is the time to stop worrying. This book will give you the tools you need to get through it all.

Wedding Sanity Savers is organized into chapters that tackle the different issues you may be facing, from family matters to cold feet. You will find that some of the sections are clearly for you, while others are not relevant to your particular situation. So feel free to skip around. Keep in mind, however, that there's a lot of good wisdom packed into these pages, so even if the questions don't relate to you directly, you may find interesting food for thought or advice that helps you think about your wedding and upcoming marriage in a different light. For example, if you are marrying someone of a different faith you may want to read the section on religion even if there are no complicating issues in your specific situation, because you might learn something about your own beliefs or gain some further insight into what a merging of faiths really means. The truth is that there's a lot more to getting married than what you read in bridal magazines, and there's a lot you can learn about yourself and your future spouse if you think about these issues and ask the right questions about how you can have a strong, harmonious marriage.

Above all, remember that it's been done before. People get engaged every day. And despite the obstacles that may arise along the way, they *do* get married and live happily ever after! So even if your mother's every opinion suddenly seems as important as world peace, and you don't want to wear the gown she wore at her wedding, and your bridesmaids are hinting that they just can't wear the dresses you painstakingly picked out, and your fiancé is bringing up the elopement idea again, read on and smile. It's going to be fine. More than fine. It's going to be the best day of your life, and you are going to be totally, utterly, absolutely, thoroughly, entirely, and completely prepared and happy.

Let's go do it.

ONE

Engaged and Becoming a "We"

YOU'RE ENGAGED! And suddenly you realize it's about more than wearing a ring. It's more than choosing the music and the flowers. You are in the process of becoming part of a "we." Even though by day you are bombarded by the choices you have to make (which ring, venue, dress, flowers, food, photographer are right for your special day), in the quiet of the evenings you may be contemplating the reality and the highs and lows of becoming a married person.

There are definite phases in the wedding process, all of which lead to being altered at the altar. Not everyone will experience these phases in the same way, but recognizing that they exist will make your life a little easier. It's OK to experience some fears and doubts. After all, it is normal to feel fear when jumping into the unknown (in this case, marriage). In the weeks and months ahead, do your best to stay in the moment rather than let your imagination run wild with thoughts of the future. Do your best to embrace the upcoming "new." And remember that no amount of frenetic racing to make all of the "right" decisions will put your mind and heart at rest. Rather, this adjustment in identity takes time and will happen within you at your own pace.

All of us have varying degrees of flexibility when it comes to change, and the process of falling in love, becoming engaged, getting married, and then living life as a couple certainly alters the landscape of your world. Moreover, since every courtship and every wedding is different, it's not easy to create a general guide to each of the various stages. There are some commonalities, however: You are being asked to make a huge change in your life; you are being asked to make a lifetime commitment; you are adjusting to becoming a member of someone else's family; and you have been thrust into the center of attention while experiencing a major change in identity. There will be days when you feel as though you are compromising a lot of what makes you the person someone wants to marry.

Take it from us: It is virtually impossible to glide through it flawlessly. Don't expect to. Do expect ups and downs. Along the way you will find out a lot about yourself, your fiancé, and about the family that raised you and the one you are marrying into. Your challenge is to stay true to yourself and at the same time remain open to what lies ahead. Becoming a part of a "we" is a process of growth.

Part of the new we is setting up a home together. If you're not already living together, this can be a major adventure. It is only when you are both in one place that you can truly begin to build your life together, creating your own rituals and routines as a committed couple. Whether you do it before or after the wedding, there are issues to be addressed. If you have some growing pains with this (if you sometimes get on each other's nerves, if you suddenly find habits annoying in your partner, ones that didn't bother you before), it doesn't mean you're not meant to be together. It is simply part of negotiating as you share the same space. Setting up the home, room by room, is one thing. Maintaining your personal space, making your own decisions, and keeping yourselves happy both separately and together takes some work. Here are a few of the common hurdles that arise when merging two lives under one roof, along with some basic troubleshooting tips:

* Are you moving into his existing space or is he moving into your sacred home? Remember that it is important that neither partner feels like a permanent guest. Make sure that both of you are reflected in your home. This may mean adding new decorative elements, rearranging the furniture, reorganizing the kitchen cupboards, or changing the message on the answering machine and the name on the mailbox. Both partners need to be sensitive that these changes are not always easy. Giving up coveted shelf space can be irritating, but the overall message is "I'm happy you're with me."

* You may be a "shabby chic" type and your intended a minimalist. Don't panic—this can be a *good* thing! Most couples realize they need to compromise. You may forgo that bright yellow bedspread while he passes on the black one. When you are conscious of another person, you may find that each of you is perfectly happy with the tan duvet cover and cream sheets. In the end, the ideal is that your surroundings reflect the tastes and personalities of both of you.

• Expect to make adjustments regarding your personal space. For example, should you share a phone line or have two? You need to find ways of balancing your separate lives while building a life together. Keep in mind that sharing the same space doesn't mean you have to breathe every molecule of oxygen that your partner does. You can and should allow for personal space and personal time. Closing the door every once in a while doesn't mean it's over, so long as you express "I love you, and I need some time just for me."

• Communication has never been more important. Habits such as leaving stockings in the shower, clothes on the floor, dishes in the sink, or crumbs on the counter can all be subtle irritants at the start and become major dramas. Try to address them as they come up and not be insulted or insulting. Just because you've both been living your own way doesn't mean you can't—or shouldn't—modify your behavior. That said, remember that you were not put on this earth to change your partner. The goal is to get along without making the other person feel diminished because his ways are different from yours.

• Whether it's planning the wedding or doing the dishes, sometimes each partner has different ideas about what constitutes a division of labor. Sometimes one partner will take over all the daily chores, with the understanding that the other partner supports their life together in different ways. This arrangement may not work for you, and if you feel that the responsibilities are better shared so that neither partner feels resentful, then make a plan. From the beginning, make sure those roles do not become your rules. Discuss what will be fair for the two of you and watch one another to make sure you stay on track.

- Suddenly your finances are no longer just about you. Will you have separate accounts, or will you open a joint one? Who pays for what and how is this decided? Are necessities to one of you viewed as extravagances by the other? When couples decided to get engaged, questions of finance always arise. These questions can be exacerbated throughout the wedding process (more on this in Chapter 11). It's worth sitting down at the outset to discuss your financial situation and priorities and to set initial boundaries.

Moving in together is just one of the things you may both have to adjust to once you're engaged. But when all is said and done, these compromises and changes will strengthen you as a couple. Throughout this time, be patient with each other, keep the lines of communication open, and focus on the real joys of being together, and particularly on the pleasure of waking up next to your best friend every morning.

THE END OF PRIVACY

Dear Dr. Dale,

I am concerned about moving in with my fiancé. I really love my privacy and am afraid that when we live together, I will have to give it up. We cannot afford a large apartment and there won't be a place for me to go to be by myself. This is a big deal for me, and I don't want my fiancé to think I don't want to be with him. It is just that sometimes I need some private space.

Private time to be with one's thoughts, feelings, books, music is essential to anyone's happiness, and yet most new couples give this up. They feel they should—and should want to—spend every minute together. But if more couples paid attention to this very primal need to have time alone to refresh and restore, we are certain that there would be many more content marriages. Perhaps you and your fiancé can arrange some time each week when one of you can leave the apartment for a few hours and you can look forward to this time without feeling that either of you is being rejected. Planning this can help ensure that each of you have the time alone that you need and that you will reunite with your partner feeling more at peace. Remember: Time for yourself benefits you as a couple as well as individually.

WHEN DO I LET HIM SEE THE "REAL ME"?

Dear Dr. Dale,

I enjoy looking my best—for me and for my fiancé. I dress nicely, and I make sure I am regularly "brushed and buffed." I have manicures, pedicures, facials, and weekly hair treatments. But I also love to hang around the house in sweats, without makeup and mousse. My fiancé has made it clear that he loves the finished product but that he has no desire to see the "behind the scenes" stuff, and once he caught me with a facial mask on and was not happy. He only wants the perfect result. Since we are not yet married and we are establishing routines that we will probably keep after our marriage, I am at a loss as to what to do: Do I change myself and keep makeup and perfection as my constant goals, or do I stay the same and let him get used to the "real" me? I feel funny even asking you, because I imagine you saying, "He should accept you as you are." Even though I think that's right, I don't know how to make him do that.

The part of you that enjoys primping and pampering needs a break—it is hard work, and time consuming. Gently let your fiancé know this, but in a fun way: Involve him in some pampering, and show him how much sexier and healthier he looks after one of your facials, or a massage. Have him slather the mud all over you, which can be a whole lot of fun for both of you. And remember, you can still keep some things secret: Mystery is very sexy, so leave him out of the loop on some of your rituals. You need to decide what is to be shared and what isn't. For some women, they have their partners participate in their grooming while others keep it all private.

The more important aspect of your question is, however, that it seems your fiancé expects you to be a Barbie doll. By that we mean he wants and expects you to be "perfect" and "on" whenever he is around. This is pure fantasy. Is he hanging around in his three-piece suit? We doubt it. Get yourself some comfortable sweats and be a normal person. Why should you live with such pressure to always appear "perfect"? If he is willing to see you as the person you are, without your face paint, then go for it. We shudder to think about you jumping out of bed before he wakes up to put on your makeup and comb your hair so that the first image he sees is you looking perfect. If he only wants the "perfect result," then we suggest he live alone with a collection of air-brushed magazine images and you find someone who appreciates the real woman behind the makeup.

MINE, HIS, OURS

Dear Dr. Dale,

My fiancé and I bought the most adorable house together, and I couldn't be happier. The problem is that this is our starter house and it's smaller than we would have liked. We lived apart before, so we both have couches, tables, and beds—everything we might need. But I'm not crazy about his taste, and he says that he thinks my things are too girly. We don't have room for everything, so do you have any suggestions on how to choose what we use without hurting anyone's feelings?

If you can afford to, put some of your items in storage, or loan them to friends until you move to a larger home. If you cannot, you will need to decide which items you want to give to charity or sell. Each of you, privately, should make a list of the items you can live without. On another list, put your most treasured or cherished items. Compare notes. See where and if your furniture can work well together and be open to the idea of making any decorative changes that can make some pieces work better when they are merged with your partner's (covering a table, changing a lamp shade, buying a slipcover for a chair).

Living with someone involves compromise as well as respect. This includes being respectful of their taste and/or attachments to their things. You may not like them, but you may find that you can live with them because they mean a lot to your spouse. Whatever you do, avoid casting aspersions on your partner regarding his things. And once you merge your things together, you will probably find that as taste changes over time, yours may combine to make a new taste—one that expresses the two of you as a couple.

NOT READY TO MOVE,
NOT READY TO STAY

Dear Dr. Dale,

I'm getting married next year, but I have already "half" moved in with my fiancé into our new house, and I'm really happy and excited with my new life. I say "half" because, although I spend most of my time there, I still sleep at my parents' home during my working week. I'm twenty-four and I feel really guilty about leaving my parents. I am an only child and have always been very close to them. We do everything together, and for some reason I feel that I am abandoning them too soon!

Sometimes I think I'm crazy, as it's my life and I need to get on with it and be independent. My fiancé tries to help me with this, but it breaks my heart to hear my dad say, "What are we going to do without you when you've gone?" I also have a very close relationship with my mother, and I know she is sad that I am "growing up," but we are trying to help each other face this transition. What can I do to ease this feeling? Is it even normal? Help!

You are not alone. More brides and grooms than those who admit to it have difficulties leaving their parents' home. The transition from single person to married person is filled with challenge and fear. Your parents know you and love you and accept you as you are. Building a life with another person, no matter how much you want to, is a venture into the unknown. For most people that means taking a risk.

Separation takes time and practice—especially when you have had as close a relationship as you seem to with your parents. It does not mean, however, that you do not move along with your life. As you move toward your wedding day, try spending fewer nights at your parents' house, so that by the time you are married you are living with you fiancé full-time. Work on shifting your self-perception from being primarily a daughter to being primarily a wife. Remember above all that you are not "abandoning" them. When your father says "What will we do without you when you are gone?" you can respond with, "I know, Dad, it will be a big change for all of us—but we will adjust."

POSTENGAGEMENT PARANOIA

Dear Dr. Dale,

I just got engaged to my soulmate. I've known he would be the one I marry since our first date. We're very compatible and have had almost no real arguments since we started dating. Now that we're engaged, however, I've become really paranoid that he's going to hurt me or leave me, and I'm afraid these concerns may put a strain on our relationship. These are things that didn't really bother me at all before we were engaged. Are any of these feelings of confusion and self-doubt normal?

Concerns, confusion, and doubts are very normal prior to marriage. After all, you are making a major, life-altering commitment to share your life with this man. You mention that from the beginning you said you two were soulmates and that you rarely argue. Just for the record, arguing does not mean you are not right for one another. It is nearly impossible to be with another person and *not* argue. Two people invariably will challenge one another's opinions and want to share differing perspectives. *How* you argue is much more important than the simple fact that you argue at all.

You are right to worry that your developing fears will potentially put a strain on your relationship. So give yourself an opportunity to try to understand why you have these fears. Perhaps you are reminded of a time when someone hurt you in your past after you'd shared your intimate self with him. You may wonder whether you will still be loved when you are really known, day after day, year after year. There are many possibilities you may wish to consider. Try to discover what is at the root of your fear. Once you discover the root of your fear you can discuss it with him and tell him you are willing to work on this with his help.

When you feel anxious about the potential of him leaving, do a simple relaxation exercise where you will "center yourself" through your breathing. Lie on the floor or sit in a chair in a quiet room, with the lights low, in a comfortable position. Breathe slowly and deeply with your eyes closed. Imagine the worst-case scenario and then allow all of your fearful feelings to flood you. Keep breathing, rhythmically and slowly. Allow the anxiety to "flow through" you. Keep breathing. Now, replace those "worst-case scenario" thoughts and feelings with "best-case scenario" feelings.

Remind yourself that even when you argue (and every couple argues), you have a history of making up and staying together. Breathe deeply and visualize the many situations when you have made up with each other and have gone forward. Breathe into each scenario you remember. The idea behind this exercise is for you to re-create the many times you and your fiancé have gone through difficulties and have come through them together and stronger. Instead of focusing on the fear of splitting up, you need to focus on the history you have together of making up and staying together. Then, when you are engaged in an argument, you can control your anxiety by breathing and reminding yourself of the normalcy of disagreements and coming together. You may have a sixth sense and indeed be right, or because of your own discomfort you may be planting the seeds for a self-fulfilling prophecy, which would be tragic.

CABIN FEVER

Dear Dr. Dale,

Ever since my fiancé and I moved in together, we've been fighting. It's wonderful to have him around all the time, but I get really irritated by his socks on the floor, his dirty dishes in the bedroom and kitchen (what is it about men that they use a dish and put it *next* to the dishwasher rather than in it?). And sometimes even the constant togetherness is too much. Is it wrong to want my own space? We are planning our wedding and this transition time is making us tense about everything else.

It is not wrong to want your own space. But you must acknowledge and prepare yourself for sharing that space. Once you have done that, recognize, too, that living together—like marriage—takes a lot of negotiation and understanding. Each of you comes to this new space and newest phase of your relationship with a different set of expectations as well as habits. Getting irritated by his socks on the floor or his dirty dishes in the sink is not going to help your relationship. And, while you are not the maid (and you are not his mother), still, you need to verbalize your expectations and your hopes for how you will live together peacefully and (more) neatly.

To make this transition easier, tackle the practical stuff. You and your fiancé would be well advised to come to an agreement regarding household chores and the level of neatness and cleanliness. Decide and agree on what is reasonable for each of you. You may wish to put money aside to hire a cleaning person or you may wish to have a few hours on the weekend devoted to cleanup. If you can afford this, it is a terrific solution to making sure your space will be clean—but both of you need to resolve to keep up your end of the relationship in terms of sharing space.

As for wanting your "own space" within the relationship—if you have the room, do reserve spaces where each of you can be yourself, to which each of you can retreat when you need regrouping. This is a very normal part of marriage. It is not an insult to the other to want this, nor is it unreasonable to want to be alone occasionally. Just remember: It is a two-way street, and you both deserve such privacy. Eventually you will find your rhythm as a married couple, with time and space for both of you.

TWO

Beauty and Body Image

W E ALL HAVE ideas and ideals about what we want to look like, and when we become brides, how we look takes on even greater importance. For many of us the image we have of ourselves as brides began years ago, in very early childhood, when we dressed our dolls in bridal gowns. Now, as you begin to plan the wedding, all those years of thinking about being a bride begin to merge with the thousands of pictures of beautiful—and perfectly shaped—brides, reed thin and looking "perfect" (whatever that means) in wedding magazines.

Enter television, which only adds to this "dream." There are now cable television stations totally devoted to weddings. *InStyle* magazine has special shows on weddings several times a year. In the past three years, even the two biggest morning shows, *Today* and *Good Morning America*, have spent months preparing for the fantasy wedding of a couple chosen by the U.S. public, with hundreds of thousands of viewers calling and writing in, voting on choices the couple must make. (And the biggest vote getter of all: *Which dress will she wear?*) Obviously, the bridal industry has quite an impact on us, and we cannot help but imagine ourselves walking down the aisle in veil and tulle, satin or lace, ball gown or sleek sheath looking just like these brides splashed across the glossy spreads.

Let's get down to reality. Buying into the belief that you must look like all these images, figuring that if you work hard enough you can "get into shape" before the wedding—no matter how much work that "shape" will be—is unproductive, inappropriate, and in some cases even self-destructive. This is the time to remind yourself—daily, and hourly, if you have to—that every bride is beautiful. Why? Because on this day you will be filled with a radiant joy that shines from within. No body is perfect, and your unique beauty stems from your attitudes about how you look and how you move, not from how closely you mirror an ideal. Remember, your fiancé fell in love with and proposed to you exactly as you are.

Having said that, it is understandable that any bride would want to present her "best self" at the wedding. Good grooming and self-care are always appealing no matter what the occasion. But you need to keep your expectations positive and realistic. Focus on enhancing all the wonderful attributes you currently have rather than striving for dramatic change. If you want to drop a few pounds, tone up, get into better shape, feel better about how you look, and likely get more energy in the process, that is terrific. If, however, you intend to starve yourself between now and your wedding, depriving yourself of the nutrients you need, eating food that is neither nutritious nor healthy on a "crash" diet that will likely cause you to gain weight when you stop—as well as probably make you unpleasant to be around—we urge you to reconsider this plan.

Remember, body image is not only about weight—it's about keeping *your* body healthy and in the best shape you can. "Beautiful bride" and "handsome groom" are terms we all use, but we are missing the point if we only consider their meaning as defined by models in magazines. What makes a bride beautiful and a groom handsome? If you think about it, you will recognize that it is the light in their eyes as they reflect the love they feel for each other; it is the relaxed, easy look that loved ones share when they know they are with the person they love and who loves them. When they feel safe and secure in that love, they feel beautiful and accepted.

As you move toward your big day, don't let your self-image be dictated by the images around you. Be true to yourself. After all, the image we develop stays with us not only for the walk down the aisle, but for the "walk" through life.

MY DREAM DRESS DOESN'T FIT

Dear Dr. Dale,

I'm writing this e-mail because I don't know what to do. I have a dream dress in mind for my wedding—it's a dress I have loved ever since I started to think about getting married years ago. The problem is that I weigh about 230 to 240 pounds, and I need to get down to at least 180 pounds in the next four months in order to wear it. I already asked the store if the dress could be made in a larger size, and they said no. So I really need to begin a diet right away. I don't know how to start or how to stick to it. And, in case you are wondering, I'm not going to settle for another dress. This is the one I love and I will wear it if I have to starve. Please help me!

OK, take a breath and sit down. Now think about this situation from a rational perspective. You are focusing solely on your dream dress and not on what may be practical (or healthy). There are thousands of wedding dresses out there, and limiting yourself to just one may be a bit unrealistic of you given the task ahead.

If you want to lose fifty to sixty pounds before your wedding, then you may be able to do so, but much will depend on your determination and on losing the weight in a safe, smart way. Crash dieting will not do the trick. These diets generally do not work, since they slow your metabolism, and people generally gain more weight than they lost after they go off the diet. The key to sensible weight loss is changing your lifestyle, making healthy food and exercise choices, and paying attention to the way you live your life.

First, find a program that is well known and that has professionals who have designed it and are supervising it, because such dramatic weight loss should not be undertaken alone. One of the secrets behind successful weight loss is to participate in a program with other people (this is why programs such as Weight Watchers™ are successful). Joining Overeaters Anonymous can be useful as well if you have an ongoing problem with food. Choose an appropriate and safe diet, start a fitness regimen, and stick to it—and buy your gown only when you *have* lost the weight.

MY WEDDING IS BRINGING UP
BODY IMAGE ISSUES

Dear Dr. Dale,

I am planning to be married in June, but I am also recovering from a serious eating disorder. What with the stress and pressure of the wedding, I find myself wishing that I could lose a lot of weight, and I know that this desire is not a healthy one. In addition to the regular stress of dealing with planning a wedding, my fiancé and I have personal and financial reasons that are forcing us to limit the overall number of guests to about eighty. As it happens, most of my family is in England and can't attend anyway, but my fiancé's mum has insisted on inviting a large number of friends. As such, I won't be acquainted with more than 25 percent of the people at my own wedding. This makes me highly uncomfortable, but his mum insists that we (mostly I) have already prevented her from inviting the ninety or so friends she wanted to invite.

I am so afraid of being judged by his family and their guests, and this is adding to my levels of stress and insecurity. I am self-conscious of both my height (6 feet 1 inch) and my weight (144 pounds). All of my bridesmaids are significantly shorter and tinier than me, and trying on dresses with them makes me feel like an elephant. Because of this insecurity I feel an earnest desire to lose weight before the wedding, but I am trying to do so in a healthy manner. However, when confronted with such huge amounts of stress, I cannot seem to maintain my appetite normally, nor am I able to look in the mirror without feeling gigantic and wanting to stop eating for days altogether. I am afraid of succumbing to the earlier problems with food I worked so hard to overcome. What should I do?

Premarriage, by definition, is a difficult time and, with the additional demands you are facing with your in-laws, it is not surprising that given your history you may be focusing on your weight and food at this time. You may be feeling a loss of control, especially given the situation with the guest list. Since you are recently recovering from a serious eating disorder, we recommend that you immediately see a counselor who is familiar with eating disorders and who can be available to offer support during this time.

The feeling of discomfort, of being judged, and a fear of being observed by strangers can be a natural result of any event that brings with it a lot of change and puts you in the center of attention. You mentioned that you are self-conscious about your height and weight. It is unlikely that you will have resolved these issues by the time you are married. However, try to work on shifting your perspective. Keep in mind that as the bride you are supposed to stand out, so people will be looking at you—not because you are large, but because you are the bride and it is your day. If trying on dresses with your friends is a difficult situation for you, steer clear of it. Try on dresses by yourself or with one friend with whom you feel totally comfortable!

Your fiancé needs to step in and talk to his parents, for while the guest list was already decided upon (apparently), his mother feels that it is OK to exceed the number of guests allotted. Now is the time to take a stand as a couple and assert your desires. Make sure your fiancé's response does not minimize what you are experiencing, which is a deep sense of inner turmoil, pain, and lack of control. Make sure he understands this by talking to him candidly and getting his unwavering support. It is critical at this time to make sure he does understand you and support you, both because it is a stressful time and because it is the beginning of your marriage.

Remember, depriving yourself of food will do nothing to restore your inner balance—but taking care of yourself in a conscious way will. Every day, commit yourself to eating right (fresh fruits, vegetables, and other healthy foods will help you maintain your health and look your best) and to spending some spiritual time by yourself (perhaps by reading something inspirational, or something about another person who has overcome an eating disorder). Get plenty of sleep and do some body work (exercise, walking, yoga) that will help relieve stress. Allow yourself to become comfortable with your body and with who you are. Visualize yourself as a confident, comfortable, beautiful bride.

BREAST REQUEST

Dear Dr. Dale,

I am a slim woman with a boyish figure. I have always liked my body, but I am engaged to a man who loves big breasts. He always notices women with large breasts and comments on those in the movies and on television. I love him and he loves me, but this is something he really cares about, and it is a part of a woman he thinks is beautiful and sexy. He, of course, loves me with my small breasts, but I am considering having breast implants before my wedding as a surprise for him. Kind of like my own personal wedding present. What do you think?

Hold on a minute! Your own personal wedding present? What happened to watches and cuff links? Undergoing surgery before your wedding as a surprise is *not* the way to begin your married life. Aside from the questionable nature of going under the knife for someone else, let's take a moment and think about what it is you are contemplating. First, you said you like your body. If you like it and have always liked it, leave it alone! Breast enhancement surgery is serious stuff and not to be trifled with, as many complications can arise. If you want to surprise your fiancé before the wedding, wear a padded bra! Your fiancé may admire large-breasted women, but that doesn't necessarily mean that he's not content with you and your figure. Don't forget, a person can admire all types of bodies without needing to be married to that particular body type in order to be happy and sexually fulfilled.

More important, however, is why you would consider such drastic measures to begin with. Our hunch is that somewhere deep down you do not think you are attractive enough to suit his tastes. If this is the case, have a heartfelt discussion about what makes you (and him) feel attracted and attractive. Listen closely to his response—hopefully he will reassure you up and down that you are the perfect woman for him. If he doesn't, then you may have a problem. When you enter a marriage you want to feel wonderful about yourself, not inadequate. If he doesn't make you feel beautiful, please rethink this relationship. Not only is it not great for your self-esteem to have your fiancé comment about how he would prefer large-breasted women, but these types of comments are highly insensitive. Even though you say your own body image is good, living with someone you love and want to please can damage that image if that person makes you doubt yourself. Remember, when you see yourself reflected in the eyes of your fiancé, you want to see a beautiful image, not a flawed one.

I DON'T WANT TO WEAR THAT DRESS!

Dear Dr. Dale,

My fiancé's mother, whom I like a lot, told me that it would mean a great deal to her if I would wear the wedding dress that both she and her mother wore in their ceremonies. I like the sentiment; I hate the dress. My fiancé simply couldn't care less. Do I have to wear this dress?

If you wear the dress you will make your fiancé's mother feel proud and wonderful. Not a bad way to begin a relationship. On the other hand, if you wear the dress, you run the risk of feeling inappropriate and awkward. Not a good way to begin your marriage. Wear what you want and whatever best expresses who you are. Explain to your fiancé's mother that you are honored and touched by her gesture, but that you have made another decision. Then ask her to give you something else (a handkerchief or a piece of jewelry) to continue the family legacy.

If you are at a loss for what to say, ask your future mother-in-law to lunch, just the two of you, and begin by sharing with her your excitement about the wedding and how lucky you feel to be marrying into her family. If you don't live nearby, make a date for a phone conversation where you each have time to talk, and try something like the following: "I wanted to share with you how thrilled I am about the upcoming wedding and how much I love your son and look forward to being a part of your family. You are so generous with me and I know your offer to wear the gown comes from your heart. I have thought about it and decided to select a new gown. The idea of selecting a gown that is perfect for me is something I have always dreamed about. I hope you understand my decision is not a rejection of you but rather is my need to feel comfortable in my own dress. I would love to have an heirloom from your family, perhaps a handkerchief or a special piece of jewelry I can wear at the ceremony."

If you want, you can ask your mother-in-law to come shopping with you to look for a wedding dress. If you don't want her there, don't ask her to come.

TOO TALL AND TOO THIN

Dear Dr. Dale,

I hate my body! And what I hate more is that everyone will be looking at me as I walk down the aisle and dance at my wedding. I am so unnerved by this that I am seriously considering *not* having a wedding at all and just going to city hall with my fiancé, who, by the way, thinks I am crazy to feel this way. My friends also think I am weird because they say they envy that I can eat anything and not gain weight.

I am extremely tall and skinny. My arms and legs are like a giraffe's. I have bad posture because for my entire life, in an attempt to "blend in" (which, of course, I never did), I have slouched to "look shorter." My mother is not much help because when we went to look for dresses she was so critical that I had to leave the bridal salon. It occurred to me that one of the reasons I feel so awful about my body is for as long as I can remember my mother has told me I am "ungainly" and "stringy." I really do not think I can get it together before my wedding. What should I do?

At this time in our culture "thin is in," but that does not address your personal torment about being in your particular body. The image you have of your body is deep-seated and will likely take much work on your part to amend. With all you need to do before your wedding, you may or may not be able to take on this task, too. It doesn't make much sense to us to plan a wedding that you are not looking forward to and that fills you with such a severe sense of foreboding. It is *your* wedding, after all! You need to be at ease (as best you can), and setting yourself up for a situation where you *know* you will be tense and unhappy just doesn't make any sense. So our advice is to create a situation that will work for you.

Discuss your true feelings with your fiancé and ask him to try to understand how you feel. Is there a scenario where you will feel less "conspicuous" as the center of attention? There is a big difference between walking down a long church aisle with hundreds of eyes focused on you and standing in front of a justice of the peace in a courtroom somewhere. Think of other possibilities and assess how anxious you feel in response to each scenario. Might you feel less conspicuous and more comfortable surrounded by a circle of your loved ones without having to walk into the room—perhaps outdoors in a garden, with everyone standing around you?

And please—don't go shopping with your mother! Her callous comments are not what you need. Her words have contributed to your poor self-image. Picture yourself in the outfit that flatters you and makes you feel the most comfortable and take it from there. Ask the bridal consultant for suggestions. Maybe you don't even want to get married in a gown, which is a perfectly acceptable choice these days. It is entirely up to you.

Having said all of this, the most important thing is not what kind of wedding you have or the dress you end up wearing, but taking care of yourself in a way that can help you to change the image that you have held for so many painful years. As you begin this new chapter in your life, consider living your life as a woman who can learn to accept and appreciate her body, tall and thin, lithe and elegant. Seek the help of a therapist who will incorporate physical as well as psychological exercises to help you develop a more gratifying image of yourself. And if you cannot do it before your wedding date, so be it. The more important thing is that you do it eventually, in your own time.

WEIGH TOO HEAVY

Dear Dr. Dale,

I'm going to be married in seven months, and I weigh over two hundred pounds. I have never been this heavy in my life; in fact, I didn't weigh this much when I gave birth to my son six years ago. I was always the thin girl, but now I have gone from a size 11–12 to 13–14 to a size 16. It's so hard to believe every time I look at myself. On the positive side, I am in a wonderful relationship, even though my mate and I have each gained a lot of weight together. The truth is, we enjoy eating all the time, and exercise is nonexistent. I'm about to get on my treadmill right now, but I know it won't last, because I get all excited about exercising one day, and on the next I admit that I truly hate it. How can we get motivated enough to stick with an exercise program?

The task you face is a difficult one, but attitude has a lot to do with it. You and your fiancé need to recognize that a healthy relationship is easier to maintain when you are both healthy and active. Together, you can develop interests and do activities that will help you get into shape. You can bowl together, take walks, ride bikes, take dancing lessons—not only get on the treadmill that you both obviously dislike.

It does not matter *what* you do. It matters *that you do something*. If your attempts at exercising and keeping yourself in shape have failed in the past, then you need to do something different. Get a buddy—online or in person. Join an exercise class that costs some money so you are more motivated to go. Attend a support meeting on a regular basis (Weight Watchers™ is great in this regard) and find an eating program that is nutritionally balanced and right for you. Healthy food no longer means lettuce and granola; there are many good and healthy eating programs available now with delicious recipes that are packed with flavor.

The key is to try to wrap your mind around your goal. Don't go crazy and "diet" just for your wedding. Think about living differently, taking care of yourself, and envisioning the kind of life and body you want to have. It will take time and effort and energy, but you will see results over time. More important, you will begin to feel success, and success breeds success.

THREE

Stress, Jitters, and Cold Feet

WHEN SOMEONE ANNOUNCES their intention to marry, the usual (and desired) response is joy, excitement, and an immediate shift into "planning" mode. Why, then, is there so much stress? It's actually pretty easy to figure out—and totally universal. Each of us has expectations about what our wedding, the months leading up to it, and the years after it will be. We also have varying degrees of flexibility when it comes to change—and the process of falling in love, becoming engaged, getting married, adjusting to someone else's family, and then defining yourself as both a "wife" or a "husband" and a couple requires much change.

Many of us are not emotionally prepared for everything that a wedding entails. The reason is a simple one: You are making the most important decision of your life! Are we overstating it? Not by a long shot. No wonder you feel as if you are on an emotional roller coaster! One day you're totally convinced of your decision, and then a couple of weeks, days, hours (or even minutes) later, you're questioning everything about your choice of a mate. Even though this is the person you love deeply and have chosen to marry, and with whom you dream about building a life, it is perfectly normal to question not only whether you are from different planets, but whether you even inhabit the same universe. You may wonder whether you really know this person as well as you should, or if it really is possible to spend your life with *one* person. Suddenly that guy at the gym looks darn good, and fantasies of an entirely different life and relationship begin to flood your brain; your fiancé works late, forgets to call, and you wonder whether you are marrying the most inconsiderate man alive; your future father-in-law drills you and assesses how you measure up against the *previous* girlfriend, and you fear you may be marrying into a nightmare. In short, your emotional life is topsy-turvy. One minute you are on top of the world feeling happy and blessed, and the next you feel sad, consumed with worry, jealousy, and confusion.

Prewedding jitters are often about becoming an adult and realizing that your role is changing. For some, the entire engagement period is about letting go, making adjustments, and coping with confusion, change, and expectations. It is about new beginnings as well as endings, and all endings are defined by separation and loss. Just think about all the transitions you are making:

- Your parents are finally having to let go of their "little boy" or "little girl."

- You (and your fiancé) are letting go of the single lives you have cultivated for any number of years.

- You're saying good-bye to your familiar lifestyle and embarking on one filled with unknowns.

- You may be changing old habits, behaviors, routines.

- There will be shifts in the way old friendships and family rituals and activities worked before, and you may be rearranging old relationships now that two people are involved.

Furthermore, stress, intrapersonal tensions, and emotional upheaval frequently result from the magnitude and confusion of the planning process itself. It is easy to misinterpret others' well-meaning intentions or find crossed wires or mixed messages fueling conflict. For example, sometimes the groom-to-be stays in the background so that his fiancée can plan the wedding of her dreams. He continues with his normal life while she becomes preoccupied, overwhelmed, and tired, and she often feels resentful about his apparent lack of either involvement or interest. She gets angry that he is not helping more; he gets angry because he thought he was being helpful by staying out of the way so she could plan the wedding she wanted. Fortunately, there are a few things you can do to alleviate tensions, jitters, and other emotional road bumps as you go forward with this process:

- Recognize stress when it appears, acknowledge it, and find ways to manage it. There are people around you who want to help and to share in the experience. Let them. Don't be afraid to ask for support.

- Understand that people handle stress, change, and loss in a variety of ways. You may not be the only stressed one during this process. Be sensitive. Put yourself in their shoes and try to discuss what is happening. Parents in particular often go through their own phases, which may leave them feeling or acting differently. Additionally, their adjustment process may not be parallel to yours. They may make a big deal about what you think are little things; they may appear to have gone "mad" by arguing about the slightest thing. Recognize that this is not unusual behavior, and handle it as it comes up.

- Plan as much as you can early so that you have some time to enjoy the process, your fiancé, and other aspects of your life (yes, you do still need to live your life!). Continue to spend time with your friends—alone. So many brides- and grooms-to-be fear becoming estranged from their friends after they marry, but this doesn't have to be the case.

- Prepare by prevention. Anticipate trouble spots and try to deal with them appropriately in a preventive way.

- Remember that worry never prevented or solved any problem. Rather than worry, which is not productive and can even be counterproductive, act on what worries you. Instead of focusing on possible problems like "I'm so worried about whether John will drink too much," enlist two of his friends to keep an eye on him and help keep him in check.

- Forget "perfect." Perfectionism is about control, and very often brides (as well as their mothers) fixate on perfection as a way to stay busy and avoid normal feelings of change, loss, and fear. It is much healteir to open up and deal with these emotions. If you loosen your grip a bit you'll be able to process these feelings in a natural way—and avoid sending your blood pressure sky-high.

- Focus on what is truly important to you. Decide, with your fiancé, which aspects of the wedding are worth the extra time, focus, and energy you will need to make them what you want. Prioritize so you know where you will stand your ground and where you will be more flexible, and be sure the two of you are on the same page.

- Stress often comes from expectations. Be careful about what is fantasy and what is reality, particularly when it comes to what is affordable and appropriate. Even though your fantasy wedding would take place in the Bahamas with your loved ones around you, consider whether this makes sense. And if it doesn't, don't brood. Plan the wedding that works and that you can afford.

- Face your fears about marriage. You may have been raised by parents who did not have such a great relationship. You may be worried about your own chances for a good marriage. Talk with friends who have been married for some time. Ask questions about what it is like to be married. Share your fears with your fiancé—you will likely find that just giving voice to these fears can diminish their power.

- Relinquish the need to control everything. So much of planning a wedding is out of your control. There are others in your life whose creativity, ideas, talents, and personalities can enhance the experience of planning your wedding if you give yourself a chance to incorporate them and their "style" into your life. *Let the experts—the florist, the caterers, the seamstress—do what they are expert at doing.*

- Understand that you cannot please everyone. If you have a history of needing to please people, standing up for yourself may be tough, but understand that everyone involved in your wedding has a vision of what they would like it to be. Your vision, however, is the one thing that you need to be clear about so you can express it and make it happen. You will be in situations where other people's needs clash with yours. If people disapprove (which they will), remain calm and do not react with anger. Everything can be worked out.

• Keep things in perspective. There are very few things in life over which it's worth losing your cool. Planning your wedding may appear to take over your entire life (and those of your family members), but the world doesn't revolve around the wedding. No matter what happens with the weather, your in-laws, your divorced parents, the children who are your ring bearer and flower girl, you and your fiancé will commit yourselves to one another and begin your life together. That is what is important.

All we can say is, hang in there—it's normal! Every bride goes through what you are going through. This is not the time to diagnose yourself as clinically insane; it's par for the course. Take deep breaths. Remind yourself that you love your husband-to-be. The small details, though important, will not make or break a wedding. Your happiness is all that matters. Remember, your goal is not to have a totally stress-free wedding, but to have a wedding that is both enjoyable and meaningful and that everyone involved can handle happily.

CAN I TRUST A GROOM WHO HAS LIED?

Dear Dr. Dale,

My fiancé and I live in London. I met him when we were both twenty, at which time he did not have a girlfriend. But there was one particular girl he had a huge crush on. It was

only after she went to study in America that he and I got together. We were together for one year, and when we broke
up, he went to "visit" his friend in America, not knowing
that in the meantime his crush had come home to London.

When he was in America, he called me every day, telling
me how much he loved me. He came back six months later
and we began to see each other again. A short while later, I
found out that he had also been seeing the "crush girl." I
guess I was suspicious, because I did something I had never
done before—I snooped around and found letters to this girl
on his e-mail. When I asked him about it, he denied everything and cried bitterly, saying he had met her once or twice
and had had an interest in her, but that nothing sexual had
happened. He begged me not to dump him, and I forgave
him. We did get back together, but since then I've found out
other details about that relationship which indicate that he
was still telling lies.

So maybe I am an idiot, but I love him, I have always
loved him, and be it a strength or a weakness, it is my reality! When he proposed three months ago I was surprised,
but of course I said yes, and we are to be married soon. But
I can't shake the feeling that something is terribly wrong.
What if I find more lies after we are married? What if she is
his true love, and something happens when she comes
around again, even if we are married? I feel suspicious in my
heart, and I know that's because of his history of lying, but
is that unfounded? And how do I deal with it?

You suggest that loving someone is both a weakness and a
strength. We would suggest that if you are in love with the right
person, it is only a strength. But loving someone is not easy. There
is always a risk involved and that is what makes deep, committed
love so amazing. Loving someone and allowing someone into your

heart means that you trust them. Moving beyond your fiancé's involvement with his former girlfriend will take time, and understanding—of him, and of yourself. You have doubts and fears, which is understandable.

If you move forward, however, you will need to work on putting these doubts behind you. But you need to be honest with yourself about what you—and your idea of marriage—can withstand. For example, if you discover, after you are married, that he had slept with her, what happens then? Is that grounds for divorce? Or is it an opportunity to go through something that you will *both* have to deal with—and discover why he thought it best to hide the truth?

It is likely that your fiancé does not know how to deal directly with the truth, and that lying is the way he deals with things. If this is the case, you will need to come to terms with the fact that you will never be 100 percent sure that what he tells you is the truth. Only you can know if you can live with this uncertainty. We can share with you that since the bottom line of most good relationships is a solid foundation of trust, you are beginning with a rocky foundation. In this case, if your gut is telling you that something is terribly wrong, you might do well to heed it. You may want to consider going into couples' counseling before your wedding to make sure that you are both in a place where you are ready to move forward with a lifetime commitment.

NERVOUS NELLIE

Dear Dr. Dale,

I am a bit embarrassed about asking this question, but I need help. I am absolutely the most nervous person in the world, and I worry constantly. I get so nervous just going to my fiancé's parents' house, sometimes I make myself sick over it. I'll either get an upset stomach or sometimes I have panic attacks. I am so afraid that I am going to worry myself sick on my wedding day, fixating on the hundred or so people who will be looking at me, and just worrying that I'll do something stupid. I don't want to be walking down the aisle as a Nervous Nellie and get so ill that I have to turn around and go to the bathroom. I do get excited about my wedding and the wedding dress that I ordered (it is gorgeous!), and I know that I'm marrying the right guy, but I just can't seem to control my nerves. What can I do?

Worry is something that takes an enormous amount of effort and time and doesn't do the person or the situation any good. Generally we say: If you have a specific problem, try to do something about the situation, and you won't have to worry. But if you cannot do anything about the situation, worrying will not help.

Our sense is that you worry because you feel you are being judged, and that somehow you will come up short. There is no such thing as perfection, and although each of us strives to be the best we can be, worrying about "not making the grade" robs us of the opportunity to enjoy life's moments as we experience them. We can choose to look at the world in a variety of ways. Imagine that each of the hundred people at your wedding is sending you messages of love and good fortune, that they are looking at you admiringly and enjoying the fact that you have found the man you want to spend the rest of your life with. Imagine that your in-laws want to get to know you better, as you are, and that they open their hearts to you and look forward to getting to know the woman their son wants to marry.

There are also ways you can control the worry and anxiety: by doing some deep breathing and some "self-acupressure." Acupressure involves tapping lightly with your fingers on different spots on your face (underneath your eyes on the lower bone; underneath your nose in the depressed space between your nose and your upper lip; and also just below your lip, between your lower lip and your chin). While tapping, take a moment and breathe deeply. You can also practice a yoga eyes exercise in which you open your eyes and slowly look up, then to the right, then down and then to the left. You make a slow circle with your eyes and then reverse the circle. By doing these exercises (the breathing, the tapping, and the eye rotation) you can usually bring that anxiety number down several notches.

TIME CRUNCH

Dear Dr. Dale,

My fiancé and I have finally decided to make things official and get married. However, in our typical style, we're getting married in a mere three months. I'm both excited and nervous about everything, because I can't imagine that I can put together a polished and meaningful ceremony in such a short time. Moreover, the wedding will be in my fiancé's hometown, which is six hundred miles away, so this makes the hiring of caterers and photographers a bit dicey. Luckily, we have a small guest list of only twenty people, but even that small number seems huge with the tight budget we have to work with.

How can I remain sane and still assure a special day for my fiancé, our guests, and me?

Just because you have limits on your time and budget doesn't mean that you need to be limited in terms of meaning and feelings. First off, you need to have a discussion with your fiancé about the kind of wedding you want. Once you have determined the mood of the ceremony and what specifically you want to convey, you can begin to apply the specifics of your budget. Which features are most important? Most costly? You will need to adjust according to both your budget and your desires.

The best way to ensure your sanity during this happy, hectic time is to enlist good, reliable help—people you can trust who also want you to have a successful wedding. Given that the ceremony is in your fiancé's hometown, perhaps his family can help with recommendations as to caterers, florists, or photographers. They might also be able to line up appointments with all of the vendors so that you can plan a visit to meet and interview them all over the course of a couple days. Take care of your dress, veil, and shoes in your own town, and if you are having any attendants, talk with them about what your expectations are, and then have them make arrangements on their own.

Much of what needs to be done can be done online—either via e-mail or through the resources of the Internet. And do not forget to take time to breathe, and to allow yourself to absorb the many changes that are happening. If you find yourself feeling as if you are on an emotional roller coaster, don't just fasten your seatbelt— stop and reflect on all that is happening and allow yourself to experience the shifts. Enjoy the pace, and don't fight it. Years from now you'll look back and marvel that you put everything together in record time.

MY WEDDING IS BECOMING MORE OF A BURDEN THAN A JOY

Dear Dr. Dale,

My fiancé hasn't been very involved with the wedding planning, and his family has given me grief about everything that I want this wedding to be. At this point, the wedding is starting to feel more like a burden than anything else. I found out about a week ago that a friend is expecting a baby. My wedding is in thirty days and I am happier about my friend's baby than I am about the fact that I am getting married. The planning of the wedding has been so stressful, and the people I had hoped would be there for me have made it more difficult. Frankly, I have been conditioned to *not* be excited about my own wedding. This worries me, because I fear that if I'm not happy about the wedding that will set the tone for our marriage. I love my fiancé, but I feel totally alone. Right now, on the eve of our wedding, I need his support the most and he is not there.

Because planning this wedding has been far from joyous, it makes perfect sense that your reaction to your friend's happy news fills you with the feelings you would have liked to have had for your upcoming wedding. But your feelings of loneliness and lack of excitement concern us. Many other brides also feel this way, but you sound as if you wonder if your fiancé is going to be there for you when his status changes from fiancé to husband. Your concern about whether you can lean on and rely on your fiancé is significant because that trepidation is for your whole life.

Whether or not he has been involved in the wedding details should not affect his larger involvement in your life, particularly considering the significance of his family's input. We suggest you talk with your fiancé, approaching him from the perspective that you cannot do anything about what has already transpired, but as you go forward, you need to be able to count on him to be there for you in specific ways. Tell him what you need and what you want regarding his behavior and his family. Listen carefully to what he says and how he says it. He may want to do what you need but may not know how, and will need you to teach him. For some couples, it takes a long time. If his heart is in the right place, and he begins moving in the right direction, you can have hope.

As for his family: If your fiancé is not involved, how is it that his family is in the position to give you grief? Are you dealing with them without his knowledge? Is he aware of and condoning their treatment of you? Clear this up right away, because your fiancé needs to back you up, right from the start, in any conflicts and disagreements with his family. This is true for the wedding planning process, and it is particularly true for the rest of your life together.

I'M SO STRESSED THAT I CAN'T BREATHE!

Dear Dr. Dale,

I generally know what to do when my stress levels get out of hand. Before a big presentation at work, I relax my body, breathe deeply, and if I can, I take a walk. I know what helps me calm down. Lately, however, nothing seems to work. I feel unbelievably stressed out as I contemplate my wedding, which is happening in one month's time. I am easily overwhelmed, almost panic-stricken. I love my fiancé, but sometimes I wonder what all of this stress means. Lately, the times I feel it the most are when I come home to my apartment after work and when I am just hanging out with my friends. I actually feel tightness in my chest. Last week I thought I was having a heart attack! I am embarrassed to tell anyone. How can I make this stop?

You are not alone. Most brides don't talk about this because they are afraid it means that they don't want to get married or that they don't love their fiancés. But the truth is that this is a normal stage of the wedding adjustment process. It does not have to do with your feelings about your fiancé, but rather with your feelings about becoming a married person. Just one month from now you will be changing your life dramatically! Your physical symptoms may be masking feelings of loss about these changes in your life and a sense of not being able to control that which is unknown as you go forward. As the clock ticks down to your wedding day, this "unknown" looms ever larger.

When you get the panicky feelings at home, after work, it may be because you realize that your home will have someone else in it from now on—all the time! Or, you may be packing up your apartment, going through your things, and realizing that your new home will not only reflect your taste but someone else's, because it will be his house, too! (Now, that's a heart-stopper right there.) Similarly, when you are hanging out with your friends, you are likely aware on a deeper level of how your social life (particularly your single life) will change after you are married.

It is appropriate and normal to grieve for your old life even as you are thrilled about the new life you are starting. Change always bring with it stress and anxiety—but that doesn't mean that change is a bad thing. In fact, many of life's most stressful changes—like getting married, or having a child, or moving to a foreign country—often yield the greatest joy.

Just to be on the safe side, visit your doctor to check out the feeling of tightness in your chest and be sure there is no underlying illness. But we are certain that this anxiety and stress, and the symptoms they bring, are temporary conditions that will disappear as you begin your new phase of life.

MELTDOWN OVER MOM

Dear Dr. Dale,

I am getting married in seventeen days and my mother has been driving me crazy since day one. She thinks it is her wedding instead of mine. I have already had a talk with her

about this being my wedding and what her role needs to be. I told her to calm down about it, but it has not worked. I am going crazy over this, and she has so infuriated me that I really fear I am going to lose it. I just want her to back off!

Angrily telling your mother to back off seventeen days before your wedding will only aggravate the situation more. You do not know (unless she has told you) what is going on in her head and heart; she may be attempting to control her feelings of loss or discomfort by trying to control what you are doing.

The simplest thing, at this point, is to go along with whatever she wants! See how simple that is? Of course it is unlikely that you will agree with her every choice and want to go this route. But as difficult as it is to have friction before your wedding, if you go full force and stand up for what you want, you run the risk of doing irreparable damage that will affect your wedding day beyond smaller disagreements over ceremony details. Instead, have a conversation with your mom (or write her a note) in which you say that you appreciate all that she is doing for you regarding the big day and that you hope to improve the way things have been going between you in these last days before the wedding. Saying *"This is MY wedding"* will not work (and it hasn't). What you can say is: These are the things you would like to have, and since you know she wants you to be happy on your wedding day, and to be able to look back and see how it reflected your tastes and sensibilities, you hope she will respect this.

At this point it is more about compromise and dealing with the emotions than anything else. If you want her to calm down (which she may or may not be able to do), then you need to be calm yourself and approach her in a soothing way. To help someone calm down, gentleness usually works better than antagonism.

WILL I MAKE THE SAME MISTAKES
THE SECOND TIME AROUND?

Dear Dr. Dale,

I have been single for five years after having been married for six years. My ex-husband was very critical of me and I never felt I could be "myself." I was always nervous about saying the wrong thing and making mistakes. When I realized it was impossible for me to do or be "good enough" for him, I understood it was impossible for me to stay married.

I am now engaged to a wonderful man who loves me and encourages me to be myself. He appreciates my opinions, and I have never felt ill at ease about his impression or perception of me—until now! We are planning our wedding, and suddenly I am feeling sheer panic that the same thing will happen again—that I will not be able to stand up for myself if the situation arises. What if history repeats itself?

One good thing about marrying, divorcing, and falling in love again is that you can learn a lot in the process. It's clear that your previous experience taught you a lot about yourself and the kind of interaction that weakened your self-esteem. And you recognize the differences between your ex and your new fiancé, as well as how your new relationship has allowed you to be yourself. You're in a very different place than you were during your first marriage. And when you truly believe you are good enough just the way you are, when you understand that you are not in a relationship to be judged or criticized, but accepted, encouraged, and supported, then you will be able to affirm, every day, the qualities of your new relationship.

Remember, everyone has times when they feel insecure, no matter how generally confident. If you remain aware and are able to learn new ways of interacting when you feel insecure, you will feel more confident over time. When you begin to feel the "old insecure feelings," take a breath and remind yourself that you are not in your former relationship. Tell yourself you have every right to hold the opinion you hold, to express it, and to be heard. You may wish to tell your fiancé that you are feeling hesitant, intimidated, afraid, whatever you are feeling, and that you could use his assistance and patience as you organize and articulate your thoughts. Remind him that you are working hard to change the behavior that used to be automatic, but that sometimes you fall into the old pattern. Talking about it for a moment or two will likely help you to get a different perspective, remind you of the different person you are with, and help you to express a different response. If you do this consistently, you will have every chance of making this marriage work.

And remember, your present-day "reflected self" (the way you see yourself as reflected in the eyes of your fiancé) is very different from your former reflected self. One of the reasons you are marrying this man is because he sees you the way you want to be seen. He sees in you a woman of substance and individuality whom he wants to be with—just as you are.

THIS ISN'T WHAT I SIGNED ON FOR!

Dear Dr. Dale,

I love my fiancé enormously, but I have second thoughts about our upcoming marriage. This is a second marriage for both of us. I am fifty-two, and he is fifty-seven. We have both been single for several years, but to be blunt, I have more of a life than he does. I have friends, hobbies, and a job (I work from home). Although he has worked his whole life and was a good earner, his company restructured and offered him early retirement, which he accepted (with little conversation about it with me). He is now unemployed and looks forward to having time to travel, play tennis, and go to the beach (we live in Florida). But when we decided to get married, I signed up for a different arrangement! I am afraid I will find him underfoot and uninteresting. I am actually afraid that when he retires, he will retire from life. Am I crazy to be thinking about ending the engagement?

Marriage *is* about change, but your letter addresses more than just that. First, let's tackle the issue of why your fiancé would have made such a major life decision without you. Sometimes, when people are single for a long time (or their previous marriages were such that important matters were not discussed), they "forget" to consider the impact of their life choices on the other people in their lives. Just communicate to your fiancé that from now on, you expect to make decisions together. Chances are he will figure out how to include you in his decision-making process.

Now, to the other issue at hand. Fact: Your fiancé is now in a totally different situation than the one you expected. But remember, the "unexpected" happens to all couples, as it would to the two of you whether now or five years from now. People lose jobs, need to move, have financial or health reversals, have children move in with them. People and change go together. Generally, the couple discusses what needs to be done to integrate the changes into their lives. *Retirement is one of those changes.* You say you did not sign on for this—that is not the point. The point is to understand what he wants now that he has made this move and see if it is a lifestyle that you can live with.

Having a husband who is not working is not the end of the world, but you will need to make adjustments in your daily lives. So sit down with your fiancé and share your concerns. Ask him how he plans to spend his time and what kinds of things he would like to do. Does he expect to play four hours of tennis each day and then hang out at the beach? Does he want you to meet him after work rather than spending time with your friends? What exactly are his expectations? He may not know them, because it is all new, but if you ask him to envision what this next stage of his life will look like, you may be able to curb some of your fears. It may be that you will both be able to maintain your individual lives and space without a problem. On the other hand, if he plans to live a life of leisure assuming your job will take care of all of your expenses, you may grow to resent him for not working, and this may come between you. This is why sharing your feelings and expectations at this time is so important.

Remember also that *whether or not he is working does not determine whether he is interesting.* If he is inquisitive and participates in the world, he will be interesting whether he works or not. If you really love this man, there are real reasons that you do, and they surely include that he is interesting, is involved in things that are of importance to you, and cares about what you care for. This will not change. Chances are that a little communication will assuage your worries and reaffirm that this marriage is something you really want.

ENERGY CRISIS

Dear Dr. Dale,

My fiancé and I are having an energy crisis. We are newly engaged, both work hard, and we both bring work home with us. Now that we are planning the wedding, we are always exhausted! We get on the Internet, we make phone calls, we go over our checklists, we make phone calls again, and then we crash into bed. The next day, the cycle begins again, except that there are additional questions, additional vendors and wedding planning people to deal with, and additional parent and guest issues. Yikes! We love each other very much, and we always talk, but the conversations aren't the passionate, heated ones we had when we first met. Something is definitely missing. And I am wondering if we will have any energy to enjoy the wedding and to deal with each other as lovers after we are married. Is this reality?

This is not reality—this is just the reality of your relationship at this particular time. Understand and remind yourself daily that most of this will pass—that you just have to take each day as it comes, breathing deeply and supporting each other, and deal with the wedding issues carefully and in an organized fashion. Organization can go a long way toward giving you confidence that everything is under control.

Now—remember these words: As you plan your wedding, take the time also to plan your life. What we mean is, pay attention to the way you are dealing with this stressful time, and if you find yourselves getting into negative patterns of crisis and exhaustion, change them now—before they become a habit. Think about your priorities. Consider whether, as a newly engaged couple, it makes sense to live in such a way that you can't find time to be together in comfort and truly enjoy your life together. No matter the stresses and demands of your lives, make a point of always finding time for just the two of you. Engaged couples have the responsibility, and the pleasure, of deciding precisely how they want to be married. This is done in the time you set aside (absent computers and phones!) to do and be only what you both want.

FOUR

The Wedding Planning Process

THERE IS SOMETHING called "process," and it has to do with getting from here to there. How you do it depends in large part on who you are, the way you look at the world, how you take on challenges, and what things mean to you. It is the act of working to achieve a goal, and it describes how you absorb, think through, and deal with circumstances along the way. Some of us process things more fully and more intensely than others. Some of us are so challenged by the process itself that we spin our wheels and don't get things done as quickly as others. Then there are those of us who are totally energized by its challenges and move ahead, checking off that oh-so-long to-do list one item at a time.

Sometimes the process of planning a wedding seems all about

stuff. Of course there's the "people" stuff (relatives, bridesmaids, friends) and then there is the more logistical "wedding" stuff (invitations, registering for gifts, selecting music, choosing photographers, deciding what type of ceremony to have and who will preside, and what kind of reception you want—formal or informal, in a ballroom or on the beach, dramatic floral arrangements or wildflowers in vases). So many decisions to make, and each one comes with—you guessed it—its own process!

It's natural, at times, to feel completely overwhelmed by the process of putting a wedding together. But you may also be one of those brides who loves every minute and can't resist jumping right into comparing venues, flipping through pages of the invitation books, listening to tapes of band after band, and modeling every dress in front of those three-way mirrors. And even if you're not, there are a few things you can do to make life easier along the way.

First and foremost, don't sweat the small stuff (whoever said that is our hero!). Understand that putting together a wedding is like putting together an enormous puzzle. There are lots of pieces, and you need patience to put them together. However, unlike a puzzle, there is no *one* way that decisions have to be made, and there is no one right decision. (Unless your heart will break if the napkins are not folded in the shapes of flowers rather than swans.) Decide early on how invested you are in the different components of the wedding. Sure, everything is important, but what are the *most* important elements for you and your fiancé? Is it the venue? Is it having really excellent food? Is it making sure that you can afford to have each and every person on your guest list attend? When you break down the process and look at each part as a distinct element, you are likely to find the whole experience less overwhelming, and you'll have a clear picture of where your energies should lie. If you make your expectations sensible and attainable, the process becomes less tense and takes on more realistic proportions.

Second, the process will flow more easily if you understand that the pieces fit together in a certain way (select your dress with ample time to have it fitted; book the venue early so you have the room with a view if that is the one you want; don't fuss about who is sitting with whom until you receive the response cards, and do your best to maintain who you are so your choices reflect you and your fiancé). Know what the timeframes are for each of the decisions and work to fit them into the time you have. The abundant number of wedding planners and other books on the market can help you keep track of all the pieces, and exactly when they need tending to.

Here are a few other suggestions for enjoying—or at least managing—the planning process with minimal stress:

* If you have a sense of what works for you, don't waste time with choices that are totally out of your range or of no interest. If you hate formal wear, don't bother looking at ballrooms. But if you have your heart set on a black-tie wedding on the beach—just go for it.

* If you are working within a limited budget, don't waste your time worrying about what you can't do. Don't you believe for one minute that you have to have tons of money to have a beautiful and unforgettable wedding! Peonies in Connecticut are plentiful and inexpensive and absolutely gorgeous, while in Los Angeles they can cost ten dollars a stem. Embroidered Asian silk at twelve dollars a yard is as striking as beaded moiré at seventy-five dollars a yard. Your eighteen-year-old disc jockey nephew will make music as memorable and as much fun as a one-hundred-piece string orchestra. Trust us!

* Trust your instincts. Pay attention to what feels right to you. Have confidence in your own taste and passions, and

don't get talked into something your gut tells you is just not you. Always wear your hair down? We promise you will hate the pictures of you at the altar with a mass of curls on top of your head. Never wear strapless? This may not be the time to start. Love color? Don't get talked into all-white tables and flowers. Make yourself happy.

- Listen, learn, and be creative—you don't *have* to go by the book. We know a creative and talented bride who visited several elegant ballrooms and restaurants as they were being set up for weddings, took notes, and when it came time to create her own elegant party, she took the best from the best, and on her own budget re-created the elements she admired. It was a great success and she spent a lot of time (which she had) but very little money (which she didn't have). You can learn a lot from wedding professionals, but also from friends who have been through the process.

- If you feel overwhelmed and unsure, don't panic. If you feel pressured or pushed, step back, take a few long breaths, and ponder the different choices. Take your time. Think it through. Develop patience and keep an open mind.

As you go through the process of planning your wedding, remember that you have an amazing opportunity to learn from every interaction and every situation you encounter. You will be learning about yourself and those around you. As you do this, you will also need to learn ways to become at ease with all of the chaos. You can manage it with grace, style, maturity, and a sense of calm. Life, not just your wedding, is filled with multiple, simultaneous events and decisions that need your attention.

Some of us do that better than others during stressful times. If you are someone who cringes at the thought of doing two or more things at once, you should make your lists, enroll in a yoga class, and learn how to breathe. You will need to do this so you can proceed without falling apart when things, well, fall apart.

Plans always change, and that is part of the process. Whether you "lose it" is up to you. When you feel overwhelmed or out of your league, get help, restore yourself, resolve to use your inner resources, take a break—do anything so that you do not turn into the dreaded Bridezilla. Since you are the bride-to-be, it is now your time to behave with the maturity and grace of a woman about to be married. And that means taking responsibility for your behavior, actions, and emotional responses. Do all that is necessary to keep your eye on the prize!

GUEST-LIST WARFARE

Dear Dr. Dale,

I'm having a battle royal with my parents over the guest list for my wedding. My parents think it is appropriate to invite a large number of their friends and business associates, many of whom I barely know, and some I haven't even met. As if that is not enough, they are requesting that my fiancé and I limit *our* guests. We are crunching numbers—and nerves. I have always thought that there was a rule—perhaps unwritten—that the guests at a wedding have to have some connection, some relationship, to the bride and groom. My parents seem to think they should invite everyone they know, as if this was a business convention or a charity function. I am truly at a total loss as to how to get through to them. Help!

Probably the most volatile problem area between parents and their soon-to-be-married children is the guest list. For many people, their child's wedding is their opportunity to have people from the various segments of their lives celebrate with them—whether or not they have any connection to the couple. Often parents lose sight of the fact (or don't care) that their children will not know many of the celebrants.

Some brides and grooms have the power to influence their parents' decisions and to impress them with their need to either keep the list small, intimate, or at least familiar. But if you do not have that kind of influence with your parents, and especially if they are footing the bill, then you need to either grin and bear it and have the wedding that your parents want to give, or lobby for control over a few, *very important*, aspects of the wedding that are crucial to you and that you want in order to remain more intimate.

Some families can be convinced to allot a specific number of invitees to everyone (for example, the bride gets fifty, the groom gets fifty, the parents get fifty) in the name of fairness and derailing any further argument.

Too many parents and children get into the ill-fated conversation in which each "defends" the value of having one person over another at the wedding. It is a painful process. Occasionally parents may believe that many of your current friends will not be your friends for a long time and they do not see the value of inviting people who they perceive as transient in your lives. If they offer that argument, you can counter with the fact that at this time in your life, you want the people who mean the most to you to witness your marriage. But try to avoid these debates. If your parents refuse to give you the number you would like, see if they will offer to have another, separate party for just your friends. And remember, you can always say thanks but no thanks and give yourself your own wedding.

FAMILIES FEUDING OVER NUMBERS

Dear Dr. Dale,

I have heard stories like this before, but I never thought it would happen to us! My family and my fiancé's family have never had any love lost between them, so I should have been prepared for arguments surrounding the planning of our wedding. But now, as we are about to send out the invitations, it's getting worse. My parents have given me a limit as to how many guests my fiancé can invite, and it is significantly less than their numbers. My fiancé's parents are furious. The friction is tremendous, and I have no idea how to lessen it. What should I do?

If your parents are paying for the wedding, it is their right to decide how many guests your fiancé's family can invite. Sometimes the parents of the groom will offer to help defray some of the costs of the wedding, thereby freeing up space to be able to have more of their own guests. This is never a sure thing, and there is always the risk that the bride's parents will accept the money but not change the number of the allotment. In some cases, the groom's family can just offer to pay for an additional number of guests and see if that is acceptable.

If, as you say, there is no love lost between the two families, then a gesture of generosity will likely not be met with enthusiasm. One option, if your wedding is close to home, is for your fiancé's parents to have their own "prewedding" party for their guests. This can be a very large "rehearsal dinner" where they can invite friends to come and meet your fiancé and toast your happy marriage. Traditionally, the groom's family hosts the rehearsal dinner and, although it is somewhat unorthodox to have people not invited to the wedding at the rehearsal dinner, it may help to at least have some of their loved ones attend.

If none of these options work, then your fiancé's parents will have to accept the allotment. Try to assuage their anger and focus on the fact that they will be there to see their son get married. This is surely very difficult for you and your fiancé as well, so talk with his parents and express your disappointment that they will not have as many of their friends and family there as they (and you) would have liked.

The two of you can also speak to your parents about your displeasure with their unequal allotment of guests, and how difficult it will be for you to enjoy yourselves knowing that your fiancé's family has been limited in such a way. You can try to offer your parents the point of view that they do not have to like his family to be fair and equitable, and that your fiancé's parents would like to have their loved ones with them to witness the marriage of their son, just as they do. Beyond that there is not much you can do. If your parents are paying, it is ultimately their decision.

WHOSE NAME GOES ON THE INVITATION?

Dear Dr. Dale,

I am the bride-to-be, and my family is paying for the wedding. My parents refuse to put the groom's parents' names on the invitation, and I am very upset with them. You can only imagine how my fiancé's family is reacting! I am afraid that this will cause a rift between our families. Help!

A wedding is the joining of two people who represent the two families who have raised them. If there is any hint of bad feeling,

I suggest your parents seriously reconsider their decision. There is nothing to be gained by their decision to omit your fiancé's family on the invitation and much to lose. If you explain to them that the potential for in-law estrangement is significantly heightened by their decision, and your relationship with *both* of the families is at risk, they may reconsider.

But there is another question here, and that is one of control. Usually, the people who are paying for the wedding make the important decisions. In this case, however, with the potential so great for so many hurt feelings and feelings of exclusion, I advise you to talk with your parents with a professional to encourage them to give up their lofty position and respect your desire to include your fiancé's family's name on the invitation. If they will not, you can have a different kind of wedding (where you and your fiancé plan and pay for the entire event) or talk with his parents and explain your inability to influence your parents.

If your parents refuse to change on this matter, remind yourself and them that although you are their daughter, you are a separate person who would have chosen differently and that their decision is a great disappointment to you and you do not agree with it at all. It is still *your wedding,* and names on the invitations, and other decisions, are really in the hands of the bride and groom. You need to have this conversation with your parents—and immediately—before the decision making and anger get out of hand.

RECEPTION ON THE ROCKS?

Dear Dr. Dale,

We have several friends and relatives who abuse drinking. Thus, my fiancé and I have to reach a difficult decision in our wedding-planning process: whether or not to have a par-tially open or a fully open bar. We are expecting two hundred and fifty guests, and the bar at the hotel we've chosen for our ceremony is very pricey, even for beer and wine. The thought of these individuals getting wasted after a ceremony that we hope will have great significance and meaning really upsets me—that's not the tone we hope to set at all. On the other hand, we do not want to punish those who wouldn't be so abusive. We have discussed the possibility of drink tickets for everyone, allowing three or four drinks per person. However, I keep reading that anything less than an open bar is unacceptable for our guests, etiquette-wise. Are drink tickets inappropriate?

Drink tickets may be offensive to those who are used to abusing bar privileges, but as this is your wedding, and you are the ones paying for it, you can decide to have any sort of restriction you deem necessary or comfortable. Of course, some people will not like your choice, but as with everything that surrounds a wedding and marriage, it is *your* choice. The people who will be attending are there to celebrate in the way *you* envision. If drink tickets will help your guests maintain a level of dignity and decorum that you are happy with, by all means go with this option.

INVITATIONS AND WORKPLACE POLITICS

Dear Dr. Dale,

My fiancé and I will be married soon, and we are facing a dilemma with our guest list. We both work at the same company and are friendly with many of the people in the workplace. However, I feel that I am on better terms with most of my coworkers than my fiancé, and, in fact, some of the people in our company have been extremely rude, nosy, and unkind to him. Still, he seems to think it is better that we invite them, as it might not be a good political move to exclude them.

Can I pick and choose among our coworkers for those I want at the ceremony? And could I then extend a verbal invitation to those I wouldn't mind having at the reception? Is there a right way to do this? Is my suggestion even possible?

The fact that you are getting married does not require that you invite everyone from work, or even everyone you know. At one's wedding, the bride and groom should look around and feel comfortable with and comforted by those around them. While inviting everyone to the wedding ceremony is a lovely and expansive gesture, you may wish to think further about why you would consider inviting people who have been rude, nosy, and unkind to your fiancé.

Generally speaking, verbal invitations lack warmth and sincerity, and it is unclear whether you really care if those invited choose to attend. Nowadays, more and more people are sending different invitations to different guests. For example, in your case, you could send invitations for just the ceremony to certain coworkers, and invitations to the entire wedding and reception to closer friends and family members. You and your fiancé can discuss how you will handle any repercussions from those coworkers you choose not to invite. Some of your coworkers, indeed, may confront you. You can speak with them kindly about the difficulty of keeping the numbers of guests under control, and if you choose to go into more depth, you can say that at some point you needed to draw a line, and although it was not an easy decision, you hope they understand.

MOM HAS COMMANDEERED THE
WEDDING PROCESS

Dear Dr. Dale,

I got engaged a few months ago. The day my fiancé proposed, my mom was already jumping on the bandwagon, constantly reminding us of all the things to be done. With the wedding at least a year away, I wanted some time to relax. But my mom immediately bombarded me with phone calls. Within weeks she had set up an appointment for me at a country club with a wedding coordinator. I kept going along with everything, but after a few weeks of all the details, I asked my mom if we could work together to come up with a schedule so she wouldn't have to feel like she needed to call me every day with wedding-related stuff. I told her that I wanted to devise a plan for working together before we paid the security deposit. Well, she completely freaked out! She told me to just go elope, along with other things that I know she didn't really mean. I just wanted her to slow down!

Now my parents have totally dropped out of any wedding planning and have refused to help us financially. My fiancé and I are prepared to pay for our own wedding, but how do we get them involved again? We have tried talking and writing letters and they won't respond to me. They even told me not to come home to sit down and talk, as they would prefer to call me when they were "good and ready." I am shocked by this behavior, to say nothing of feeling angry and disappointed.

The truth is, your mother jumping on the bandwagon may have been a result of her desire to get all of the important reservations in place early on so that they were secured, and then take the time to kick back. Your desire to relax may have been interpreted as not being involved, or not understanding the world of weddings (needing to book the venue, photographer, florist, band, etc., well in advance to prevent being shut out on the day you want to get married). Whatever the root of the misunderstanding and miscommunication, unless you want to elope or plan and execute the entire wedding by yourself, it would be a good idea to reach out to your parents again, because the road to reconciliation is a long one, and your wedding is in less than one year.

Right now, you must respect their "do not call" instructions, but in the meantime, think about what you might put into a carefully thought-out letter to help the four of you get onto the right track. You can inform your parents that your desire to work out a plan was in no way a condemnation of your mother's desire to help you, for which you are—and were—grateful. You can add that you also appreciate her desire to hit the ground running, but you had envisioned something different, with a more relaxed pace.

If your mother is totally off-limits and unavailable, try your dad. Even though it is not usually a good idea to divide and conquer, you don't have much leeway. See if you can make a date with your father and approach him with an olive branch philosophy. Without condemning, tell him you and your mother got off to a bad start and you want to find a way to plan the wedding together, as a family. Ask him for his advice regarding the best way to make this happen.

Another approach is to reach out to another member of the family or a close friend of your parents' who likely knows what is going on and might be willing to serve as a mediator. If these do not work, and there is limited time, have a backup plan. You cannot be held hostage in a no-win situation. Decide with your fiancé what type of wedding you and he can afford, and plan it now. Send your parents a letter explaining your decision and requesting their attendance. Waiting until your mother and father are good and ready to talk also leaves you waiting; if your parents remain unresponsive, you need to move ahead and plan your own wedding.

WE HAVE TO TRIM OUR REHEARSAL DINNER NUMBERS!

Dear Dr. Dale,

Our rehearsal dinner is turning out to be one of the sticking points in planning our wedding. We are only having nieces and nephews in our wedding party—sixteen in all, ranging from a few months to nineteen years of age. I come from a large family (one sister, five halves, and four steps) while my fiancé has four siblings. Add to this many aunts, uncles, grandparents, and so on, and it's a general zoo, totaling very close to eighty-five people. And that's just family!

In short, we are on a budget, and we cannot decide who to invite to the rehearsal dinner and who to exclude. If we include the bridal party (and accompanying parents) we will have so many little kids! My fiancé and I were hoping to avoid kids under ten at the rehearsal dinner, but are afraid that this is rude. In addition, my parents want to invite the out-of-town guests as well (which, I think, is always proper etiquette since these out-of-town guests have traveled a long way to be there the night before). While we would like to have everyone included, it simply doesn't seem very feasible, from an economic point of view. How can we make sense of this? We are totally lost.

If you are not prepared to have a rehearsal dinner for more than eighty-five people, you have to draw the line somewhere. It is perfectly acceptable to invite the bridal party to the dinner but only those children over the age of ten. Or you can leave out the kids altogether, and hire a few babysitters for the younger children at another location, and plan games and a dinner of pizza or sloppy joes to keep them entertained while the parents are at the formal dinner. This may give you more room for the guests. Generally, out-of-town guests are invited, but nothing is cast in stone. Your parents may feel that they want to have something special for their friends and relatives who are making the trip. If there is some flexibility in this issue, you can explain that the numbers are large, and you can give out-of-towners the names of a few restaurants in town and suggest that different groups of friends and relatives go out together so they have a bit of a festive feeling. They could, perhaps, join you at the party afterward for dessert or for a cocktail.

Alternatively, if you absolutely can't trim the list, you can offer to host a casual picnic, provide the main course, and ask some of the local guests to bring potluck platters of salads, breads, desserts, and fruit.

WITH MANY REGRETS— AND TOO FEW GUESTS

Dear Dr. Dale,

It's about three-and-a-half weeks to my wedding date, and while the whole process has been pretty exciting, fun, and positive for my fiancé and me, we're feeling dejected as we see our RSVPs come in.

We chose to have our wedding on a Sunday, as our Jewish faith precludes us from marrying during daylight hours on a Saturday. The Sunday we chose fell within the Memorial Day weekend. We weren't too concerned at the time, as we'd heard that people who have Sunday weddings often choose holiday weekends—to save their guests from having to travel late on a Sunday evening. We tried to hedge our bets by sending out save-the-date cards six months beforehand to at least half of those on the guest list. We also calculated our guest list based on an estimate that 25 percent of the people would decline. So we invited one hundred and twenty people (counting single friends bringing guests), thinking ninety guests would be ideal.

Unfortunately, it's starting to look like we will barely have sixty people coming! We can chalk this up to a number of things—like the holiday weekend, and our single friends almost unanimously deciding not to bring guests—but we can't help but feel disheartened by the small number of people planning to be with us on our day. Like any couple, we've put an enormous amount of time and effort (not to mention expense) into making this day both the best for us and the most accommodating for our guests. We are trying to channel our thoughts into being extra grateful for those friends and family who did make time for us on their holiday weekend, but it is sometimes challenging to remain upbeat as we see many other old friends bow out.

Do you have any advice on not getting bogged down in feeling sorry for ourselves?

Whenever you choose to have a wedding on a holiday weekend, you take an inordinate risk of having people unavailable or unwilling to attend. Having said that, the way to keep from being disappointed is to alter your expectations and to focus on who will be there and how you can make this wedding a more special, intimate affair. It will not be the wedding you thought you were going to have, but it is the wedding you do have, so focus on what is going to happen and who is going to be there. This might be an opportunity to mix it up a little and do things you wouldn't have been able to do before—such as taking time to be with each guest and introducing each guest to the larger group. One of the most wonderful experiences you can indulge yourself in at a smaller wedding is to hold the microphone and go around the room, introducing each guest with a few sentences or a special story about them that will help everyone know who they are in your life. This allows for an intimacy that is impossible at a larger wedding, because you declare your appreciation for each of your guests, and they feel special.

This, by the way, is a great life lesson. Staying present, in the moment, conscious of what is surrounding you at the time rather than what is missing, will be a great help to you and your fiancé as you build your life together. Much of life is not about dealing with what you expect to happen, but in approaching the surprises.

CORDIALLY UNINVITED

Dear Dr. Dale,

One of my out-of-state wedding guests has informed me that she and her husband will be divorcing soon, so she will be bringing a date with her. As my fiancé and I are paying for this wedding ourselves, we have had to make a number of hard and fast rules—including "no dates." I had been aware of trouble in her marriage, but I had nonetheless invited her husband to attend with her, primarily because I viewed him as a guest who could be trimmed from the list— not as a slot that could be filled by another. I have known this woman since college, and I don't think she realizes that I am not holding an "open house" wedding with unlimited space and funds. What should I do?

It is entirely up to you and your fiancé whether or not you want to limit your guest list, and you should feel free to tell your friend that you would prefer that she attend alone. Explain the intimate nature of the wedding, and hopefully she will understand and comply. However, keep in mind that she may not, at which point you will have to explain in more detail your financial constraints, your inclusion of her husband as a courtesy and not as a slot to be filled, and your discomfort at her bringing a date. Be up front about the fact that *no one* else is bringing any dates by your specific request. You may be forced to exhibit some extreme sensitivity in this matter, since your friend may be uncomfortable attending a wedding alone so soon after a divorce. Only you can decide how far to press her on this, and how your friendship will respond as a result.

CATERER FROM HELL

Dear Dr. Dale,

My mother's friend is a well-known caterer in our area. Her food and presentation are both excellent, but I find her personally impossible to deal with. There is a perpetual mood of chaos and frenzy surrounding her, and timing never seems to matter to her. I know that she would go out of her way to make everything beautiful for me on my wedding day, but it is not worth it to me to worry that she may show up late or with insufficient help. My mother says the result is always beautiful, the food tastes great, and I should just let my concerns go. What do you think?

You certainly shouldn't "let your concerns go." You are perfectly right to be concerned; after all, do you really think that you can change this person? Every bride should be able to relax before and during her wedding, and you won't be able to do this without knowing that everyone working for you is doing his or her best.

It appears that your mother is more concerned with the feelings of her friend than she is with your desire for contentment and satisfaction. Talk to your mother calmly about your worries and, if possible, talk with the caterer herself. Can she offer anything to reassure you that the timing will be exactly as you want it? If you still feel unsure, choose your own caterer or look into the possibility of using a meeting place, banquet facility, or hall that has its own catering service. If you choose either of these routes, then invite your mother's friend to the wedding to show there is no ill will.

MY FAMILY IS FAR AWAY

Dear Dr. Dale,

My parents feel left out because they have not been consulted much in the planning of the wedding, largely because my fiancé and I live in my future in-laws' hometown. My mother, in particular, feels left out. She wants to be supportive but does not know anything about this region of the country, particularly its customs or its costs. My sister even complained that she doesn't know what kind of dress to wear or which beauty parlor to go to. How can I incorporate my family into the planning without insulting my fiancé's family?

Take into consideration how each of you were brought up. For many, the bride's family does the whole planning and the groom's parents plan and host the rehearsal dinner. Some families want to pay for everything so that they can have the final say. Others expect that the costs—and thus the input—will be evenly split. Discuss with your fiancé and his family the fact that your family would like to be involved in some way. Do this in such a way that his parents do not feel threatened that your family wants to have a say in the decision making but rather that they would appreciate being part of the joy prior to the wedding itself. Then suggest that both you and your fiancé and your fiancé's family set up times to talk with your parents about various details so they can feel a part of the process. These days, e-mail also makes it easy to swap ideas, photos of potential sites for the ceremony, and so on. Be sure to also pass along recommendations for salons in the area, and to discuss the "type" of wedding so that your family can obtain the appropriate attire.

EVERYONE WANTS TO BRING THEIR KIDS!

Dear Dr. Dale,

I am getting married in May. We just sent out the invitations a few days ago, and already we are noticing that people assume their children are also invited to the wedding. We did not put "Adult Reception" on the invitations, but we addressed the invitations to include only those who are invited. My fiancé and I would love for everyone to come, but we have limited funds for the wedding and had to cut the guest list. What is the best way to let these people know that we only want adults to be there even though we didn't specify it?

The best way to handle this is directly. It is fine to have a card printed that is sent to all of the guests simply stating that the wedding is an adults-only affair and that you would appreciate guests making child care arrangements. If you feel you would like to have children at the ceremony, you can indicate that they are welcome at the ceremony and that child care arrangements during the reception would be appreciated. Since you have already sent out the invitations and did not include this reminder, you must contact the guests who have indicated that they are coming and let them know that the invitation was addressed only to the invited guests and, therefore, children are not included unless they were specifically invited.

FIVE

The Bridal Party

BRIDESMAIDS!
What is a bridesmaid, anyway?

Is she the girlfriend who gives you support, wisdom, and advice, particularly now, when you are making the transition from being single to being married?

Or is she the girlfriend who holds up the questionnaire at your wedding shower that asks your friends to guess what your fiancé will do on your wedding night? Or the one in charge of making the hat out of those ribbons taken off your shower gifts of sexy lingerie?

Some bridesmaids are both. Some are neither. There is something about the history of this role that ends up, many times, with more friction than warm feelings of love and friendship. One would think that your "best friends"—your bridesmaids—would be there for you with grace and style while they listen to your worries, your ramblings, and your obsessions, and hold you up when the stress on you is just too much. Indeed, it seems like inviting your friends to be your bridesmaids is a chance to honor all you have done for each other throughout the years.

So what happens along the way? Why do bridesmaids—and brides—often end up feeling pulled apart during the process, when all is supposed to be joyful and fun filled? Why does your best friend's anger over situations long past suddenly rear its head when she tells you she thinks your wedding gown is a totally unflattering style? Why does your sister pick this time to tell you she just can't be a bridesmaid if you don't let her wear the dress she prefers?

It can become too much. More often than not, the bridesmaid ritual brings with it tension, irritation, and arguments that you don't need at this time. And how do you feel? Sometimes betrayed, often let down, and almost always shocked at the changed behavior of women you considered to be your closest friends.

It is difficult to know exactly why this happens. Some of your friends may feel threatened by your upcoming marriage, and wonder how your life (and friendship) will change (for more on this, see Chapter 7). Financial concerns may also play a role. Sometimes, when the bridesmaids' roles are unclear, there can be misunderstandings and resentments that build up along the way. If you want to keep this relationship smooth on the road to your big day, here are a few things to keep in mind:

- Be a gracious bride and always do your best to think of your bridesmaids' needs and wishes, and to consider their lifestyles, financial situations, family obligations, and so on. Your timing and decisions may not be good for all of them.

- Always be grateful for your bridesmaids' efforts. Don't become someone they don't know—a shrew who only considers how their actions affect *you*. Remember that your bridesmaids are spending time and money (and may have little of both) to help you.

- Have a clear conversation early on with your bridesmaids about what you expect from them and what they may expect, especially when it comes to financial responsibility and expectations. That way you can all make informed decisions about what their responsibilities can and will include. Here are a few things to figure out up front:

  - Do you expect your bridesmaids who are working full-time and living on a budget to plan and pay for your dream "girlfriends' weekend" in the Bahamas?

  - What about hosting a shower for you? Do you expect one or more of them to plan and pay for it?

  - Will they be paying for their dresses, plane tickets, and hotel rooms at your destination wedding?

  - If there are several showers planned, do you expect them to attend each one? Do they participate financially in all of them? Do they bring gifts to all the showers?

There is no way around it.

It is complicated. But don't despair. The Q&As we've included here will help you navigate a variety of situations that can threaten to derail your perfect plans. To keep your relationships with your bridesmaids intact, keep the lines of communication open throughout the process. Above all, remember to tell your friends how much they mean to you and how much you appreciate what they're doing. If you're smart and thoughtful, you'll be able to minimize the opportunities for disappointment and maximize the opportunities for a meaningful wedding experience that you and your friends can share and remember for a lifetime.

A WEDDING ALONE

Dear Dr. Dale,

I have no siblings or extended family, and my fiancé's family is completely indifferent to our getting married. We have moved to a new city, and neither of us really has any close friends—we have good acquaintances, but no "best friends." The issue is that I have no one to ask to be in my bridal party, as I don't have any girlfriends here. My fiancé can have his brothers stand for him, but that wouldn't work if I have no bridesmaids. Will I look like a fool if I have no bridal party? Do we have to have a bridal party, or can we just stand up for ourselves?

This also means that there will be no one to throw a shower for me, as my mother lives in another state, and even if she were to throw one, there would be no one to invite as I have no girlfriends (I'm not sure how to explain that to Mom, as she'll think I'm pathetic and crazy!). Maybe we should just elope and have a small dinner afterward? Why even throw a wedding if we have so few people to participate? My parents are imagining a princess wedding, but we just don't have the guest list to justify it. Please help!

First and foremost, you need to plan the wedding that is right for you. As far as a bridal party goes, if you do not have any friends you feel comfortable having around you, then you can definitely stand up for yourselves. You will not "look like a fool," to use your expression. There is a difference between doing what is right for yourself and doing what is right for someone else. If it is not right for you to have people whom you are not terribly close to be part of a wedding party, then don't.

Now for the question of a bridal shower: Instead of a shower, you may wish to go away for a weekend alone with your mom, or ask if she might like to invite her friends in her town to celebrate your marriage. You do not have to have your own friends in order for your mom to give you a shower. It is up to the two of you. In some traditions, the older generation of women (your mother and her friends) gives a shower and the bride is expected to be there to receive the wisdom of these older, wiser women.

As to the question of a large or small wedding, you may wish to have the ceremony in a clergyperson's study or at city hall, with a small and elegant dinner or lunch afterward to celebrate with your families. Of course, you can always elope. Our experience with elopement and families is that the parents often have a very hard time when their children elope because, princess fantasies or not, they usually prefer to see their daughter or son get married (and their adult children usually prefer to have their parents with them as well). But you need to look inside your own heart and decide for yourself.

AND THE HONOR GOES TO . . .

Dear Dr. Dale,

I was recently engaged, and given that it was the dream of my life, that was the easy part. The hard part lies before me: choosing my maid of honor. I have one friend whom I've known since we were in the eighth grade, but our relationship has always been one in which I was more of a caretaker of her. My second friend is someone I've known for only two years, but our friendship is far more equitable in terms of our sharing emotions and life experiences. Who do I choose?

Your decision on who serves as your maid of honor needs to be based on what you feel is right for you and your friendships. Follow your instincts and your good judgment. Keep in mind that the role of maid of honor is often given to someone who is and will continue to be extremely important in your life. Your choice is also a statement about who you value and what you value about them. Your friend of long-standing represents your past and your growing into womanhood. Even though your relationship is characterized by you taking care of her, you have been important to one another, and perhaps considering her is more a reflection of the loyalty you feel to her as your girlhood friend and the promises of being one another's maids of honor rather than of the adults you are now. The more recent friendship reflects who you are now and the kind of friendship you have: one of equals. This friendship likely embodies the adult qualities you value. Your decision may be based on whether you want your maid of honor to be representative of your past or your future. Whoever you select, be sure to talk with each of them to discuss your rationale, and at all times be aware of their feelings.

BRIDESMAID BAILING ON MY BRIDAL SHOWER

Dear Dr. Dale,

My bridal shower is in two weeks, and one of my bridesmaids just informed me that she won't be attending because she and her husband are going to Europe. My shower was planned several months ago—long before her trip. This woman has not really participated at all, either with me or the other bridesmaids, and I'm sure she was aware of the shower date.

For some time I excused the behavior of this woman (her mother passed away, which caused her to be absent from some of the planning for the wedding). I even talked to her to make sure she was serious about her decision to be in my wedding, and she was very enthusiastic. And now this! She says there is no way to change the plans, and while she's sorry, she is not attending the shower. Can you advise me on how I should deal with her?

A large part of planning a wedding—and getting married, for that matter—is dealing with the disappointment you feel when your life and your plans intersect with those plans made by others. You do have a choice in this matter: You can have the relationship that you clearly have had with your friend for some time take precedence over her lack of involvement in the planning of your wedding and her nonattendance at the shower, and then welcome her to your wedding. Or you can focus on the fact that she did not help and is not attending, and allow that reality to dominate your life. You have shared your feelings with your friend, she has apologized, and now it is up to you to accept her and her situation and forgive her. If you choose to take the high road, then enjoy the shower with those who are present and accept her at the wedding. Or, if you care more about her living up to her word, you can ask her to step down from her obligation—but be prepared for this to put a strain on your friendship.

THE BACKSTABBING BRIDESMAID

Dear Dr. Dale,

Isn't a maid of honor supposed to be a bride's best friend? I certainly thought so, but now, four months before my wedding, I have learned that my maid of honor is saying terrible things about me behind my back. My feeling now is that I don't want her in my wedding. What should I do?

Focus first on the positive news: You have four months to deal with this situation, and you don't know for sure that your maid of honor has actually said anything negative about you. Talk to her and learn the truth, and keep in mind that you clearly thought highly enough of this woman to give her the honor of being with you on your wedding day. The strong sentiment attached to your decision to make her your maid of honor is stronger than any emotion revolving around gossip. Give her the benefit of the doubt.

Having said that, if you do find that your friend has been saying negative things about you, and may harbor unpleasant thoughts, then you have every right to reconsider her role in your wedding. Keep in mind, however, that something may have been exaggerated, and that it may be dealt with—after which you can both focus on the preparations that lie ahead. If you do decide to ask her to step down, invite her to a neutral place for a cup of coffee (not at either of your houses) and say you have been giving the wedding a lot of thought and have changed your mind about her involvement. Because you have already discussed this and heard her side of the story, you can say, "I understand your points. Thank you for telling me what happened. I am disappointed and will surely miss having you involved. But I am no longer comfortable with you as my maid of honor. Let's think about what it will involve to repair our friendship. Right now I need to focus my time and energy on the wedding."

BRIDESMAIDS MISSING IN ACTION

Dear Dr. Dale,

I asked two old friends to be my bridesmaids. My wedding is in two months, and one woman hasn't even picked up her dress yet. I have not seen her in about nine months. The other woman picked up her dress, but we haven't spoken in four months. What should I do? Can you un-ask friends to be bridesmaids, or should I just wait until the last minute before we print the programs to pin them down?

Why add to the stress of your wedding planning by waiting until the last minute? Do you really want to risk the possibility (or, more likely, the probability) of feeling uneasy, upset, and disappointed when they bow out? That said, we would caution that you never know what is going on in your friends' lives, so rather than jumping to any conclusions or making quick decisions, call, write, or e-mail them and ask how each is doing. Give them an update regarding your wedding planning process and suggest a few times that might be convenient for you to meet with them or talk with them. When you do, inquire whether they are well and still interested in serving as your bridesmaids. If they are, give them an idea of what you will need from them (even if all you need is a weekly conversation between now and the wedding day and the assurance that your friend has picked up her dress). If you find that, for whatever reason, either or both of them cannot serve as your bridesmaids, allow them to remove themselves gracefully and then pick your new ones quickly!

MY BRIDESMAIDS HATE
MY COLOR CHOICE

Dear Dr. Dale,

My mother and my bridesmaids don't like the color I picked for their dresses, which is Victorian lilac. They all want navy. Should I have the color I want, or make everyone else happy and get navy?

It is your wedding, so of course it is your prerogative as to the color of the dresses. Most brides (and grooms) have a particular vision of what they desire insofar as colors, flowers, and music are concerned. But you may need to think about some compromise. There is definitely a distinct feel to a wedding that features navy as opposed to one that highlights Victorian lilac, and since most bridesmaids buy their dresses (and would later like to wear them again on occasion), you might want to think about another color that affords you the same desired vision, but also serves your mother and bridesmaids better. However, if it is Victorian lilac you want, then go ahead and ask that everyone support you on this special day.

DRESS MESS

Dear Dr. Dale,

I have several friends who were offended that I did not include them as part of my bridal party, but it was only because I had not gotten around to them yet. Now that I have asked them to participate, I cannot get them to help choose the dresses, or even to gather in the same place together. They are all different sizes and are already complaining that the dresses will be either too fitted or not fitted enough. The larger women want two-piece dresses and the thin ones want slitted sides, with the back and arms showing. How can I get just the right look for all?

You may not be able to get the right look for all, but you probably can get one look that will be great for some of your attendants and pretty good for others. There is no such thing as perfect when you are working with such a variety of shapes and sizes. Explain to them as gently as you can that the challenge is finding dresses that will flatter a variety of figures. You should know, however, that more and more brides are choosing a variety of dresses in one color scheme, or dresses that are different colors but made out of the same or similar fabric, for just this reason.

As far as getting them all together in one spot, offer a series of dates to meet at the bridal stores and go with the date that works for most of the women. The ones who cannot make the date will have to understand that you will select for them, but they will be able to do their fittings on their own schedule. With most of your bridal party at the store at the same time, you will have the opportunity to see your friends in a wide selection, and then you can make your choice.

HANKY-PANKY IN THE BRIDAL PARTY

Dear Dr. Dale,

Help! One of my bridesmaids had an affair with one of the groomsmen before our wedding. Almost everyone knows about this affair except her husband (obviously). There are a few people who are not happy with the situation (which is not their business, but that's life). I am very scared that someone is going to look at someone funny, or slip, and there is going to be a big war at my wedding. What do I do?

Talk candidly with your bridesmaid prior to the wedding about your concerns, and tell her that you support her as a friend and want her to be a part of your wedding day, but that you need her to use very good judgment and help you to keep things from getting out of hand (you will have to emphasize the good judgment part because, one might say, she did not think about good judgment when she had the affair in the first place!). She can do this by spending the wedding with her husband and *not dancing with that groomsman*. In addition, you can make sure that your friend and that groomsman *do not walk down the aisle together*! Regarding everyone's behavior at the wedding, you have no control over the fact that many adults sometimes act in a way that does not rise to the occasion.

HONORING TWO SISTERS: BY BIRTH AND BY CHOICE

Dear Dr. Dale,

My best friend and I made a pact a long, long time ago to be each other's maid of honor. We have remained the best of friends for sixteen years. I would love to have her as my maid of honor, and I was recently her maid of honor when she wed in September. However, I have only one sister and I am very close to her as well. I think both would be hurt if I didn't choose one or the other. Who do I pick? I love them both dearly. Help!

Consider yourself lucky. It sounds like you have two sisters: one is by birth and one is by choice. You find yourself in the difficult position of "choosing" between them. Nobody can or should tell you whom to have as your maid of honor. Your selection has to come from your heart. Whichever woman you choose, you must talk openly with the other about your dilemma and the reason for your choice. My hunch is that you will choose your sister by birth, mostly because of tradition and family issues, both of which might be difficult to ignore.

You are fortunate to have two such close friends in your life. If you choose your sister and are having other attendants, you can have your best friend walk down the aisle just before your sister (or the reverse if you choose your friend). Often there are several specific roles held by the maid of honor. You may wish to ask the two of them if they would like to share these responsibilities.

If you do choose both, you may make it easier for yourself and each of the women if you delineate the specific things you would appreciate each of them doing for you. In this way there is no overlap of duties, and there are distinct responsibilities and privileges for each. You can also meet with them and learn what things they would most appreciate doing, and also which things are best suited for them. Their involvement can be based on their interests—as well as your friendship—and you do not have to feel that you are comparing them.

HOW DO YOU FIRE A MAID OF HONOR?

Dear Dr. Dale,

How do you fire a maid of honor? I asked my best friend to stand up for me and she eagerly agreed. Months later, she hasn't done a thing, not even bought her dress. The wedding is now only two months away, and I have talked to her several times, and she says she is going to get it done, but she never follows through. I'm getting desperate, and now we are not even speaking. What do I do? What would be the right way to go about this in a *hurry*?

First, you must take responsibility for sharing what your expectations are and were for this friend as your maid of honor. Make sure you have made it clear what she is supposed to do. If you and she did not talk about what her role was to be when you first started to plan your wedding, then it is not too late for you to clarify and agree on it, and you can move forward together.

If you have made it clear in the past, then you can now ask her to lunch or dinner at a neutral place (try not to do this on the phone) and explain that you are concerned about her apparent lack of interest in being your maid of honor. You can ask her if something happened that prevents her from following through on her responsibilities, thereby giving her a chance to explain to you why she has not acted as she should. Who knows? You may not know all the facts. She may have some difficulties with the idea of her best friend getting married, or she may be going through a trying time in her own life. It is worth going into your meeting with her with an open mind and listening to her responses.

You can then explain that you do not want to have a strained relationship with her, as she has been so important to you. You can tell her that you are disappointed because you had assumed she would have gotten her dress by now and shown more interest in your forthcoming marriage. If she then tells you that she does not want to participate, for whatever reason, then you will have to deal with that response as directly as you can. Remember—you do not have to determine the fate of this relationship at this time. Just deal with her response, and then move on.

PAYING FOR DRESSES

Dear Dr. Dale,

I was married two weeks ago and had seven bridesmaids in my wedding. When we ordered the bridesmaids' dresses, my mother paid the total invoice up front so that the girls wouldn't have to come up with the money right then if they weren't able to. We didn't want an embarrassing situation for anyone. The dresses were two hundred and fifty dollars each, but because we chose to be married in the Bahamas and the bridesmaids were coming, we only asked for one hundred and fifty dollars from each girl, to reduce the cost. I then sent a letter to all the girls letting them know the cost of the dress, provided my mother's address for them to send their checks, and just asked each to send the checks whenever each girl was able to.

Now that the wedding is over, I have only one bridesmaid who hasn't paid. It makes me extremely mad, and at this point I just want to forget it. But on the other hand, out of principle, I feel like she needs to pay, since all the other girls did. I hate that she has put me in this uncomfortable situation! I tried to take the "easy way out" and e-mailed all the girls saying that "we haven't received all the checks, so if you haven't sent a check to my mother, please let me know when you can." That was four weeks ago. Still no check from the one bridesmaid. Please advise me on how to handle this situation politely without sounding like I'm ganging up on her.

Write a separate letter to your friend and tell her that your mom has not yet received the check for the dress and that you wanted to inquire about it. You can say that if there is a problem with sending the entire amount you would be happy to help her with offering a payment plan, perhaps half of the cost now and half two months from now (as an example). Stay away from any reprimands or any feelings that you have of disappointment or anger and "take the high road." Give her a respectful, adult way to handle the situation.

MAID OF DISHONOR

Dear Dr. Dale,

My maid of honor is a cousin with whom I have been close since birth. We are the same age and we have many things in common, but on a recent trip to look for bridesmaid dresses, my cousin seemed disinterested and bothered by the whole "wedding thing." While my other maids were there and having a wonderful time, my cousin rolled her eyes and made sarcastic comments. I love my cousin like a sister, but I'm beginning to feel, as my wedding plans become more intense, that she's jealous. My first reaction is to stop inviting her to any activity that involves wedding plans, but then what would be the point of her being my maid of honor? I don't want to hurt anybody's feelings, but this is my wedding day, and I don't want anyone to ruin it for me.

Your cousin has chosen a particular way of expressing her discomfort that is not only indirect but is also obvious. It is possible that she feels jealous; it is also possible that she has some ambivalence about you getting married. When someone close to us marries we are faced with the unknown. We can't know how "our" relationship will change, and since you've been close to this cousin since birth, her place in your future may now be unclear.

Rather than not invite her to future events, why not invite her to one very special event—a lunch or dinner with you only. Talk with her about her feelings and your wedding. Later, write her a sweet letter about what she means to you, what your relationship means, and express your concerns that she is having difficulty with your marriage. Let her know that if she is feeling uncomfortable with her role in your wedding, you will release her from any obligation—as sad as that would make you. Your desire to not have anyone ruin your wedding day is understandable, and perhaps your reaching out to your cousin can prevent this from happening.

NO CROWDS AT THE ALTAR, PLEASE

Dear Dr. Dale,

I have a big problem. I have two friends, one of whom introduced me to my fiancé. She and another friend insist on being two of my bridesmaids. But that is not possible, because we want a small wedding. We only want three people in the wedding party: my best friend, who is my maid of honor, my sister, and my fiancé's sister. I don't want any more. Please help!

You need to assert yourself to your friends in a loving way about what you and your fiancé want for *your* wedding. Remember, this is your wedding and it should be a reflection of what each and both of you want. If you want a smaller wedding party, then that is what you have.

Go out for a quiet cup of coffee with each of the friends who want to be a part of the wedding party and explain to them what you and your fiancé are planning. Be sure to let your friends know that you understand they were looking forward to being a part of the wedding, you suspect that they will be disappointed, and you understand that. Emphasize, however, that you and your fiancé have discussed and decided on what will be best for the two of you, and you look forward to having these dear friends with you to celebrate your wedding.

Sometimes we try to put the desires of our friends ahead of what is best for us and those who are dear to us. It takes time to realize that we cannot make everyone happy. Being considerate of their feelings is important, but not at the expense of what you and your fiancé want for your wedding.

THE OVEREXTENDED BRIDESMAID

Dear Dr. Dale,

My cousin, whom I chose to be a bridesmaid in my wedding, recently told me that she is moving to Tennessee in two months. I was only told of her decision to move when I was on my way to obtain measurements for her dress, but now she tells me that she is unable to order her dress for at least another two weeks, due to financial restraints associated with the move. I would really prefer that the dresses be ordered as soon as possible, but I don't have any extra money to lend her. What should I do?

There is really nothing you can do at this point other than to understand that your cousin has financial constraints that prevent her from purchasing her dress at this time. You might wish to tell a store manager or designer about the situation, and then see if it might be possible to hold the dress if a small deposit is made. If this is not possible, you need to let it go and accept the situation as it is. Life gets in the way while we are making plans. Your plans to have the bridesmaids take care of their dresses early is noble and speaks to your sense of organization and planning, but sometimes the rest of the world doesn't follow suit.

THE PREOCCUPIED MATRON OF HONOR

Dear Dr. Dale,

I have a very sweet but somewhat preoccupied matron of honor. She is more than willing to help, but we are both mothers of two young children and don't have a lot of free time. I have a total of three attendants for the wedding, and since all three are on the heavy side, I've asked my matron of honor to give me her advice on the choice of the dresses. I really want all the girls to be comfortable and not feel like large Easter eggs rolling down the aisle.

Although we have approximately nine months before the wedding, I am finding it almost impossible to get my matron of honor to come with me to help make these decisions. I have spoken to my fiancé for advice, and he only says, "She's really busy with the children. Pick the dresses yourself and be done with it." But I know it's more complicated than that. With their figure problems, if we cannot find any dresses on the rack we will have to get them made and that takes time—sometimes a lot of time. I want to take charge and be organized about this so all will work out smoothly, but I don't want to make waves with my matron of honor. Am I being too cautious about asking her to get going on this?

No, you are not behaving inappropriately. It seems to us that you are very organized and are being smart about planning ahead and considering contingencies. Your fiancé should be proud that you have taken charge of the process with your bridesmaids, and that you are sensitive both to their needs and their looks.

We have to take your word for it that your friend wants to be there for you, because she does seem to be distracted, even though we are sure she knows how important being a matron of honor is.

But if for personal reasons she just cannot step up to the plate by herself, go to your friend's house and sit with her while her children and your children are either busy or with a babysitter. Share with her that you understand how busy she is, and how little time she has to give you, and that that is the reason you are only asking her for one thing and that you hope she can accommodate you. You need to tell her that you will pick her up at a specific time and bring her with you to the bridal store to look for a dress. If you must, ask your mother or friends to help look after the children. You will need to spell out the dilemma about the time crunch and tell her that if you do not have the dresses selected by a specific date, you will not have the option of having them made. After you explain everything to her, explain further that you know she wants to be a part of the planning for the wedding, but if she cannot do it, you will select the dress for her. If that happens, you might consider going onto the Internet to view some dresses together so you can get an idea of the kind of "look" she would like.

SPENDTHRIFT BRIDESMAID

Dear Dr. Dale,

One of my good and close friends promised to be there for me at my wedding, to help out whenever I needed her, and to be one of my bridesmaids. Now she has changed her mind about being my bridesmaid because she can't afford the costs, since she is currently paying for college herself. She says she still wants to help, but I have some doubts about her story, because every time I call her she is out at the movies or shopping at the mall.

I have to say that it makes me angry that she seems to have money to go out all the time but not to be part of my wedding. Moreover, I am already paying for half of the cost of the bridesmaids' dresses because the dresses were a little expensive. How am I supposed to handle this?

It seems to us that it is clear that your friend has decided what her priorities are, and her decision is that she will not be able to afford what she feels it will take to contribute to the planning of your wedding. You need to honor her decision, which does not mean you have to agree with it or like it. But it is her decision, after all. If she chooses to go to the movies and the mall, those are her choices.

Now, if you want this friend to participate in the wedding in any way, you can structure her involvement for her and tell her exactly what you would like her to do. For example, perhaps there are things she can do that do not cost money but that require time and energy, and are therefore also valuable to you. Alternatively, if all the other women are pitching in for the prewedding festivities and she is not, you may wish to reconsider whether it is fair for her to participate, since there are others who are also on a tight budget.

Whatever you decide, if you care to bring this up with her, do it with respect and appreciation for the fact that she still wants to participate in your wedding.

DO I HAVE TO RETURN THE FAVOR OF BEING A BRIDESMAID?

Dear Dr. Dale,

I have been a bridesmaid in two wedding ceremonies, once in 1996 and the other in 1997. It has now been years since I have spoken to either of the girls who were the brides. Am I committing a faux pas by not asking either of them to be in my upcoming wedding? I have already asked my three sisters and three of my close friends to be brides-maids. What do you think?

If you are not friendly with them anymore, then you are under no obligation to ask them to participate as a member of your wedding party. Relationships change, and in the intervening years it can happen that you have not maintained your closeness. You may still have a special feeling for these women but just have not seen them. Perhaps you may wish to consider why these women who were at one point close enough to ask you to be an attendant at their weddings are no longer in your life. Planning a wedding offers us an opportunity to examine ourselves as well as those we are and have been close to. If you find yourself wishing you could renew these relationships, asking them to be a part of your wedding party is a great way to do so. If not, move on; simply include them as guests and choose your closer friends to take part in your wedding.

SIX

Parents and Relatives

YOU KNOW THE FEELING: Aunt Sally responds with regret—and everyone heaves a sigh of relief. Then Uncle Charlie (you know, the one who drinks too much and always makes a scene) is looking forward to coming. Then there is cousin Betsy, who has not yet recovered from her falling-out with your father and lets you know that if he is there, she won't be. Cousin Mary insists her seven kids (the same seven kids who masterfully sabotaged your birthday party last year) would be absolutely heartbroken if it was an adults-only affair. Meanwhile, your mother is going great guns planning the wedding of *her* dreams—it's just too bad her dreams look nothing like yours!

Can't these people behave? Can't a family be normal?

Well, guess what? It is normal to have all of these characters as part of the family, and the real challenge is not only working alongside your parents to plan a wedding you can all be proud of, but welcoming all of your diverse relatives to the event and still managing to feel comfortable.

There are very few families in which the mere mention of at least one relative's name doesn't lead to eye rolling and name calling. Understand now that you will not be able to resolve all the long-standing family dramas before your wedding day, nor will your wedding be the event that brings everyone together. Animosities, jealousies, and all kinds of previously held feelings may emerge, and you will need to decide—beforehand—how you will handle them if they do. Will you call a good friend and ask her to "babysit" your uncle so he takes it easy on the cocktails? Can you have a heart-to-heart with your favorite cousin before the wedding, imploring him to give his family clown role a rest for the occasion? Will you welcome children with open arms or politely request that Mary leave them home with a sitter? Is your uncle Sal going to stand on a chair and sing Italian love songs as he has for every other family event? And if so, will you manage a good laugh (after you wring your hands in the ladies' room, rather than ring his neck) and just say, well, now my wedding is official in the eyes of the church, the state, and Uncle Sal?

Sometimes with family you need to give a lot. Unless you are willing to have a very small wedding, you run the risk of the relative from hell doing what you fear most. Remember, it is not a reflection on you, so if you can, grin and bear it, and do your best to enjoy the wedding you've been dreaming about.

One of the largest decisions you will make is whether kids will enjoy this day with you. So, what is the deal? Do kids belong at a wedding or not?

Frankly, it is entirely up to you. Kids can enhance the wedding and add a whole different feel to it, or they can take away from a totally elegant and adult aura. What is *your* dream? Do you have in your mind a very elegant, black-tie, candlelit event at the country club with a string quartet playing, a totally sophisticated and mature celebration? Or do you want a sunset clambake at the beach with multiple generations surrounding you, with children and babysitters and parents who both add to the feeling of a family celebration and bring to the party the prospect of watching and dealing with offspring and babysitters and all that they bring?

Obviously, the choices are actually very distinct. Perhaps you are marrying into a family whose culture dictates that everyone in the family and neighborhood (sometimes that could number into the hundreds!) is invited, and they all show up in traditional garb with many, many children in tow. Then your decision is clear. Kids are coming, and you just need to prepare for them. You will choose a wedding site that is appropriate for children—that country club may be out, but a hotel ballroom or local restaurant may be perfect. You will naturally have some music for them, and plan for one or more babysitters to care for them (you can hire those or have the parents bring their own). Even with this choice, you can still plan for the kids to stay through the ceremony and part of the reception and ask that they go to bed early so as not to end up exhausted and cranky at your late-night affair. If, of course, you are planning a daytime wedding, it might be easier to accommodate the children, and you can even hire a separate "babysitter/companion" who will be in charge of amusing the kids.

If, however, you are concerned that a level of decorum may be compromised, and your choice was really that more elegant and adult wedding, plan a wedding without them—and don't feel bad or guilty. Such a decision is often difficult because it can give people with children the feeling that you are rejecting their progeny. So what? This is your wedding, and you are entitled to make any decisions you want concerning children and their place in it.

No matter which road you take—with children or without—it

is important to inform your family and friends so they know, in advance, what your decision is. But try not to feel that you have to explain, rationalize, or excuse it. Do not be defensive about your choice, nor intimidated by people who may disagree with it.

And remember, we guarantee that *everyone* will have an opinion about your decision; many will threaten that they won't come and insist that their opinions prevail. Your own mother may be against any kids at the wedding she is paying for, while your wishes are to invite all your nephews and nieces and even the children in your classroom. Conversely, you may want that elegant black-tie affair without any kids, and your parents or in-laws or other friends and relatives may try to insist that they won't come without their kids. Your answer: So be it.

Above all, be realistic and understand that no family can undergo transformations specifically for your wedding day. What you can and should control is the attention to whatever aspects you fear the most, treating each one carefully and with consideration—as you should the people who are behind or part of these situations. The main event is your wedding, not the excess baggage brought to it by your families or their kids. The questions and answers that follow will help you ensure that this is the case, and that at the end of the day you remember why it is exactly that you love those crazy folks.

MANAGING FAMILY OPINIONS

Dear Dr. Dale,

My fiancé and I are getting married in eleven months. Although we both agree on everything, we're having a slight problem with our families. Each of our parents wants certain things at the wedding, and the problem is that we don't want them. We keep telling each other this will be our day, but we don't want to hurt them, either.

The biggest problem is that my aunt wants to be in the wedding, but I don't want her there. She has been cruel to me for as long as I can remember, and now she wants me to include her in the most important day of my life. She is only nice when she wants something. My father (her brother) suggests that it won't kill me to have her take care of the registry book. The truth is that I don't want anyone doing my book at the ceremony. What should I do?

You are experiencing what many soon-to-be brides and grooms experience. Simply, it is the quandary of standing up to your parents! Your parents have specific desires for the wedding and ceremony, and they are clearly somewhat different than yours. At this point, it is a good idea to sit down with each set of parents and share with them your vision for the wedding. Ask them to listen and try to envision what you describe, without criticism. Then, offer to listen to what their visions are and, if you can and feel it appropriate, consider attempting to integrate that which you can feel comfortable with. Compromise usually plays a major role in planning any wedding.

Regarding your aunt: If you do not want her to be involved as a participant, then you do not have to have her. Your father's comment that her participation will not kill you may be an important door opener for this discussion. Surely her potential involvement would not be the end of the world—but that is not the point. The point is that you have a specific vision for your wedding that includes surrounding yourself with people to whom you feel particularly close and connected. Talk to your father and explain that while you can appreciate his point of view, you are putting your foot down. You can be equally firm—if diplomatic—with your aunt when she broaches the subject. She is not going to be part of your wedding and she will have to accept that and get beyond it.

ADOPTIVE MOM VERSUS REAL MOM

Dear Dr. Dale,

My wedding is in four months and there are many points of confusion. First of all, I am adopted, but I was adopted when I was fifteen, so I am still in regular contact with my birth family. My adopted family is paying for the entire wedding, with no financial help from my birth mother. However, I wish to honor my birth mother at the ceremony. How can I do this without insulting the person who has supported me for the past seven years and who is paying for my wedding?

To make matters worse, I am not getting along with my adopted mother at all; we are barely on speaking terms. My sister literally has to act as a go-between. Because of this conflict, no planning is getting done! We have four months to go and we don't have a caterer, the dress is not paid for, no fittings are scheduled, I have not purchased lingerie, shoes, a veil, or wedding rings. How can I work with my mom before this wedding falls apart?

You and your mother would do well to speak with a professional counselor who has both distance and objectivity. When a bride is about to be married, she often has mixed feelings about whom she wants to honor. It sounds as though you are conflicted about the roles your birth and adopted mothers should have at this wedding.

A wedding is a rite of passage, and you would not be able to take this passage were it not for many people in your life. One of those people, whether your adopted family likes it or not, is your birth mother. If you and your birth mother have been in touch for the past seven years, and your adopted mother is aware of it, then it is not surprising that you would want to have both of your mothers at your wedding. Instead of looking at it as an insult, try to explain to your adopted mother that one could look at this desire to have both of the important mothers in your life as a compliment to each of them (at least a recognition of both of them). The difficulties you are having with your adopted mother are not unlike the very common difficulties many brides-to-be have with their mothers in the wedding planning process.

Now, it could be (as it often is) that these difficulties are not about the wedding planning, but about letting go and beginning a separate life. It is likely that this has made the arguing worse (and that your adopted mom may feel more threatened because of the presence of your birth mother). You may not be able to get them together, but we commend you for your desire and for any previous attempts to help them reconcile. Peacemakers are surely reserved a place in heaven, but appreciation for your effort may not be noted while here on earth.

RUDE AUNT

Dear Dr. Dale,

Our wedding is quickly approaching and our families will be flying in from around the country. One of those coming to the wedding is my aunt, who is going through some rough times and now pretty much hates everyone. She's openly rude and has no guilt about it. She is my mom's sister, and the two of them haven't spoken in years.

I feel conflicted about this situation because, despite her rifts with the rest of the family, this aunt babysits for me and has become close to my son. But despite my sense of loyalty, I'm afraid she'll cause a scene. She has already told me that there are some guests who should be eliminated, and others whose lifestyles she finds repugnant. She has threatened to leave the wedding (with my uncle) if these guests are there. I have cried and begged with this aunt to simply be there for me on my day, but she won't budge. I don't know what to do, or how to prepare my fiancé and his family.

Ah, family! For some reason your aunt feels she has the right to offer her unfettered opinion to anyone about anything. We suggest that instead of crying and begging your aunt to behave appropriately, tell her straight up that she does not have the right to do or say anything at your wedding. You can tell her this kindly but firmly, and remind her of how much your wedding day means to you. Your wedding day is not a place for the airing of personal grievances; nor is it the time and place for her to pass judgment on your friends and family and their lifestyles. If your aunt can agree, great. If she can't, tell her you will miss having her at your special day and withdraw the invitation.

HONORING A SPECIAL AUNT

Dear Dr. Dale,

My mother passed away recently, and now my aunt—my mother's only sibling, her twin, actually—will be helping me plan my wedding. The amazing thing is that my aunt is my mother's identical twin—and I mean in every way—so that it is almost like having my mother around again. They looked exactly alike, but they also talk alike, act alike, walk alike, and have the same wonderful personalities. So you can understand why it is especially important for me to have my aunt with me, and to have her feel as special as my mother would have.

Would it be proper to have her sit with my father during the ceremony and reception? I want to acknowledge her, but I also don't want to offend my other aunts, with whom I am not especially close. And for some people, it may look kind of strange to see my mother's identical twin by my dad's side. I really don't care about that—I just want my aunt to be happy.

It is fine to honor your aunt in this way, and if you feel you would like to have her support "up close and personal," then by all means do that. There is no one who can or should replace your mother, and you, and others, will surely be conscious of her absence. Instead, even with the special circumstances of your mom and aunt being identical twins, your aunt's participation in the wedding will be a wonderful way to help you to honor your mom. Of course, you should talk this over with your dad to see if he has any objections—he is perhaps the one person whose needs you should consider as strongly as your own.

As for your other aunts, out of consideration to them, and given that they surely know how close your mother and aunt were (not only in genetics!), you can write them a letter explaining your decision. They will surely understand, and your aunt (and your father) will be touched and moved by your plans.

DAD'S GIRLFRIEND DOESN'T LIKE ME

Dear Dr. Dale,

I am getting married next spring. My mother passed away five years ago, and within a month of her death, my father met a recently widowed woman and they moved in together. I do not like this woman at all—she has been quite mean to me, sending me nasty letters for no reason. It's quite upsetting to me, especially because I tried so hard to get to know her and like her when they first met. She never lets my father visit me and doesn't invite us to their home. The last thing I want is to have her at our wedding (which will be quite small—fifty people) but I know she won't let my father attend without her.

I know I have to invite her—how do I deal with her once the big day arrives? At a recent family funeral, I dealt with the situation by ignoring her—probably not the best route, but it worked at the time.

This is a particularly sensitive and difficult situation. Your wedding is likely a time (both in the planning and in the actual celebration) when you will feel the loss of your mother quite intensely. Having your father's friend around, whom you do not care for, may also contribute to making that loss feel even greater than it is. However, ignoring your father's friend will be difficult since your father is sure to play an important role in the wedding ceremony and reception. And, with only fifty people present, it will be difficult to avoid her.

You may wish to write to your father and this woman explaining how you envision your wedding and that you hope you can count on their being present to wish you and your fiancé great joy. You can also frankly bring up the fact that you realize the relationship between you and this woman has been less than stellar, and that you hope in the months between now and the wedding you will be able to find a way to have a truce or, better yet, a healing and defining of a new and better relationship. You will need to appeal to your father on this front, as it is his responsibility as well to help heal the rift. If this doesn't work, do what you can to put her from your mind on your special day—be pleasant and cordial when you see her but focus your attentions on your fiancé and all your other loved ones who are present.

FATHER AND SON RIFT

Dear Dr. Dale,

My boyfriend (fiancé) and I are only nineteen, but we have been dating for two years and are really in love. We realize that we are young, so even though we are newly engaged we are waiting two years before getting married. He is very close to my family and I was once close to his. But his father isn't a trusting man, and when we went on a weeklong vacation to my grandparents' house, my boyfriend told his father that he was going away with friends. Unfortunately, his father found out and now says that if my fiancé doesn't break up with me forever he will be kicked out. My boyfriend does have a job, but he hasn't saved up the money to be on his own quite yet. Furthermore, his father now says that if we were to get married, he will not support it or come to the wedding. I don't want to be the cause of a father and son losing a relationship, but I don't want to lose my relationship either. What should I do?

Clearly there was already a troublesome relationship between your future husband and his father, since your fiancé thought it necessary to lie about going to your grandparents' for the week. Why couldn't he tell him the truth? Clearly your fiancé's father is struggling with the fact that his son is serious with you (or it could be the fact that he is serious with anyone, since you are both young). Whatever the reason, however, your fiancé needs to take a stand, assert himself as an adult, and decide what is best for himself, you, and your burgeoning relationship and marriage. His having a job is excellent. When you begin a marriage it is important to begin on the right foot, and having money saved to be able to support yourself is a good first step. As to his father coming to your wedding—that appears to be a couple of years away, and a lot of healing can occur during that time. Reach out to his father in conversation or through counseling, and make the effort to let him see not only how much you love each other, but how responsible you intend to be about the road ahead.

HISSING COUSINS

Dear Dr. Dale,

Lately my mother has been constantly expressing her disapproval of my choice to invite her second cousin (my aunt) to my wedding. Unfortunately, I have already invited this aunt and she has eagerly accepted. My mother was the one who initiated our family's relationship with her, but she now complains that this cousin was always jealous of her and only wants a free meal. My fiancé and I are paying for the entire cost of the wedding, and to this end, I realize I can invite whomever I choose, yet I want my mother to feel comfortable. She's constantly nagging me about this, and now we're not talking.

I don't know what to do: Should I not say anything to my aunt and let her come, or should I explain the situation to her and see if she'll back out?

In this touchy situation, you need to remind your mother that the family connection was something that she initially promoted, and that she knew your aunt would be invited, and it is too late to rescind the invitation. Talk with your mother about your desire to honor her wishes, and explain to her that while you understand her level of discomfort you hope she will be able to allow your aunt to enjoy herself at the wedding and limit her own interaction with her, save for being polite and gracious.

MOM THREATENS TO BOYCOTT MY WEDDING

Dear Dr. Dale,

My fiancé and I are currently living in the same area as my parents, but we have both lived for years in a city in another state where we met and where all our friends still live. We have been planning to have our wedding in our original "hometown," especially since we are planning to move back there, but my mom is furious and feels that the wedding should be held in the original hometown of the bride and her family. I've explained that I don't consider this place to be my home, and now she is threatening to boycott the wedding. She thinks that I should ask all my friends to fly up here and spend money for hotel rooms, and I refuse. I'm not going to ask my friends to do that just so she can invite all of *her* friends to the wedding. It's my wedding and, besides, my fiancé and I are paying for it. I don't think I'm wrong, but I would like to make peace with my mom and have her at the wedding. How can I do that?

Whether we like it or not, most weddings are not only for the bride and groom. Parents, who also have waited for and dreamt of this time, have their wishes too. One of these wishes is to have their friends and family with them—the people who have been important to them while they raised you, the people who have given them support and who have known them as they matured through their lives.

It is difficult to ask your mother to give up her wish just as it would be difficult for you to give up yours. At the same time, you question the reasonableness of expecting your friends to travel at great expense and some distance to join you on your wedding day. Some brides and grooms in your situation decide to split the celebrations and have a large party in the "other" city, before or after the wedding, for those who will not be able to attend. Although it would be wonderful for your mother to say, "Yes, honey, that will be fine. Get married wherever you like and I will help you and be there," she is probably waiting to hear something similar from you. "Yes, mom, I am looking forward to getting married at the club where we grew up and which all of your friends call home." Reminding your mother that you do not feel that her "hometown" is your home isn't going to advance your position. It is possible that your mother is struggling with feelings about your growing up and moving away to start your own family, and her lobbying to have the wedding at her home is a way for her to give you a "proper" send-off.

You need to decide which is more important for you: to have your friends at your wedding, or to have your mother at your wedding. If your mother is serious about her threat, then you may well be getting married without her. Try to reach a compromise like the one suggested above. Be sure you express your empathy for your mother and tell her you can understand how difficult it will be for her to see you get married without her friends with her in a familiar surrounding. Think about the idea, and if you are comfortable with it, suggest that you have a celebration party in her hometown for her friends before or after the ceremony that you will have in your city with your friends. Because of situations similar to yours, many couples are celebrating their unions in more than one place, with an engagement party in one place, the wedding ceremony and party in another place, and a reception in another place, so family and friends from different geographical areas can celebrate with the couple. It is not easy, but it can help smooth ruffled feathers.

MY ESTRANGED MOM MAY NOT COME

Dear Dr. Dale,

I'm thirty-three years old, and I'm getting married for the first time to a wonderful man. That's the good news. Unfortunately, my mother and I have a very strained relationship and, in fact, we haven't spoken for more than two years. I am inviting her to our wedding, but I'm not sure she'll attend. Should she choose to avoid my wedding, can you offer any advice on how I might take my mind off this uncomfortable situation on my big day? What should I say about her absence to my guests? How do I prepare for this emotional disappointment?

As important a life passage as your wedding is, it may not be the event that allows you and your mother to heal what has transpired between the two of you. You will no doubt feel her absence if she chooses not to attend your wedding, and nothing will change that. However, you can help yourself through that difficulty by making sure that you have people around you who demonstrably care for you and are able to participate in the ceremony in a way that makes you feel supported and loved.

When your guests ask where your mother is, simply say, "She wasn't able to come." You don't have to explain her absence any further unless you choose to do so. If you feel you might get through your wedding day more easily by opening up to your guests, you might say something like "As you know, Mom and I have a difficult relationship and she was not able to bring herself to attend. It is unfortunate and I am deeply sorry that she is not here." It is possible, still, that you and your mother may be able to heal what is troubling your relationship, but in its own time. Right now, that timeframe doesn't seem to be consistent with your wedding date, and you should not try to rush it.

And, always, when there is something troubling you, focus on the good of that day, let your heart fill with the love from those around you, especially your fiancé, and that in itself will shoo away the pain.

HOW CAN I HONOR MY MOTHER IF WE'RE NOT CLOSE?

Dear Dr. Dale,

I am getting married in June and am having trouble incorporating my mother into the event. I grew up with my grandparents on my father's side and am very close to them and want to honor them. My grandfather is walking me down the aisle, and I want Grandma and the mother of the groom to light the unity candles. Do you have any suggestions on how to include my mother?

How about giving your mother something special to read during the ceremony, such as a particular prayer or poem that means something significant to you? It is also not out of the question to have your mother participate in the lighting of the unity candle. Nowhere is it written that there can only be one or two or three people who participate in that ceremony, although you may wish to leave that task to the relatives you've already chosen.

You might also consider asking your mom what her preference

would be as far as her participation. You may not wish to do this because you want to choose (or limit) her involvement. If, however, you are open to exploring other possibilities with her, you might ask her either what she would like to do or give her a choice of two or three options and let her choose.

MY SISTER'S SECRET IS COMPLICATING PLANS

Dear Dr. Dale,

I am getting married, and I asked my only sister to be maid of honor (I was her maid of honor for her wedding). She initially said yes, but then called me a few weeks later to tell me that she did not have the money to afford the dress. I offered to buy it for her, but she still would not accept. She said that if she couldn't afford it herself she wouldn't be in the wedding, and that she didn't want anyone else to know of her financial problems. I told her that people would ask questions because I had already told people she was going to participate. I know I shouldn't worry about what other people think, but it really has hurt me to think there will be gossip on the day of my wedding with people—including my parents and other siblings—assuming that I didn't want to include my only sister. I feel like I need to advertise that I did ask her—even though she doesn't want me to let others know her financial problems.

We have since agreed that my sister will be the personal attendant, but it is not the role I intended or wanted for her.

We have to wonder why your sister's pride stands in the way of her allowing you to buy her a maid-of-honor dress (or loan her the money so that she can repay you whenever she has the funds) in order for her to be next to you at your wedding. Try to offer this again, couched in the reason that you cannot imagine getting married without her present as your maid of honor. If she cannot bring herself to do this, then you have two choices. You can agree to go along with whatever story she wants you to tell, or simply say that she chose to be your attendant and keep it at that. You do not have to take responsibility for her hiding the truth, but at the same time, it is not your prerogative to share her personal situation with anyone without her permission. Be discreet and she will respect you and appreciate your help through a difficult time. Ultimately, which relationship is more important—the one you have with people who will gossip about your sister not standing next to you, or the one between you and your sister? Likely it will be your sister's bond.

PROBLEM DAD

Dear Dr. Dale,

I am getting married in four months, and everything is going wonderfully—with one exception: my father. We have never been close. In fact, when I was a child he was very abusive. I have been able to put the past behind me and let it go, but I will never forget the pain that was inflicted upon me by him. My mother died ten years ago, and my grandmother, who was an angel and saved my life, also recently passed away.

My problem is: Do I invite my father? I have tried over the years to form a relationship with him. I reach out and he never reaches back. So I decided to leave him completely out of my wedding and have my brother walk me down the aisle, or to just walk down on my own. This has caused endless sleepless nights. The reason is that my brothers and sister accept my father for who he is and don't care that he has never done anything for us. If I don't invite him or include him in my wedding, they will not come.

What do I do? Do I have to invite my father to the wedding even though the only thing he ever did for me was cause me endless pain and humiliation? I want my family there, but I also want a peaceful, beautiful wedding. How should I handle this?

Just because your siblings have accepted your father for who he is and have no expectations of him in the relationship department does not mean that you must follow suit. You imply that you came to terms with your past and your father's place in it. At some point you obviously decided that enough was enough. And it is unfortunate that now your brothers and sister have forced another confrontation with your dad, and surrounding your wedding, no less. Still, you are the only one who can decide what is best for you.

Sit down with your siblings and tell them that you are not ready to have your father at your wedding because it will be too hurtful. Also explain to them that you feel they are punishing you for asserting your right to make an independent decision that you feel is right and healthy for you, regardless of their decisions about how they have reconciled their relationships. Ask them to make an effort to see your side, explaining that it appears they are taking sides with your father, thus rejecting you. They are not you. Their choice is not yours. Adult siblings have a luxury that children who are siblings do not have: They can make their own decisions, as adults, without fear of their parents' reprisals or punishments. They can stand on their own feet and do what is right for them and their relationships—unless, of course, they are still fearful of their parents, in which case, although they may look like adults, they act like the intimidated and frightened children they once were and may still be. Hopefully your siblings will take a hard look at their own motivations and weigh what is really important.

You deserve to be comfortable at your wedding, and if having your father at your wedding is so uncomfortable for you at this time, then your decision is obvious. If your siblings decide not to attend, that is the result of a difficult choice. Only you can decide which is the lesser of the two evils, and which is the higher price to pay: having your dad present or your siblings absent?

SCHEMING SISTERS

Dear Dr. Dale,

I'm a forty-year-old single mother about to be wed, and my fiancé is a thirty-one-year-old single father. My problem is with his sisters who, every time there's a family party, event, or gathering, want to have it at his ex's house. My fiancé has told his sisters that he feels this is insensitive and disrespectful to me, and he has frequently objected to their efforts. But it is clear that they have an agenda about his ex, and truth be told, I'm reluctant to even invite them to the wedding. What should I do?

First the good news: You have a fiancé who is willing to stand up to his sisters. Now the bad news: These sisters are not willing to listen to their brother and respect his wishes and desires. You say that the conflict has not interfered with your relationship, and yet you are considering not inviting them to the wedding—so, in fact, it already has interfered. Of course you are not wrong to feel the way you do about having these women at your wedding but it is unlikely that you will be able to have your wedding without them if your fiancé wants them there. That said, there are things that you can do outside of the actual wedding to work on changing the relationship between you.

These women seem to be oblivious to the fact that their brother has fallen in love with another woman, has moved on with his life, and is making plans to marry. Whether they are in denial or are just being hopeful that they can manipulate him into resurrecting his former relationship, we can't say. And if they want to continue their friendship with her, that is up to them. However, you and your fiancé can make it clear that if they want to have family gatherings that include their brother and his family, they will need to alter their behavior. Whether they do so or not, you and your fiancé can begin to plan your own family gatherings and you can invite his sisters to participate if you like. If, however, they spurn you or treat you badly, mention to them that although you know they would have preferred that their brother remarry his ex, that you are the woman in his life and that you would appreciate the opportunity to build a relationship with them that is based on respect and consideration. If they are not willing to participate, you can keep your contact with them to a minimum.

RELATIVES OF FRIENDS

Dear Dr. Dale,

I have a friend whom I've known for twenty years. She is my best friend. We met in grade school and she moved across the country when we were only ten years old, but we managed to keep in touch and ended up going to college only two hours from each other, and we visited often. Though we live on opposite coasts and rarely see each other, we are very close and talk often.

This best friend has a sister a year older than us. I've always considered her merely my best friend's sister, and we never really developed a friendship separately. However, we were friendly; we even celebrated occasions together, such as birthdays, my best friend's wedding (she made me one of her bridesmaids), her child's baptism, and so forth. But we aren't very close as far as sharing secrets, dreams, fears, etc., and we don't really talk or see each other unless her sister is around.

When I first began dating my fiancé, my friend's sister, her husband, and infant daughter came to stay with me for a week while they planned for their move to the area. My then boyfriend and I were more than happy to help them, but she was not very nice or welcoming to him, and even told me he didn't need to be around. I was very hurt by her comments and felt she was ungrateful for all that we did for her while she was here. Since then, my fiancé proposed and we are now engaged to be married. Now, suddenly, my best friend's sister has been calling and e-mailing. I hear from mutual friends that she wants to be invited to the wedding. I don't want her at our wedding, and my fiancé does not care for her presence either. But I am afraid I will disappoint my best friend if her sister is not there. My best friend is aware that I was not pleased with her sister's behavior during that visit, but we haven't had to really deal with my dislike for her sister because there was no reason to broach the subject. Now, with these important events coming up, I don't want to invite her sister to the parties, showers, or wedding, but I know that it will not end there. There will have to be explanations and confrontations. Can you help?

Honesty is called for here. You are under no obligation to invite your friend's sister, but since you are close to your friend, you may feel more comfortable confronting the situation honestly and with compassion before things move too much farther ahead. Call or make a time to meet your friend's sister if you can, and explain the feelings that you have harbored since her visit. Tell her that you were unhappy about the way the last visit transpired and that you felt hurt by her dismissal of your boyfriend, now your fiancé. Explain that you are uncomfortable with the idea of her participating in the festivities because the previous interactions were never directly addressed (you can take some responsibility here), and that you want to celebrate with people who you know wish you well and have your best interests at heart. Listen to what she has to say and be open to hearing her perspective.

These kinds of talks can be helpful in not only clearing the air, but in moving you to the next level in a relationship. You do not have to invite this woman, but you may find that talking things out and sharing how you feel will help you to make up your mind, let go of an old hurt, and decide you want to give friendship another try. However, if you feel strongly that you do not want her at your wedding, nor does your fiancé, the most important thing is to honor *those* feelings. And if your friend is as close to you as you say, she should understand.

FEUDING SIBLINGS

Dear Dr. Dale,

I have three brothers who really don't get along. My oldest brother has done things to the family that were not very nice (he stole money from my dad, he is abusive in his language—and those are the only two things that are printable!), and my other brothers are not as forgiving as my mother and I. My mother and I both want my oldest brother to be at my upcoming wedding, but I am nervous on account of the tension that will exist. The two younger brothers say they won't attend if my oldest brother is there (he also is cruel and taunts my other brothers every chance he gets). They are terrified that something will go wrong or that my oldest brother will embarrass me in front of my fiancé and my wedding guests. That said, he is family, and I just can't get my head around excluding him. Can you give me some much needed advice?

Sibling rivalries show up at the times we least want or need to deal with them. It is admirable that even though your oldest brother has problems, you still see him as part of your family and want him to share your day, but it is understandable that your other brothers are protective of you, given your oldest brother's history. Speak to each of your brothers separately, and tell them that, no matter what the issue, the thought of not having them at your wedding is one you can't entertain. Tell them you hope they will put their differences aside to support you and behave like the gentlemen you know them to be. Ask each to decide if they can do this; if they cannot, you may have to exclude one or all from your wedding.

As far as your wedding guests go: You do not owe them an explanation, should one or both of your younger brothers opt not to attend. But you might want to let your closest friends and family know that your brothers don't always get along and you are concerned about their behavior, so they can be on guard and deflect any tensions that flare. Enlist their help to make sure your wedding day goes off as smoothly as possible.

MY SISTER WON'T LET HER
DAUGHTER PARTICIPATE

Dear Dr. Dale,

I'm having a problem with my oldest sister. She has a daughter who is twenty months old and an absolute doll. She is a wonderful niece and I love her very much. It would mean a lot to me if she could be a part of my wedding, but her mom apparently has a problem with it. I say apparently because she absolutely refuses to talk about it, either with our mother or me. She keeps saying that she has to talk to her husband about the idea, but I think nine months is plenty of time to have had such a conversation. I don't know what to do. I would bring it up more directly with her, but the only time I see my sister is when I babysit or she brings my niece over to visit, and I don't want to fight in front of the baby.

If I had to guess what her objection is, it might be: 1) that my niece is too young (she will be two and a half at the time of the wedding); or 2) that we have different religious beliefs. The first isn't really a problem, because I was planning on having two other flower girls, so that if my niece is having a bad day and doesn't want to do it, she wouldn't have to. But it is the second point that is more likely the source of her anxiety. However, our wedding ceremony itself is not going to have any specific religious affiliations so as not to offend anyone's sensibilities. What can I do to untangle this mess of conflicting views and enable my niece to be a part of this special day?

It is not unreasonable to want your niece to be a part of your wedding party, but you do need to respect your sister's discomfort with both the prospect of her participation and the discussion. Rather than fight, write her a letter and calmly spell out what you suspect are the two issues that concern her, along with your responses. You can tell her exactly what you plan to do regarding the ceremony if, as you surmise, she may be uncomfortable with the religion aspect. Let her know that you will honor her decision but that you would appreciate knowing her reasoning if she insists on keeping her child from participating. Keep in mind, however, that your sister does not *owe* you any explanation, so let her know that you understand this but that it would be helpful for you to know just the same. You need to proceed with your plans, and it does not seem as if a discussion in person is likely to happen, so pen and paper is the best resort.

BROTHER IS UNRELIABLE

Dear Dr. Dale,

I am in the process of planning my wedding. My father passed away several years ago, and when that happened, my brother told me that if I ever got married, he wanted to be the one to give me away. He is very set on doing it, and in theory it is a great idea—I love my brother and want him to have some special role. The problem is that recently he has shown signs of becoming an alcoholic, and I'm worried about him being dependable and accountable. It pains me to say it, but I have no idea about the condition he'll be in on the day of the wedding, and I don't want the ceremony to be disrupted if he should fail to show up.

I have thought of using my grandfather as a backup, but with the wedding already costing so much I hate to rent a tuxedo if it won't be needed. What do you suggest? I love my brother and don't want to take this away from him, but I'm afraid of what might happen.

You cannot be certain about anyone's last-minute behavior at a wedding, especially someone who may have an alcohol problem. Invest in a caring conversation with your brother and explain your concern. Tell him you, too, are looking forward to him escorting you down the aisle, and how much it means to you to have him participate in this most honored role. Tell him you want to be able to count on him and you have reason to be concerned about his recent behavior. Mention your concern about his drinking and how much it means to you that he get this under control before it gets out of control. Ask him if there is any way you or any other family member can be helpful to ensure his ability to be in good shape at the wedding. Our advice is that you institute a backup plan for the worst, but do everything you can to insist on the best. As to your plan for a backup: Go ahead and rent a tuxedo for your grandfather, and consider it wise insurance.

ADULTS-ONLY AFFAIR

Dear Dr. Dale,

My fiancé and I will be getting married on New Year's Eve, and both the wedding and the reception will be very late affairs. As a result, the only children we want in attendance are the two who will play a role in the ceremony. We also feel that, given the late time of the festivities, it simply won't be a good place for kids. Tell me, can we write something on the invitation that politely states that only adults are invited? We both have a lot of younger cousins, nieces, and nephews. Is it improper or in bad taste to do something such as this?

It is neither improper nor in bad taste to delineate the type of wedding and guests you desire, since you have the right to invite whoever you want to your wedding and reception. If you want an adults-only wedding, you can and deserve to have it. You may wish to place an insert into the invitation in which you state that you look forward to having your friends and relatives with you at your wedding, and that you have decided that, given the time of the wedding as well as the time of year, you would prefer that it be an adults-only affair. At the bottom of the invitation (underneath where you have printed "festive dress" or "black tie") you can also have printed "adult reception" or "reception for adults" in either the lower left or lower right corner. Such an insertion should prevent any confusion and make your preference clear.

PROBLEM CHILD

Dear Dr. Dale,

My fiancé's brother's five-year-old son is going to be our ring bearer. Both his brother and sister-in-law, who are also part of the wedding party, think their son can handle this responsibility. But I see him in a different light, and my fiancé has expressed concern about his disrupting the ceremony. Any ideas?

Having a child walk down the aisle can be adorable but also nerve-racking. Designate someone (not a member of the wedding party) to be in charge of your nephew. You might want to select a good friend of the family who has a comfortable relationship with the boy. This person can take him to the bathroom before the ceremony, and make sure his shirt is tucked in, his shoes clean, and his body and mind ready to perform this responsibility. Ideally, this friend will keep your mind off your nephew, and keep the nephew from running wild—and roughshod—over your wedding. Remember—it is not your responsibility to worry about this on your wedding day. By simply delegating responsibility, you can put your own mind at ease.

DISAPPROVING SONS

Dear Dr. Dale,

I am getting married for the second time, and it will be an interracial union. My sons, who are twenty and twenty-four, are very much opposed to this wedding, even though I have been with my partner for ten years. In fact, their opposition has a history: Five years ago we were going to be married, but my sons' opposition led me to cancel the ceremony. I very much want my sons to be a part of this special day. What can I do?

You have already shown extraordinary and admirable sensitivity toward your sons by postponing your marriage once before, but you may be erring honorably, in that your sons are unlikely to alter their feelings any time soon. There is no reason to wait to begin this union with this man, whom you clearly love and with whom you've shared your life for ten years.

You mention race as a reason for intolerance from your sons, but we wonder if there is something more involved. Try talking to your sons to reach an agreement. If it happens that racism is the root of their resistance, then there is nothing more for you to do than to go ahead with your marriage, live a loving and open and tolerant life with your husband, and continue to invite your sons to be a part of this happiness. Set an example of tolerance that they will hopefully learn from. If something else is bothering them, you will need to weigh these other issues accordingly. But either way, it's your life, and since your sons are now adults, you are perfectly entitled to make decisions independently from each other.

SISTER STRUGGLES

Dear Dr. Dale,

My fiancé and I have spent two years planning our wedding, and will tie the knot in less than two months. My fiancé and my maid of honor have both been terrific. It is my sisters who are driving me crazy. One decided to drop out of the wedding, giving some lame excuse about needing to go on a business trip *on a Saturday!* (She has never worked on a weekend before.) When I questioned her, she changed her story and said she needed oral surgery *on the day of the wedding,* which is two months away. My other sister consistently complains (about the dress, the shoes, the other people in the wedding party). This really makes me sad, as I had hoped this would be the happiest time of my life and sharing it with my sisters means a lot to me. Help!

Usually, when people behave like this, they are telling you that they are not happy with some aspect of your relationship. And in this case, your sisters' dissatisfaction is coming out in their behavior relating to the wedding. You may have hoped that this would be a joyous occasion for all of you, but the reality seems to be that they are having a very hard time with the fact that you are getting married.

Sometimes, sisters feel threatened by another sister's marriage. They wonder how their relationship will change; they may not like their future brother-in-law; they may feel jealous because of the attention directed toward you during the two years that you have been planning your wedding; or they may feel envious that you are making choices that are different from the ones they would make and they may resent that you did not ask for their guidance or approval. Sometimes, sisters feel that their roles (as they define them) are not being respected. In your case, the sister who is complaining may wonder why you chose a friend instead of a sister to be your maid of honor. There can be any number of reasons and issues, some of which you may be able to deal with, and others that have been there for your lifetime and are just now coming to the fore.

Instead of simply hoping that things will improve, why not sit down separately with each of your sisters and quietly, respectfully begin a conversation about how you feel (sad, disappointed, concerned). Tell each of them that you sense something is quite wrong and that you want to know what it is and are there to listen. Don't be afraid to tell them that you wonder why they seem unable to participate and be happy for you. Tell them that you would like to begin to relate to them differently, with the goal of improving your relationship. And then listen to what they have to say. No matter what their reactions, do your best to uphold your end of the bargain and be as considerate of their feelings as you can be. You can't control how they behave, but you can help to create an atmosphere where good feelings and positive interactions can flourish.

SEVEN

Divorced Parents

No matter how you say it, "divorce" is a difficult word, and when it turns up during your wedding it's even worse. All the complicated feelings and histories that go along with it now threaten to contaminate one of the most wonderful moments in your life. No matter when your parents were divorced—recently or long ago—once or multiple times—chances are it is still painful for everyone. And the reality you must face is this: The pain will surface with a vengeance during the wedding planning process.

When divorced parents are part of the wedding, complex questions will come up. The answers are not simple because the situations are not simple. The first and most important question that will come up will be: Are your parents willing (and able) to put their differences aside? Can they leave behind their baggage and traumas from the past?

The issues surrounding parental divorce are often so stressful that for many brides concern about their parents can supersede concern about themselves and their wedding. So, if you feel resentful that you have to deal with all of this, you're entitled, because here you are, about to embark on the most important journey of your life, and the two people who hopefully love and support you the most are posing one of the biggest challenges. Not to mention all the other family dynamics sparked by the divorce: Your sister (your maid of honor to boot) has yet to forgive your mother for having an affair; your brother still sides with your father every time you want to talk about a family issue; your dad lost his fortune and then made it back *after* he and your mother split and now is living a life of luxury while she struggles to make ends meet. It's a lot to deal with!

Never fear—you are not alone. In fact, this is the reality for *millions of brides and grooms*. And even given that everyone's divorce is unique and that the "fallout" (or aftermath) for every family and every bride is different, there are no simple solutions. And it's not just worrying about how Mom and Dad feel—it's about how *you* feel as well. Your own feelings will depend on the circumstances, on how much time has passed, and on things like:

- Have your divorced parents built new social lives for themselves?

- Are they dating?

- Are they friendly?

- Have they remarried?

- Do you like their new significant others?

- How do your parents feel about each other's choices?

- What are your parents' relationships with you regarding the divorce?

- Is either parent envious of the kind of relationship you have with the other?

- Are your parents people with egos that need to be considered every step of the way?

- And, most important: Do your parents understand and respect your feelings about their divorce and about your plans for your upcoming wedding?

Start your wedding planning process by carefully answering each of these questions candidly. Now, take a deep breath. You can deal with this. The most important thing is to *keep your eye on your goal*, which is to make the event and the time leading up to it as *stress-free* as possible. Write to or talk with your parents, alone or together, or both. *And not once or twice.* This is a process, and it starts immediately. Be mindful of informing and including each of your parents in what is going on as soon as you make the decision to marry. Share decisions with them, and float your ideas and concerns, especially if they are paying for any part of the wedding process. This is particularly true if it is your own parents rather than your fiancé's who are divorced, because every decision can be fraught with competitive and hostile feelings that have nothing to do with you.

You need to think of what your goal is. At a minimum, that goal is to feel calm and secure in the knowledge that your parents will help you plan and attend your wedding, celebrate with you, put aside their differences, and focus on your joy.

Even if you have a fantasy that your parents, who have not uttered a kind word about or seen one another since your high school graduation, will somehow greet one another warmly and dance a waltz, you must face reality and accept that this is highly unlikely. Once you know that, and acknowledge the loss of a part of your wedding that you may have longed for, you'll be better able to accept what *is* possible. What *are* these two people able to do, and what aren't they able to do?

Whether they're willing or able to sit in the same room and discuss wedding plans in a civil manner is *not* a reflection on their love or devotion or support for you. It's a reflection on them. Once you realize your divorced parents' attitudes toward your plans and decisions are more about how they deal with each other rather than how they feel about you, you'll begin to separate from them in a healthier way. You will be better able to understand which behaviors and attitudes are possible instead of those that aren't.

For example, even though you would like a "family photo" with your dad's girlfriend *and* your mother, it may just be too difficult for your mom to stand that close, let alone smile for the camera, next to the woman for whom your dad left her. So, even though it's not your dream, you may need to settle for one with your dad and his girlfriend and one with your mom.

If your goal is to involve them both in the planning of the wedding, and they have a hard time communicating, you'll likely be in the middle delivering messages back and forth. Discuss with each of them how *you* would like to proceed, given what you observe are the challenges in their relationship, and propose a plan: "Dad, I know it is tough for you to talk with Mom about the nitty-gritty decisions, so I propose you be involved in _____ and _____ and she will do _____ and _____."

If your goal is to "get through" the ceremony and reception without "a scene," then have an honest, heart-to-heart with all of them and express your concerns, if you have them, that they will not be able to "keep it together." Ask if they can try to hold on, as a gift to you, and assure them that you will do whatever you can to help.

A good way to help ensure there will be an easier flow between your divorced parents is to be sure everyone knows the plan. You don't want either your mom or dad to be surprised, caught off guard, or embarrassed.

Consider one bride-to-be whose father gave her a certain amount of money to spend and said, "Do whatever you want; just don't go over budget." He was furious when he discovered that unbeknownst to him his ex-wife had "chipped in" a difference of several thousand dollars. The bride had not been aware that the majority of the problems between her parents, who had divorced when she was six years old, had been about money. Now, conflicts more than a decade old were suddenly playing out again in the arena of her wedding, and she was caught in the middle.

Being in the middle is certainly not the most comfortable place to be. Most children of divorced parents have been there before and don't want to be there again. But if your parents' relationship is still full of anger and unresolved issues, you may find yourself back in that all too familiar and uncomfortable territory. The challenge is to *not* become a little girl again. The same goes for your fiancé if his family is the one creating conflict. These issues can seem insurmountable, but it is possible to pull off your wedding unscathed if you remember to *keep your focus on the goal* (or *your eyes on the prize*). That is your main job.

Pay attention to the potential minefields and talk about ways to avoid them. If you are frank and open with your parents, you can achieve your goal: to be that relaxed, calm, and happy bride with both of her parents at her side sharing in her joy. You are certainly entitled to tell them what you need from them to make this happen. But you should also ask them what they need from you—within reason—so they can make this happen.

And finally, keep reminding yourself that this is *your* wedding, and at the end of every day, *it is your happiness that is most important.* If your parents can also keep this in mind, issues will be resolvable. If not, continue emphasizing in your own heart that you come first, that you have done your best, and that your wedding will go on with your wishes first and foremost.

THE DIVORCE SNAG

Dear Dr. Dale,

I just got engaged, and I've started thinking about the kind of wedding I'd like to have. However, there is a bit of a snag: My parents were divorced three years ago, after thirty-six years of marriage, and there has been a great deal of animosity involved—there was another woman, and my father walked out, leaving my mother to fend for herself and to assume many of his debts. My fiancé feels strongly that my father should be involved, no matter what he has done, because he is still my father. I feel the same way, although having him and his new, young wife at the wedding will upset my mother and my siblings terribly, and I don't want my day—or theirs—to be ruined.

To make matters even more odd, my father's new wife doesn't like us to be in contact with him, so there is still more tension to deal with. I am feeling that my father doesn't deserve to walk me down the aisle. How do I deal with this mess?

Unfortunately, your "bit of a snag" is more and more common these days, and you are trying—honorably—to be respectful of both your parents. You should understand that it will not be easy for either you or your parents, or for many others attending, and try to maintain realistic expectations of what you will be able to accomplish. The damage done by the divorce is not likely to be repaired by your wedding, or even by a noble gesture. As far as "ruining your day," it is possible that your day may be marred, but it does not have to be ruined. The way to minimize the distress is to acknowledge each of the separate issues and to address them individually.

You and your fiancé should sit and talk with your family members (including your mother and siblings) and explain what you see as the potential problem areas, and stress that you welcome their input toward a workable solution. You can tell them that your wish is to have your father in attendance and that you know you cannot have him there without his new wife—and you also cannot have them there without your mother's and siblings' cooperation. Explain that it is your desire to minimize contact among your mother and siblings and your father, but that you want a joyous event. Everyone must agree—and cooperate—to make this work, by keeping *you* and *your happiness* as the goal.

You should also sit down with your father and his wife and explain your desire to have a civil wedding and your expectation that they will work hard to make sure that nothing they do gets in the way of your happiness. Work out the particulars—who sits where, etc.—as you go along. The most important thing is that you reach an agreement that everyone involved will be respectful of the value of your wedding and of family, so that you and your fiancé can begin your new life together with as much love surrounding you as is possible. Perhaps the process will be made easier if your father's new wife decides that they should not attend, but in this scenario, at least you have been the bigger person and reached out to them as graciously as you could.

MOM DOESN'T WANT TO INVITE DAD—
AND SHE'S PAYING

Dear Dr. Dale,

My parents have been divorced for years, and needless to say, they absolutely hate each other. My mother is footing the bill for my wedding, and she has asked my father if he would like to contribute anything. He declined, saying that he would prefer to give us a monetary gift. When I told my mother, she declared that since he won't pay his share, neither he, my stepmother, nor my two half-brothers will be invited to the wedding. Obviously, since my mother has paid for the wedding, she has the final say on the guest list, but I feel trapped between these two grown adults. Why can't they both grow up and simply be happy that I'm getting married? What should I do?

Your mother, unfortunately, is holding you hostage. It was entirely her choice to pay for your wedding, and if it was her assumption that your father would share in the expenses, then that is her shortsightedness and not a fault for which you should now suffer. You may be in a no-win situation; however, there are some things you can do that may help the situation.

The first conversation to have is with your mother, as she is equating paying with total control of what happens at this wedding. Unless you can resolve this issue with her, and make her understand that paying for the wedding is a generous gift that doesn't necessarily mean she gets to have final say over all the details, you will, unfortunately, have to deal with having a wedding without the rest of your family. Emphasize to everyone that nowhere is it written that the person paying for a wedding has the final word on the guest list. There are many who would argue that the final say rests with the bride and groom no matter who is footing the bill.

If this doesn't change her mind, you may have to play hardball. Present her with the choice that either your father and his family must be invited to the wedding, or she forfeit the money she has spent on securing your wedding plans thus far. You could then plan your own, small wedding service, at which your father and his family would be in attendance. Yet another possibility is that you use the monetary gift from your father to help your mother with the expenses.

Unfortunately, there is only so much that you yourself can do about this, as much remains in your mother's hands. If you are willing to take control and redesign and plan another wedding, taking the risk may be worth it—this is, after all, your wedding, and you should do what will make you and your fiancé happy.

WHO WALKS YOU DOWN THE AISLE: DAD OR DAD?

Dear Dr. Dale,

My mother and my "real" dad divorced when I was only a year old. Although I have maintained contact with my father through the years, I don't feel comfortable with the prospect of him walking me down the aisle at my wedding. I would prefer to confer this honor on my stepdad, who bothered with the details of raising, advising, and educating me, and participated in every part of my childhood all the way to becoming an adult.

I have no desire to embarrass or hurt my father (or his current wife). I want everyone to be happy at my wedding. Luckily, my dad has told me he's comfortable with whatever decision I make. My brother has offered to walk me down the aisle instead, so that no one is singled out. But I still feel, in my heart, that I want my "dads" to be part of this ceremony.

Can you offer any suggestions as to how I might handle this?

The rite of passage in which a father walks his daughter down the aisle is one that is emotional and symbolic, the act of having the man who raised you present you to the man with whom you will, hopefully, share the rest of your life. Keep in mind the power of "symbolism." Have you thought of having your birth father walk you part of the way down the aisle (since he delivered you into the world and has maintained a relationship with you), and then having your stepfather bring you to the altar, which takes you to the next phase of your life? This seems to work for many couples, as long as family relations are amicable, and makes everyone feel as if they had an important role in this part of the ceremony. Brides who have chosen this path also say that they feel doubly blessed that both these men were able to literally hold them at a moment in life when that embrace meant everything.

However, if this scenario is still uncomfortable for you, then you might want to have your stepfather walk you down the aisle and have your father recite something meaningful to you when you arrive there or at the reception. You could even have both your dad and your brother walk you down the aisle together, if you are close to your brother, and that makes the honor seem less focused on your father. There are really no rules about who walks whom. The most important thing, particularly since your dad has supported any decision you will choose to make, is that you are comfortable with your decision. Talk to both of them and make the decision that is best for you and your groom. Look deep into your own heart and decide what will mean the most to you both for that moment in time, and for later in life when you will remember the roles both these fathers played.

DOES DAD DESERVE THE ULTIMATE HONOR?

Dear Dr. Dale,

My parents are divorced. My father was really never in the picture until I was about sixteen years old, when one day he called. Over the past few years my father and I have worked on getting to know each other.

When I got engaged, my dad suggested that he wanted to walk me down the aisle. I would prefer to select who would walk me down the aisle from among my grandfather (who has lived next door to me all my life), my brother, or my mother.

Since my father first raised the issue with me, I have been in an extremely uncomfortable position. He has tried to bribe me with money, and his sisters (my aunts) have been bombarding me with e-mails asking me if he will be walking me down the aisle. How can I handle this with a little grace and still keep my sanity? Ideally, I would like my mother to walk me down and still have my dad in the receiving line. Is this appropriate?

To start, let's be clear about one thing: Bombarding and bribery are hardly ways to reestablish a relationship that was in such poor shape for so many years. It sounds as if your father (and his sisters) are eager to have him accompany you in part so that it will appear that all is well and your relationship has been healed—and that all is forgiven.

It takes time to build (or rebuild) your connection, and a relationship such as this needs to be based on trust and openness. We suggest that you talk with your father quietly and explain to him that you are pleased that he is back in your life and you look forward to sharing many wonderful life experiences together from this point on. But you need to be clear that offering money or having his sisters barrage you with e-mails will not help you feel closer to him, and that you are not quite ready to have him walk you down the aisle because you believe this role, at this particular time in your life, is better suited for your mother.

The person who "gives you away" is generally the person who played the most significant role in raising you. Traditionally, it is one's father, but in many families, if the relationship is strained, or if in fact the father was not a significant part of the bride's child rearing, then it is perfectly acceptable for another person (family member or not) to accompany the bride to the altar.

It is true that you honor your mother by choosing her to accompany you down the aisle, but it is not true that you dishonor your father by not choosing him. You can honor your dad by asking him to receive your guests as he stands near you and your husband in the receiving line; this is a perfectly acceptable, and graceful, alternative.

HATEFUL PARENTS ON BOTH SIDES

Dear Dr. Dale,

This may sound like a bad movie, but unfortunately it is my life! My high school sweetheart of eight years and I are getting married next year. My problem is with all three sets of parents, who have known each other pretty well over the years. His parents have been divorced for eighteen years, and his dad, stepmom, and mom all *hate* each other. I don't use the word "hate" lightly—they can't even be in the same room at the same time. To make matters worse, my mom doesn't care for any of them, and has made it known over the years.

How do we handle the wedding events and seating arrangements? We want our day to be relaxed, given the animosity between all the parents.

First and foremost, you need to recognize that you will not be able to "cure" the ills that are deep-seated and have lasted for the better part of your life. Instead, you should focus on getting through this wedding with your happiness intact.

First, speak to each of the "parties" individually, and tell them that you appreciate that they all have difficulties with each other, and that you want to try to honor each of them and their "space" so that they each are able to enjoy your nuptials. Tell them you hope that they will behave maturely and respectfully at the wedding *as a gift to you and your fiancé.* Tell them that you would appreciate their putting their *very substantial and understandable* differences aside for this one day only.

It is important that you avoid getting into a discussion about the reason for the rift and who is right and who is wrong. Repeat that this is not what you are doing. Rather, what you are attempting to do is appeal to these people to give you the support you need on your wedding day and the related celebratory events. Think about concrete ways to make this easier for them. It will be useful to ask your mom, for instance, to plan to be with (and nearby) a dear friend of hers so that she feels she has support with her.

As far as seating is concerned, seat each of the parents at his or her own table with their friends or family. Arrange yourself and your fiancé either at your own "bride and groom table" or at a larger table with your friends.

We would also recommend separating your fiancé's mother and father, even though they are technically on the same side of the family—do not risk them having arguments in your immediate presence by sitting them at the same table. If at all possible, take the safer route and just seat all these people far away from each other!

MOM VERSUS DAD'S NEW GIRLFRIEND

Dear Dr. Dale,
My father and mother have been divorced for six years. My mother has remained single and my father is seriously dating another woman. My mom is convinced that my father's relationship with this woman was the reason for the divorce and, therefore, she is adamantly opposed to attending any of my wedding festivities if "that woman" is "allowed" to come. I have explained to my mom that I expect my dad to honor and support my relationship with my fiancé, and also for us to extend the same respect toward his relationship choices. Therefore, it would seem hypocritical to deny my father the chance to bring the woman he is dating. Of course, this has not gone over too well, and I have yet to make a definitive decision. My father feels my mother is being absolutely unreasonable and offers no further input. Both parents are waiting for me to make the move.

You have done the right thing by trying to show compassion for both your mother and your father, but realize that ultimately the decision is theirs to make: They must both decide if they can put aside their differences for one day and participate in their daughter's joy. Let them know that you plan to invite both parties, that you love them, and that you sincerely hope they will attend. Promise to keep their interactions limited, and should they decide to swallow their grievances, keep to your word on this point. If your mother refuses to come you will have to live with her decision. You need to share with your mother how devastating her absence would be for you. But you cannot force her to do something she perceives she is unable to do.

TRYING FOR PERFECT ETIQUETTE WITH A NOT-SO-PERFECT FAMILY

Dear Dr. Dale,

My parents have been divorced for sixteen years. My mother is still single, but my father has a serious girlfriend. I'm not sure what etiquette says I should do in this situation, but my mother thinks that she and my father should be introduced together and sit at the head of the table together— in other words, to assume the entire honor of being parents of the bride.

I understand my mother's desire, but I don't want my father's girlfriend to be excluded and uncomfortable. Also, since the divorce, my parents have hardly spoken, so the idea that they assume their parental roles side-by-side is jarring. What should I do?

It is common today for brides and grooms to sit together, alone, at a specially decorated table just for them or, perhaps, for them and their friends. This way, your mother and father could sit at separate tables among their own family and friends. If, however, they both agree that they would like to behave, theoretically they can sit together; etiquette-wise, it is perfectly permissible. But in this case there is a third party in the equation: your father's girl-friend. For this to work she needs to be okay with the decision as well, so by all means discuss this with her beforehand, and make sure (regardless of the seating) that you make a point of introducing her to people, so that she won't feel stigmatized. You might also want to assign some of your guests or members of your wedding party to make sure she feels included and comfortable.

With all that said, you—and your mother—need to realize that the best solution might just be (particularly since your parents have hardly spoken in sixteen years) to have your mother sit at one table with members of her family and with her friends, and your father and his girlfriend at another table with theirs. It seems ambitious to try to bring them together in a symbolic way under such emotionally charged circumstances. Sitting them separately in this scenario most likely will result in everyone enjoying themselves and you not having to worry about how they will get along.

I DON'T LIKE DAD'S NEW GIRLFRIEND

Dear Dr. Dale,

My fiancé's mother is deceased and his father has a relatively recent girlfriend who is rather odd and selfish. So far in the process she has called me long distance to request that she be seated with my fiancé's father and given a corsage; she has also called and asked about the color of her dress, where she will stand in the receiving line, how many pictures she will be in, and many other annoying questions. Because she is only a girlfriend, how should she be treated? I don't want her in my pictures, nor do I want her in the receiving line. How do I introduce her, or should she be introduced at all? My own stepmother graciously said, "This is your mother's day to be mother of the bride. It's my place to sit this one out." Why should I give all this attention and recognition to a girlfriend I don't even like?

It appears that your future father-in-law's girlfriend has unrealistic expectations regarding her involvement in the wedding. Even though she is your fiancé's father's girlfriend, she is a guest, with no particularly "favored" status in the wedding or reception. The decision rests with you and your fiancé as to the role, if any, that she will play, and how to deal with the attention and time she requires before and during the wedding. You will need your fiancé's help in this matter, since he can both support you and work as a liaison with his father. Either by letter or e-mail you can let your fiancé's father and his girlfriend know how the wedding, and her role in it, will proceed. This, of course, is entirely up to you.

As for introductions: If you are asking about formal introductions to be made in front of the guests, we see no reason why she would require any introduction at all. Regarding introductions to other guests you may be interacting with, ask your fiancé's father and his girlfriend how they would like to be introduced—as "my fiancé's father's companion," or "significant other," or simply, "girlfriend." Do whatever you need to do to remove the pressure from yourself, and simply ask them for their input.

As to her other questions: Members of your immediate and stepfamilies are those who are generally part of a receiving line, and not a girlfriend of a family member. Moreover, among the many things a bride-to-be is concerned with, one should not be the apparel of every guest. Therefore, urge this "odd" woman to wear whatever pleases her and hope for the best.

DIVORCING PARENTS

Dear Dr. Dale,

My fiancé's parents are going through a very nasty divorce, and we're trying to include both in our wedding. So far there have been no problems, but I'm worried about a feature of the ceremony: the lighting of the unity candle. I'd like for my parents to light one side, while his parents light the other, after which my fiancé and I would light the center candle. I am terrified that my fiancé's mother will make some catty remark during this ceremony, and that the father will return a comment. Do you know how we could avoid any unpleasantness while still maintaining the ritual?

Your plan will likely work if you gently explain your concerns to each set of parents (both yours and your fiancé's). If you like, you can write them a letter and explain what you hope to accomplish through this ritual, and then ask *each* person (so as not to assign blame and incite rancor) to think about his or her role in this important part of your ceremony.

In particular, explain to your fiancé's parents that you understand their uncomfortable position right now, but that your wedding is not a time for it to find expression. Agree to call them after they have received and reviewed the letter, so that they can release whatever initial emotional response they may have. Once this is done, you can then fully focus on the unity ceremony at its truest.

If your fiancé's parents cannot agree to participate in a civilized manner, tell them you are not willing to risk a catastrophe at the altar. If they agree to "behave" but cannot seem to do it and exchange snide comments, squeeze your fiancé's hand, look into his eyes, and remind yourself you are marrying him to build your own relationship, separate and distinct from his parents'.

EIGHT

Stepfamilies

REALITY CHECK: Being part of a stepfamily is never easy. In fact, get ready for a ride that will bring you great joy and—at least at this point in your wedding process—some real challenges.

How do we know? Not only do we have many friends who married people with children from previous marriages, but Dr. Dale sees many patients in her practice who are contemplating becoming part of a stepfamily. And, for the most personal of examples, Dr. Dale married a man with two sons who were twelve and fourteen when she and her husband met. The only way she and Rob could plan their wedding was to consider not only their own needs, but those of his young boys. To add to that, Rob was a widower (which brought added challenges), Dale's father had Alzheimer's and was not going to be the kind of grandparent the boys would have loved, and there were many new relatives who suddenly appeared in everyone's lives. Dale quickly found that they all had a lot to learn, about themselves and each other. Sometimes they did it willingly, and other times reluctantly. But they all knew that they were there for the long haul. Establishing the new family took time, a lot of patience, work, and love on every person's part. And the price of this new combined family was that Dale's fantasy wedding was not going to happen. Instead, and to everyone's great joy, they had a warm, intimate, quiet wedding ceremony in Dale's parents' living room, and four months later, a celebration for friends and family. By that time, the new family was well on its way to becoming a whole new—and happy—unit.

As you plan your new beginning with your fiancé, and you go through the normal ups and downs of the wedding planning process, be prepared to confront the many issues that naturally unfold when you bring stepfamilies together. There is no such thing as "blending" families. Families are not fruit drinks. They take time to grow. Relationships develop over time, with experiences—lots of them. New and future stepparent relationships, especially in the beginning (and perhaps for a long while afterward), work best when they are more like friendships. Understand that it takes a long time to build a relationship with a child (even if that child is a teenager or an adult), and if they are not "in your camp" as you plan the wedding, don't write them off. Remember, you are the adult in this situation. Stepchildren, quite understandably, wonder if your new marriage will last, and may react to you with some suspicion and reserve. They are often hesitant to get too attached, since they see the stepparent as an interloper, someone who wants to replace their other parent. Even if the children are happy that their parent found someone to love, and even if they like or even love you, they may still feel somewhat distant and need to take their time. Your relationship may go through a new or different phase as you plan the wedding. The reality that you are going to be a definite fixture in their lives looms large. So reach out. Make time to be together that is unrelated to the wedding plans. And make sure your fiancé has time with his children without you, so they can be comfortable with the knowledge that they will still have alone time and access to their parent.

Understand also that even though you think you know your fiancé and his children, when you spend the weekend with him and the kids, you may see sides of everyone that will make you rethink this entire arrangement. You may find yourself thinking, "If he would only do this, he would avoid that kind of behavior from his daughter." Or, "Why does he allow his son to treat me this way?" Your future stepdaughter may threaten to boycott the wedding altogether; your future stepson may get into trouble with the law as an attempt to derail the wedding plans. When your fiancé changes his mind about having your brother as his best man in favor of his teenage son, who finally agreed to attend the wedding, you need to remember to think about things from a long-range perspective. Your brother can be a groomsman; his son needs to be by his father's side. Or more to the point, your fiancé may need to say to the world, as he embarks on this most important journey with you, that his son is by his side. These are the subtle and not so subtle messages you need to pay attention to as you plan your wedding and start to lay the groundwork for your lives together. The truth is that there are more than the two of you to consider now. You have the kids, and sometimes the "exes," to include, or if not include, at least pay attention to. Patience is probably the most important characteristic you will need to count on and hang on to in order to persevere.

But wait a minute—this is your wedding, right? Why do you need to spend time tiptoeing so carefully around the kids? The answer: Because it will help you smooth the transition to your new life as a family. Consider:

- Often when people marry someone who has children, they are not used to kids being "around," and may resent them. Or, they simply forget to take them into account, making decisions that directly affect the kids without consulting them. Kids can pick up whether or not they are respected, and you'll need to work on making decisions as a family. Some of what you are doing will be fun for the kids and some of it they will want no part of. Don't push. Just move forward, and if they give you grief, try not to take too much of it to heart.

- Even if they like you, kids may have mixed feelings about the whole wedding "thing," so be careful when you enthuse about the colors and textures of the linens and the flowers. They may or may not be onboard with the same level of enthusiasm as you.

- With some careful inclusion in the planning, you can help stepchildren adjust to the larger idea of a wedding, which will make the transition smoother. Spend time talking with your future stepkids about their role in the wedding, and ask them what they would be comfortable with. Give some options that are age and personality appropriate. Bridesmaid? Flower girl? Ring bearer? Best man? Standing around you with other members of the family? Reading a poem? Registering guests? Consider the options. Maybe they can weigh in on a choice of food or flowers. Ask for their input; it will allow them to feel like they are playing an active, important role and thus have some control over the situation.

- You may consider inviting one of their friends or that friend and their family. That way they will feel they have support from people other than family members. It also demonstrates that the way they enjoy and experience the wedding is important to you.

- Parents who do well as stepparents often put energy into working toward developing a *parenting coalition*. In other words, they *coparent*. A good place to begin is when planning the wedding.

- It is a good idea to communicate with your fiancé's "ex" about what the children will be doing: what you are planning for them; in which activities they will be participating; what they will be wearing; and so on. When parents and stepparents cooperate with the children's other parent the child's loyalty conflicts are minimized, which makes it easier on everyone involved (and may even contribute to the new marriage having a better chance of surviving). Thus, when planning your wedding, if at all possible, include the other stepparent in some of the arrangements, scheduling, and decision making that involve the children in any way. Try to have harmony within your household as well as across households during this process.

- Knowing you are not the primary parent can make you, as the future stepparent, feel less valued, and that can put more pressure on the wedding planning. You may need more reassurance from your fiancé. You may find that you are needier than usual. While he may feel it necessary to reassure his children they are not going to "lose him" to you, you may need reassurance that you are not losing him to them!

One final word: So many newly married stepparents forget about the importance of their time alone as a couple. Remember, one of you was in a relationship that did not work, and very likely the kids have witnessed more than you would have liked them to during its demise. Now you have a chance to offer them a good and loving model. That does not mean that you should fawn all over each other or be inappropriate. Most kids are uncomfortable with that. So ease into it. Yes, kiss and hug and hold hands, but also make sure that they see that you have your own time as a couple. When you nurture the marriage you help nurture the family, and demonstrating your love for one another throughout the wedding process is a way to communicate the love you bring to the family as a whole.

HOW CAN I INCLUDE MY STEPMOM?

Dear Dr. Dale,

Both my and my fiancé's parents are divorced, and all—except for my fiancé's mother—have remarried. Both of us actually feel closer to our stepmoms than to our biological mothers. This is going to be a Protestant wedding, but other than the unity candle, how can we include the stepmothers as part of the wedding ceremony?

Too often stepparents (and stepmothers, in particular) get little or no positive recognition and feel the sting of the stereotype of "the wicked stepmother." You both have a golden opportunity here to honor positive aspects of your relationships with these women. You can honor your stepmothers by asking them to read a special passage, prayer, poem, or significant reading during the ceremony. The pastor can mention them by name during the service, when he refers to the families and to the joy felt by every person who has participated in the rearing of the bride and groom. After the ceremony you can include them both in the receiving line, so they can greet and manage the guests along with your biological parents.

STEPMOM VERSUS REAL MOM—WHOM DO I HONOR?

Dear Dr. Dale,

I am getting married in three weeks, and am concerned about how to handle issues that involve my stepmother, who has low self-esteem. My mother is deceased, yet I was planning to find ways within the ceremony to honor and remember her by having my aunt (my mother's only sister and my godmother) fulfill certain roles of the bride's mother (i.e., lighting the bridal taper for the unity candle and sitting in the pew with my father).

While I have an OK relationship with my stepmother, I feel it is important to pay respects to my own mother and remember her as part of my life (my stepmother had no part in raising me as my father married her only a few years ago, after I was out of college). However, I am feeling some pressure to have my stepmother fulfill the mother roles involved with the wedding. Shouldn't this day be about how I want to honor family and friends?

Fortunately, it is not difficult to solve this dilemma. In most wedding ceremonies, there are ample opportunities to honor the people who are and who have been important to you. In some cultures, weddings are a time to invite and include all of the couple's deceased ancestors so that their spirits can be present to bless the union. Certainly, honoring your mother is in line with such a tradition, and having your aunt participate is a lovely way to include someone who was not only important to your late mother but remains important to you today. The ways that you have chosen to honor her will be both appropriate and memorable to everyone.

That said, although you are right that this is about how you want to honor your family and friends, you do not live in a vacuum. By excluding your stepmother you may be showing her (as well as your father) disrespect. Even though your stepmother did not participate in raising you, she is still a part of your and your father's lives, and leaving her out of the wedding seems unnecessary. Why not find another role for her? Talk with your stepmother privately and explain your desire to have your aunt be present as a representative of your mother, both as a way of honoring your mother's memory and making you feel that she is with you at your wedding. Then suggest some other ways that your stepmother can participate, perhaps by hosting the guest sign-in book or reading a special prayer, as an assurance that you intend to honor her role in your life at this point.

HOW DO WE DEAL WITH MY FIANCÉ'S WICKED STEPMOTHER?

Dear Dr. Dale,

How do I deal with my fiancé's stepmother (he hates her) who insists on planning the rehearsal dinner (her husband is paying, after all)? She moved in on his dad while he was married, had an affair with him that devastated my fiancé's mother, was spiteful to his mother (made the divorce just awful, trying to leave her with almost nothing!), and was generally a witch. You can understand why my fiancé can't be around her. But she has been his stepmother for almost

ten years now, and his father feels that we have to deal with
her. On the other hand, my future mother-in-law, who always acted with great dignity throughout the messy divorce,
has not made any demands on us, never asking us to leave
the "wicked stepmother" (my words, not hers) out of the
wedding. So dealing with the rehearsal dinner is all we have
to consider. Any advice?

It's easy. You deal with your fiancé's stepmother with respect.
She is your future father-in-law's wife, and traditionally the
groom's parents host the rehearsal dinner. Yes, your fiancé hates
her, and it seems like he may have good reason, but you all need
to get through the wedding weekend intact. His stepmother may
be using this event as an opportunity to be in the limelight, to
show her support and caring for her husband and/or his son, or assert her position as sort of a family matriarch. Whatever her mo-
tivation, you do not have to buy into it, but you should allow her
to proceed with her plans. Just try to appreciate the experience of
being together with the people you love around you on the night
before your wedding. Sometimes, it pays to be a bit philosophical
and keep the bigger picture in mind, and this is one of those
times.

That said, in terms of specifics, it is perfectly appropriate for
you and your fiancé to call your future father-in-law and stepmother and say that you would appreciate talking with them
about the rehearsal dinner. Be sure to highlight your gratitude for
their generosity in hosting the event and that you would like to
share with them what you hope will be included. For example, if
you are concerned that your fiancé's mother may feel slighted, be
sure to mention to your future father-in-law that you are looking
forward to a respectful interaction between them. If you know of
a friend who has prepared a toast, let them know so they can include him or her in the plan of the evening. Additionally, you can

tell them that you hope your father-in-law and his wife will include you in the planning, seating, and organization of the evening, since you know the members of the wedding party well and your input will be valuable.

You and your fiancé can agree to help one another during the evening by being sure everyone there feels as comfortable as possible, introducing each of the guests to everyone else, and preparing (and practicing) a well-thought-out thank you toast to his father and stepmother for hosting the dinner.

MARRIED . . . WITH STEPCHILDREN

Dear Dr. Dale,

I'm thirty-six and am engaged to a spectacular man, who also happens to have two great kids, ages seven and ten. My fiancé has been divorced for about four and half years, and we've been together for two years, so I feel very comfortable with his kids, and I think they like me as well.

I consider it fortunate that the kids' mother is very much a part of their lives, and even more fortunate that she's not threatened by my becoming their stepmother. My fiancé has custody, so the kids will live with us and see their mother every other weekend as well as one evening during the week. My only concern is that there won't be enough private time for me and my fiancé to build our marital relationship when not focusing on the children. Any ideas?

Even if you choose to marry a man with children, you can still have an adult, loving, and devoted relationship. In fact, it is helpful for children to see their parents involved in respectful, healthy, affectionate partnerships. Having said that, it is a great challenge for a couple (particularly a newly married couple) to carve out private time for themselves in such a way that the children can appreciate.

Typically, children of a newly remarried parent need reassurance that they are still loved and valued, as well as involved in a loving family. Don't be surprised if the children object to demonstrations of affection, or if they develop a stomachache just as you and your husband are about to leave for the movies on a Saturday night. It takes time to find the right balance, but be assured that the children can adjust and will ultimately benefit from parents who take care of their own relationship as well as take care of them. As long as you are thoughtful with the children and with your fiancé, you will find the right balance between the two. And since you already know that private time between the two of you is precious and must be planned for, carefully and continuously, you will find it easier to make it happen.

MY FIANCÉ DOESN'T LIKE MY SON

Dear Dr. Dale,

My fiancé and I are both in our forties, and we have each been married before. We recently decided that after ten years of dating, we could not live apart any longer, and so we got engaged and moved in together. My fiancé has three grown children, all in their twenties, and his youngest son, a full-time college student, lives with us. My eldest son also came home to stay last year, after a job didn't work out.

I was a single mother for almost all of my boys' lives, and we are extremely close. I have always felt that wherever I am, my kids are always welcome. If they are having trouble with work and finances, they should feel free to come home while getting back on their feet. My son is not a slacker; he is a very hard worker who has been caught in the terrible economy. However, my fiancé is very upset that my son's stay has been longer than he expected, and now they barely speak to each other. At first I thought it was just the two of them being men—claiming territory—but they can't seem to get past their hostility. I am at my wits' end, as the stress of these two actively hating each other is too much for me. If I appear to favor one, the other is upset. I don't know whose side to take, and even though my fiancé is a wonderful man in every other aspect, I am considering calling off the wedding. How can I marry a man who does not like my kid? I am so torn.

You ask, "How can I marry a man who does not like my kid?" Well, your fiancé does not have to like your children. Of course it is better when stepparents and stepkids do like each other, as it makes the combining of the families a whole lot easier, but it is not mandatory. And, frankly, difficult feelings between the new stepparent and the children are more common than not.

So if he does not have to like your son, what *does* he have to do? He has to treat your children with dignity and respect. If he objects to your philosophy that your home should be available to your sons when they are having hard times, then he needs to deal with this difference of opinion with *you*. It does not give him license to insult your son or to give him the cold shoulder or to treat him disrespectfully. At the same time, you can discuss with your son how hard it is for you when there is such tension between the two of them. The other part of the equation between you and your son involves examining ways you can help your son to get back on his feet in a timely fashion. If things are too cushy at home, he may not be that motivated to more forward. If, however, he is actively seeking work, networking, following opportunities, and working around your house and/or at something or with someone while waiting to land the right job, things may be better at home. If your fiancé sees your involvement in helping your son become independent again, he may be more patient with the whole process (and kinder to your son).

The real difficulty is that you are in the middle of two men whom you love, feeling as if you need to choose one over the other. This is a no-win situation, and hopefully you won't have to make that choice. Instead, you and your fiancé need to work out a way for him to be civil to your son and to be supportive of your role as mother. You can accomplish this with the help of a counselor who is experienced in working with stepfamilies. You have already devoted ten years to this relationship, so a bit more time cannot hurt. It will be worth it, and it is very possible that with some mediation, this will work out.

MOM MIGHT CAUSE A SCENE WITH STEPMOM

Dear Dr. Dale,

I have recently severed all ties with my biological mother and do not wish to invite her to my wedding. She has been a source of embarrassment to me for most of my life. She often showed up drunk and sloppily dressed at my school. She flirted with all my boyfriends. The last time she ran into my stepmother she initiated a catfight. She is fifty years old and still doesn't realize that her actions have consequences; nor does she understand how to behave like an adult.

My stepmother, on the other hand, is a wonderful, caring woman, generous and thoughtful, who has been there for me—a great source of balance, as I have had to deal with my mother's shenanigans. Because she *has* been there for me most of my life, my stepmother will be acting as the mother of the bride. If my biological mother shows up unexpectedly at my wedding, I do not want a scene between the two moms, and I don't want any scene where my mother acts insane. How can I prevent this?

It sounds like not inviting your biological mother is a kind of punishment for the past disappointments and hurts you say were inflicted on you. This is not an unwarranted reaction on your part. It just may not work with a person who, as you say, takes no responsibility for her actions and basically acts in whatever way she wants. She may indeed show up uninvited, and it doesn't sound like you can stop her. You just need to prepare yourself as much as you can. We suggest that you talk with a trusted relative who you can rely on, who will be prepared to act if she shows up. It will be his or her "job" to stay with your mother and to keep her occupied and distracted. Talk with this person and appeal to his or her desire to help create and/or maintain peace in the family. Then, if your mother does show up, you will not have to worry that she is going to do something outrageous without anyone watching over her. As difficult as it is to understand, you are not responsible for nor can you predict your mother's behavior.

You can also talk privately with your stepmother about your fears of what might transpire if your mother shows up at your wedding. Share your fears with your stepmother and let her know what your hope is about how that situation would be handled. Determine how you can be helpful to each other. Even though it is your wedding, your stepmother will be in a sensitive position, and although you cannot prevent a scene, you can tell your stepmother how much it will mean to you if she acts respectfully toward your mother (if she shows up) as she proceeds with her most honored role.

I DON'T WANT MY HALF SISTER
IN MY CEREMONY!

Dear Dr. Dale,

I'm thirty years old, and I'll be married in Hawaii in about a month. My parents had a very bitter divorce ten years ago, and they aren't cordial. My father is now married to the woman who was his secretary. My mother is paying for my wedding, while my father is contributing nothing.

My father has asked that his five-year-old adopted daughter serve as a flower girl in the ceremony, although I already have four flower girls, as well as a ring bearer. The girls I have selected are nieces and nephews, and I have been with them for every birthday and holiday, and I have always intended for them to be in my wedding. I have only met my father's daughter twice, and while she is a sweet girl, I don't want her in my wedding. However, I also don't want to hurt an innocent child's feelings.

My father and his wife have pressed the issue aggressively and, as a compromise, I have let him know that his daughter could be a lei greeter. This is unacceptable to him, and he has complained to others in the family that I am selfish. I think he is the one being selfish. Any suggestions?

Weddings often have an unfortunate way of bringing out the fantasies that people want while also exposing the difficulties we have in accepting reality. In this case, it sounds as if your father wants all of his children to be treated equally, with no regard to the extenuating circumstances of your family's situation. Further, he seems to be directing from the sidelines and applying pressure without offering any aid, financial or otherwise. This is unacceptable. So talk to him. Explain that you understand his wish to have your half-sister participate in your wedding, but that you are only comfortable with her in the role you have assigned. Add that you see this invitation as a means of expanding her role in your life and that you expect that, over time, you will come to know her better. However, right here, right now, you can offer no more. And be prepared for him to either withdraw from the wedding or try to keep the pressure on. Don't let him continue in his position. Make it clear that either he accepts your terms, since it is your wedding, or not—but that you will not negotiate or discuss this further. If he declines to accept the role you are offering, you will look forward to either seeing them both as guests, or to spending time with his daughter once the wedding has passed.

Remind yourself that there is always some fallout from family decisions. And stick to your guns. You are right and appropriate in your desires and how you are dealing with them.

NINE

In-laws

WHEN YOU GET ENGAGED you are not only gaining a husband—you are signing on to become a part of a new family. And it is one that you may or may not already know something about. But you do know one important thing: This is the family that raised the person you have chosen to spend the rest of your life with. And that is reason enough to feel grateful, appreciative, and respectful of these folks you will soon be calling your in-laws. Hopefully you will embrace them, they will embrace you, and you will have a lifetime of caring and sharing. But, even when this happens, it takes time and effort. You and your future in-law family have different habits, customs, ways of setting the table, celebrating holidays, talking about feelings.

Whether there are cultural, religious, geographic, educational, or social differences, you have a lot to learn about your future in-law family, as they do about yours. From the start, open yourself to listening, learning, and observing. It is all part of the package and the family that helped to form the person you have fallen in love with. That said, people can behave beautifully and badly (and every way in between) when their precious son or daughter, sister or brother, finds the person they are soon to call their "wife" or "husband." It takes time and mutual respect to raise the comfort level to one of love. It is a process that begins the first time you meet and will continue even after the wedding. You may have a fantasy of one big happy family, but the truth is that this rarely happens right away, if ever. Think of the different roles your in-laws can play in your wedding and discuss them with your fiancé to see if he thinks your ideas are realistic. You need to stay real, grounded, and away from preconceived notions. If everyone is simply pleasant and getting along throughout the wedding process, that itself is a major first step.

As the future bride (and future daughter-in-law), you need to realize, first and foremost, that your future mother- and father-in-law are not *you* and that their boundaries and comfort level about all sorts of things may be quite different from yours. They may be comfortable seeing you and their son openly express your affection, or they may not. They may have expectations for you and their son—and your wedding!—that you don't think you can abide. They probably have their own traditions and cultural values. And they may have a different sense of what "being family" involves—such as dropping by unannounced for a visit. When these kinds of differences and issues surface, you and your fiancé need to talk openly about what is going on and how you feel about it and, together, how you will handle it. Remember, you are investing in a long-term relationship and the process takes time.

In our culture, there are a lot of mother-in-law jokes and, believe us, they don't do much to present a healthy and happy picture of what a terrific relationship this can actually be. Don't believe all the bad press. Many mothers- and daughters-in-law adore each other. That said, there are reasons those jokes exist. Mothers-in-law, in particular, often have a hard time making the transition from being the primary woman in their child's life to taking second place, or as they often put it, moving to the backseat. Most mothers generally feel that they know their own children better than anyone else, and giving up the ease of frequent contact, of not knowing the daily life of one's child, and of not being consulted about helping with major decisions, can be tough for a lot of parents who have been intimately involved in their adult children's lives. Many parents operate under the assumption that their standards and practices are universal and, if not universal, then, at the very least, will surely be easily accepted and embraced by anyone their child would consider marrying. Not accepting their practices can be viewed as a rejection of them, their values, their culture, or their life, and can result in friction.

So how to deal with issues as they come up? Do the best you can to start off on the right foot. Don't be afraid to make the first move and simply pick up the phone. You cannot go wrong if you are open and gracious. If his parents and yours have not yet met, go ahead and arrange an outing. Remember, families who stand too firmly on ceremony often miss out on a lot, so you and your fiancé should be the force that draws everyone together. If you have not already done so, spend some time telling your parents what it is you love about this person who you have chosen to spend the rest of your life with, and why you feel he is a good partner for you. Have your fiancé do the same, and tell his parents about all the wonderful qualities you possess that make you a perfect fit *for him*. You will want your folks and his folks to extend their hands in friendship, and the likelihood of that happening is greater if they understand what it is about each of you that makes your hearts sing. When parents can see their future son-in-law through *your* eyes, they are more likely to be open and receptive. You can also offer suggestions to your own parents about how to make their first meeting go well and have your fiancé do the same for his parents.

If you are miles away, and your folks have not yet met or spoken and it just isn't possible to get everyone together, try to arrange a "first" conversation between your two sets of parents, so that they can share in your joy. This is when the work you've done prepping your parents can really come in handy. So often in-law parents know nothing or very little about their new in-law child, and have not been told by their children what it is about this special person that they love so much. If you've filled them in, they can exchange generous observations about how happy the two of you are and all of the things you share.

When it comes to actual conflicts, we receive more letters about mother-in-law issues than any other, particularly with regard to what the role of the mother-in-law should be in the planning of the wedding. This can be very sensitive. It used to be that the bride and her mother simply planned everything, and although this is still done in many families, times have changed. A lot depends on who is hosting the wedding and how involved the bride and her mother want the mother and father of the groom to be, no matter what the arrangement. Talking about what your future in-laws have in mind is helpful, and asking for your mother-in-law's opinion on certain items can go a long way. Keeping your fiancé's parents informed will enable them to feel a part of the process, even if you are handling the actual details and decisions. Here are some other tips for handling in-laws throughout the planning process:

- If you are lucky enough to have your future mother-in-law offer to be helpful, give her a specific role. But make sure she knows that she must honor the bride's and the couple's wishes.

- The mother and father of the groom usually host the rehearsal dinner. But this, too, can be negotiable. As more and more couples pay for their own weddings and festivities, these old rules don't apply, and the in-laws' position on this can and may vary. Make sure you and your fiancé discuss your intentions up front and explain your wishes in a clear and respectful manner.

- One of the most frequent problem areas is the total number of guests and how the number is to be divided— bride's side, groom's side, the couple's friends. Sometimes the mother of the groom can interpret their number as a reflection on how the bride's family feels about them and their family, their value, their importance. Some parents of the groom will offer to pay for the difference of the increase in the number of guests. It is entirely up to you and your family regarding whether you want to accept this.

- However, sometimes the venue cannot accommodate more people, so having an offer to subsidize the difference does no good. Usually we advise people to accept the number and move forward. If your future in-laws (or your own father or mother) refuse to honor your desire, then you will need to address it with them directly. Acknowledge their disappointment about not having the number of guests they would have liked.

- If you want to, you can explain the limitations and how you decided on the numbers. If not—and you are under no obligations to do this—you can just listen to them and reiterate that this is the number, and you know it is difficult to choose from all of their many friends and family, but you hope they will select those folks they are the closest to and who know you well. We know of some families who, when they find out there isn't going to be room for all of the people they want to invite, host their own celebration. It can be an engagement party or a prewedding celebration for their friends. There are many ways around the numbers game, but the reality is that someone may still feel slighted.

- One of the worst-case scenarios occurs when an adult child feels conflicting loyalties between her fiancé and her family. If you do not like your fiancé's parents, you can deal with that. But you must be respectful to them. After all, they *are* the people who raised the person you have chosen to spend your life with.

- Be conscious of not using your fiancé as a go-between.

- Engage your in-laws. As a future in-law child, you can help forge a meaningful relationship by initiating discussions about their individual life stories (where they are from, their own family backgrounds, their education, work, life experiences, what is important to them—getting to know who they are). And, share your own life story to help them understand who you are and what is important to you. This helps build respect. Ask them about themselves and tell them about what you are doing, what is interesting to you, and above all make sure your conversations include topics other than the wedding. Remember, the wedding is *one day* (albeit a great one), and they will be your in-laws for life.

- If you find that you are getting a lot of unsolicited advice and opinions from your mother-in-law, it may be that she is used to giving her opinions openly and doesn't know that you prefer to ask for advice. The best way to deal with this is to sit with her and explain to her that you love talking with her about all of these issues, and that you would be grateful to have her advice when you ask for it. Remember, your mother-in-law may be used to guiding her own children (no matter how subtly). One way to approach her is to say: "We come from such different orientations. I am used to asking people for advice when I feel I need it, and you are used to giving advice when you think someone needs it. I appreciate that when you offer advice, it is out of love and a belief that you have the right answer or approach. That is terrific for you. Honestly, though, it does not work as well for me. Usually I like to work things out on my own, to problem solve and consider my options before seeking advice. I know this is my quirk. Do you think you can try to wait to offer advice until I ask for it? I think I will be more open to hearing what you have to say if we can try to do it this way."

• There is one thing you can certainly expect, and that is that your mother-in-law will want to be appreciated. For example, if she gives a gift, or is helpful, she should be thanked just like you would a friend.

In the event that heated conflicts do arise, deal with them directly—and respectfully. Above all, keep the communication lines open. Sit with your in-laws and listen to what they are upset about and share where you think there have been problems. Do not accuse. Begin any conversation with an open heart. Try to understand who your in-laws are and why they behave the way they do. Get to know them. They're not your parents, so you have a chance to interact differently with them than your fiancé does. Explain that you want to have the best relationship that is possible, and you need their help, and then describe the situation from your own perspective. "I am troubled by this." "It bothers me when . . ." "I would like to improve our relationship."

One of the greatest in-law hurdles can be a difference of opinion between you and your fiancé regarding what constitutes acceptable behavior and involvement from your in-laws. Perhaps your fiancé's family was more tightly knit than your own, and whereas he is used to regular calls and unannounced drop-in visits, this may be too much for you. You're going to have to figure out how to support each other's needs.

If you find yourself in the situation where your fiancé always takes his parents' side, and you are "sure" they are not always right, you need to have a talk with him about why he does not allow your opinions to have the same weight as those of his parents. It may be that he just does not want to ruffle Mommy's feather or receive Daddy's glare of disapproval. Sometimes separating from parents means standing up for yourself, and he may not be able to choose you over his parents. He may feel guilty if he suggests something different from what they desire. He may not yet feel comfortable "standing up for himself" as part of a couple, and this may manifest itself in caving in each time he has an opportunity to assert himself. Deal with this gently, but firmly. Use examples so he can see what you mean. Do not get overly emotional, because that may cause him to tune you out and turn you off, dismissing you as hysterical and not really understanding your point. Or there may be a part of him that secretly wants you to fight for him against his mother. Who knows? The important thing to remember is, each of you needs to remain true to each other and to listen to your parents, and then make the decision that reflects what you want or what you have agreed to.

In-law relationships take time to develop. During the time when you are planning your wedding, there are countless opportunities to fall off the high road. Resist! During this time, make an effort to get to know them and understand how they are dealing with this tremendous change in their lives. Remember, parents are often struck with the reality that "before they turned around," their baby was all grown up, and now is about to be married. Realizing their child is an adult, and an adult about to commit to someone they really do not know, can be terrifying as well as wonderful. Sometimes these feelings come out in ways that are far from joyous or caring or endearing, but if you become a person who remembers it all, is unforgiving, and will get them back for what they said or did, your wedding planning will be filled with caution, anger, and sadness. Better to opt for developing a sense of humor and a forgiving attitude, and discover who these people are. Remember, they are the people who gave life to your beloved.

AFRAID OF MY FIANCÉ'S PARENTS

Dear Dr. Dale,

My parents absolutely love my fiancé. He has been attending church with us ever since the beginning of our relationship, and this is one thing that was important to them and they are very happy. In many ways, he's like the son they never had. With his parents, however, it's a different story. I don't know if his parents even like me, let alone love me. We don't really spend much time with them, since my fiancé lives on his own and has for some time. I take every opportunity I get to spend time with his folks to get to know them better, but every time I get butterflies in my stomach and I feel like if I screw *anything* up, they'll hate me for life. I was thinking of asking his mother to help with my bridesmaids' dresses, because it felt like his parents need to be involved in planning somehow. How can we go about asking them to be involved, and how can I start feeling comfortable around his parents? Is it me?

To begin, you need to put aside your fears that his parents will be instantly turned against you if you screw anything up. Take it from us, we *all* screw things up from time to time. But here's the news: You are not on trial, and his parents are not the judge and jury, waiting to sentence you for any infraction. You are the person their son loves, who will be building a life with him. Naturally you want to get to know the people who raised the man you love. And it will be easier than you think once you have sharing the wedding process as a place to start.

Start by asking if they would like to be involved and if they have any ways they might like to contribute. Explain that you would like them to be involved and give them some options—one of which could be helping with the bridesmaids' dresses—along with some other ideas. Tell them that you look forward to spending more time with them and getting to know them, and vice versa. Then, once the planning process begins, keep them in the loop on a regular basis.

You may also want to take a closer look at why you are so petrified of these people. Are you afraid they won't like you (why wouldn't they?) Are you overanxious to please them (do you tend to do that with other people?)? Or has your fiancé hinted that they are "difficult" and thus predisposed you to react this way? Think about your own place in this, and discuss your reactions with your fiancé so he can help you begin dealing with it. If you find that this fear is all in your own mind, and that they have given you no cause to be so frightened of them, make a new start—assume and act as if they like you, and proceed from there.

ALOOF MOTHER-IN-LAW

Dear Dr. Dale,

Ever since my fiancé and I told his parents about our engagement, his mother seems to be treating me differently. In the past, we used to get along really well and always had something to talk about, but lately she hardly speaks to me. When I am at her house for Sunday dinner, she only looks at her other daughter-in-law and never makes eye contact with me. When I call her, she never returns my phone calls. I'm not sure where this is coming from or why she is acting differently. Whenever my fiancé asks her what the problem is, she just says she's busy with her father, who is quite ill. But I really don't think that explains her behavior. This has really hurt me, especially since we started out with such a nice relationship. I'm tired of feeling like I'm constantly "sucking up" to her and suddenly being made to feel as if I'm not good enough for her son. Help!

Parents often go through a variety of feelings as they anticipate the marriage of a child. After all, they are "losing" their child and someone else is going to be number one. Having said this, however, many parents are unaware of the emotional effects of their behavior. They are aware that they are feeling strange or different (or more angry, sensitive, alienated, fearful, sad, depressed, scattered, and so on), but they do not realize that this is manifesting in their behavior or make the link to this dramatic change in family structure.

Since you do not have a clue about what might have precipitated her change toward you, it seems like a good idea to talk with her, alone, about your perceptions and feelings. Without "sucking up," you can sit down with her and describe the changes you have experienced and talk with her about what she thinks might be the cause. Respectfully share your observations with her and let her know that if anything has happened between you to hurt her or alienate her, you are unaware of it and would appreciate being told. You can also tell her that you can appreciate how she may be wondering what kinds of changes there will be once her son marries, but that you have every intention of continuing what you had thought was a close and positive relationship.

If your future mother-in-law bristles, then take a deep breath and say you would appreciate her helping you to solve whatever the problem is. Let her know how much you love her son and plan to build a loving relationship with him and hope to do the same with her. Tell her you feel her change toward you is due to something, but you don't know what. If she says you don't know what you are talking about and that you are dead wrong, tell her you wish that was the case, but that you have come to trust your feelings and perceptions and thank her for listening. Ask her if she wants you to point out when it next occurs so you can deal with it at the time. If your future mother-in-law says no, tell her you hope she will think about what you said and be aware of your feelings. You can tell her you would like to think that once she knows that her behavior was hurtful to you, even if it was unintentional, that you hope she will try to be more mindful of your feelings.

If after all of this, your future mother-in-law is still dismissive or exclusionary, your fiancé will need to step in and talk with his mother about being more respectful and inclusive.

CONTROLLING MOTHER-IN-LAW

Dear Dr. Dale,
My future mother-in-law wants to control everything my fiancé and I do with regard to our wedding. I try to include

her in our decisions and ask her to give us her opinion, but that is not good enough. The funny thing is that when I first got engaged, she told me how she hated the fact that her mother-in-law had controlled everything from soup to nuts, and that it was especially hurtful because her in-laws paid for *her* wedding and that was their excuse. Now she is trying to control *our* wedding, even though she is *not* paying; my fiancé and I are paying. Occasionally, she offers to pay for certain things, but only if she can pick them out.

My fiancé fights with her constantly, telling her to leave me alone and let me make my own decisions. But she is very stubborn, doesn't listen to anyone, and could care less about what her son says. Thus, she still calls me and tries to make decisions for me. I tell her in a nice way that this is her son's and my wedding and we are going to do what we want. I explain that I don't include my own mother in every decision because my fiancé and I feel that this is our wedding and our decisions count the most. What do I do to get her to leave me alone?

Some future mothers-in-law are not easy to deal with. Unfortunately, yours falls into this category. The fact that she is not listening to you says more about her than about you. If you give her the benefit of the doubt, you could say that she wants to be involved, and may be calling you and selecting things for you as a way to become closer to you and to "share" the experience with you. It is possible that having lived through her own in-laws doing *her* deciding, she now sees an opportunity to do what she could not do for herself. Your fiancé yelling at her is not working, and may only spur her to try to become *more,* not *less,* involved.

So start by suggesting that he back off. Then, sit with her and tell her that you want to go forward with your wedding planning in a way that will suit you, and you *need her help to make this happen.* Ask her how she felt when her mother-in-law selected things for her, and see if she can recall how she felt. Stick to the question and don't get off track. When she tells you how she felt (disappointed, pushed aside, angry), you can offer a response like "That must have been terrible for you, a young bride-to-be wanting to express herself by planning her own wedding and not having a chance to do so." Then make the leap to "I know it is difficult for you *not* to be involved. But perhaps you don't see that what you are doing makes me feel as if you are taking away the pleasure I have looked forward to for so long—that of planning my own wedding and making my vision and my dream become my reality. I appreciate your desire to help me, but I really do want to do it all by myself. If there is anything I want your help with, I will feel free to ask. What you are doing is not working for me and I do not want our relationship to suffer. Please help me with this."

See how she responds to this approach. Be gentle. When you notice *any* improvement in her behavior, tell her how much you appreciate her trying. Chances are that this will work. If not, you just have to move on and do what makes you and your fiancé happy, and weather the storm while it lasts. Hopefully, after your wedding you and she can develop a more even-keeled relationship.

IN-LAW FRICTION

Dear Dr. Dale,

I am currently living with my fiancé at his parent's house (it's a long story!), and his mother and I have a lot of conflict and friction between us. I desperately want to be friends with her, but it seems impossible. Our wedding is only three months away, and I need some advice. Help!

You and your future mother-in-law are both going through major changes in your lives, and you also happen to be undergoing them while under the same roof. You and your fiancé are about to be married, an experience you are approaching with joy, elation, and maybe some trepidation. Parents, too, endure an array of feelings, including sadness at realizing that their child is about to become someone else's husband, partner, chief concern. We don't know the circumstances that have led you to be living with your fiancé's parents during such a potentially stressful time, but those conditions would be difficult even for a long-married couple with a strong foundation of love and trust from which to operate. In addition, there will be tension surrounding routines and rituals whenever people of differing generations live together, even when not planning a wedding.

Whatever the source of these frictions, sit down with your fiancé's mother and try to simply talk about how you are feeling, then ask for her feelings and concerns and advice. Begin by asking her if this is a good time to talk about something important that is on your mind and about which you could use her help and advice. Tell her you are concerned about the relationship between the two of you and want very much to improve it but do not know what caused the distance. Acknowledge that you know it is difficult to have someone new living in her house and how much you appreciate how difficult that is. Perhaps you did not talk about the living arrangements and boundary issues (who cooks when, who cleans the bathrooms, who does the laundry, who pays for groceries, etc.) and maybe this is bothering her. Who knows? You won't know until you ask and hear her answers.

If she is rude, do not be rude back. Tell her you are coming to her with the hope of making things better, and you need her to help you. Explain that the very least you two can give one another is respect, and you cannot have her talk to you in a disrespectful way. (You can only say this if you are respectful to her.) If she is defensive, ask her to tell you what bothers her about your living there. Ask her to tell you the specific areas that trouble her and share with her the areas you feel are filled with conflict. Tell her you are eager to work out ways to live together under one (her) roof more peacefully.

And remember, it is still her house. Do whatever you can to move on and move into your own place with your fiancé. It is hard enough to begin a life together without having to live in the same space as a mother-in-law who lets you know how put out she is by your being there.

MY IN-LAWS IGNORE ME— AND OUR WEDDING

Dear Dr. Dale

I am getting married to my best friend, with whom I have been in love for four years. He is wonderful, and there aren't enough kind words to describe him. He is also the most well-mannered and thoughtful person I have ever met. Unfortunately, he did not learn his kindness and good manners from his parents. I don't know if they are just self-involved, cheap, ill-mannered, or all of these, but here is how they have behaved thus far:

- They have never acknowledged that their son is getting married, either to him or to me.

- When they call my fiancé they never ask to speak to me. When I answer the phone at our home, they just ask to speak to him.

- When we had our engagement party, they didn't even RSVP. My fiancé had to call them to see if they were coming!

- When we got engaged, they never called my mother to congratulate her. We have been together for over four years, and the only time they have ever met my mother was at our engagement party.

- They have never once offered to help with any of the planning of the wedding, nor have they shown any interest when we try to share the plans with them. Sometimes they even change the subject, as if the conversation about our wedding bores them!

- They have already told my fiancé they will not help out financially with the wedding. They are not rich, but they are not hurting either. My mother took out a second mortgage on her home to pay for the wedding.

I try to pretend this behavior doesn't affect me when I see his family, but it is killing me and I know how embarrassed my fiancé is. What can we do?

The reality is that your in-laws are going to be a part of your life forever. They may have put you in an uncomfortable (and inappropriate) position, but you still have choices. You can be angry as all get out, and build up resentment and disappointment that can linger for years. Or you can take the high road and make a point of reaching out to them and inviting them to participate in some of the planning, and see how they respond.

Let's start by giving them the benefit of the doubt. If they have not offered to become involved, it may be because they are waiting to be asked their opinion regarding some of the planning. Most people do not wait to be asked to contribute, but there are exceptions. They may feel that they do not want to barge into the bride's family's domain. They may be intimidated by all this hoopla, and their way of dealing with it is to withdraw from the process or just ignore it. So asking them to help with planning (and make it something specific) may be in order.

OK. Now you have given them the benefit of the doubt. But what if they really are just not interested? And what if they really do just have bad manners and are self-involved? The best you can do in this situation is to try not to read anything into their apathetic responses and just move ahead and pretend that they are not behaving this way—ignore how they are acting and instead act, yourself, with the dignity and well-mannered behavior that is part of who you are. Here are some suggestions:

- Present concrete invitations to participate in the planning by inviting your mother-in-law to come along when you look at flowers or favors.

- Continue to invite your in-laws to all prewedding events, and have your fiancé call to get their RSVP.

- Send them notes—via e-mail or letters—with updates about the plans.

- Invite your mother-in-law to lunch with you and your mom.

- When they call your home and immediately ask for your fiancé, ask how they are doing and continue the conversation, keeping them on the line with your own stories and updates.

- As far as their offering to pay for anything, the only thing to do is to speak with them with your fiancé about their possibly paying for the rehearsal dinner, which as you may know is usually a gift from the groom's family.

If your future in-laws don't "take the bait" or don't respond to your extending your hand, stop asking and focus on the people who really want to be there and be involved in this joyous part of your life. It is always better for you and your fiancé to take the high road. That way you will not have any regrets about your own behavior.

HIS FAMILY DISAPPROVES

Dear Dr. Dale,

My fiancé's parents have always adored me, but now that we are engaged they have told him that they think we're not right for each other. Both of us have spent a long time thinking about this, and we very firmly believe we *are* right for each other. Adding to my discomfort is the fact that his is a very family-oriented clan: They all live within one mile of each other, and Sunday is considered family day, with everyone attending church together. I have been going with them to services since early in my relationship with my fiancé, but now I feel terribly uncomfortable attending with them, since I know how they feel. I want to be the mature one in this situation, and I think we should talk with them about their feelings. How can I possibly convince them that their son and I are right for each other?

You are absolutely right that you should sit down and talk with your future in-laws, but your mission is not to convince them that you and your fiancé are right for each other. That has already been decided by the only two people who could know that—you and your fiancé. Be yourself, and let your fiancé's parents know *why* you both feel you are a perfect match. Do not be defensive: Simply offer them the opportunity to hear why you love their son and why you want a wonderful future with him—and them. If you are willing and comfortable, invite them to share their specific concerns, which you can then both address.

As to your concerns about family activities, all couples need time alone to develop their own connections and ways of dealing with each other. Marrying is the beginning of a new family, consisting of you and your fiancé, and while time with his family is important, the time with your new husband is more important. Make sure that your fiancé understands this, and that he doesn't fall into the trap of immediately moving you into his family's routine. The two of you need to make your own routine; otherwise, you will lose your individuality as a couple. Developing a firm identity for the two of you will enable you to meet any challenges or disapproval of your union from a position of strength.

PREJUDICED RELIGIOUS VIEWS

Dear Dr. Dale,

I am about to get married, and my fiancé and I have been together for over four years. We are madly in love, and are truly soulmates. But we have a huge problem, which has been there since the beginning, and that is my future mother-in-law. Simply put, she is prejudiced. However, she is also quite religious and uses many old-time phrases and beliefs that have, in most worlds, been discarded. Not with her. For example, my family is of Hispanic descent, and this woman uses stereotypes when discussing me and my family, but always couched in terms of God and religion. She also attacks other religions and races. I get very upset by all of this, not only because I hate prejudice, but because this comes under the guise of religion, sent in long-winded letters in the name of "the Lord," telling me how to plan my wedding, and how I will (should) live my life.

You are going to ask how my fiancé deals with this. Not well! He doesn't really stick up for my reactions and feelings. It's not that he is a bad person. I just think he is so used to hearing these views that he doesn't take it as seriously as I do.

You seem like you already know the answer! Yes, you and your fiancé first need to work this out on your own. And that starts with him sticking up for you. Your fiancé should talk to his mother. He must be *clear and forceful* about his support of you, about his feelings that prejudice and demeaning stereotypes have no place in his life, and that her interference in his new life will not be accepted nor tolerated.

You are also going to have to talk with your future mother-in-law, no matter how daunting that may seem. Tell her that you appreciate how strong her faith and opinions are, but that you are comfortable with your own faith and means of raising a family, and are uncomfortable with any proclamations that insult your family, your history, your nationality. As to her letters, realistically, you can either accept these letters as gifts and read them, or you can simply toss them out as irritants when they arrive.

THE OTHER WOMEN IN MY FIANCÉ'S LIFE

Dear Dr. Dale,

In three months I am marrying a wonderful man. That's the good news. Unfortunately, my fiancé's mother and ex-girlfriend have decided that this is their time to bond—and to be nasty to me. His mother liked me up until he asked me to marry him, and then the attacks began. On Christmas, she yelled at me for "outdoing" her present to my fiancé's daughter; on Mother's Day she told my fiancé's daughter not to eat the cookies I sent because they might be poisoned; and when my fiancé talked to her about our wedding, she told him that the only reason she is coming is to let my family know that she objects.

Then there is my fiancé's ex-girlfriend, the mother of his child, who took her daughter to a psychiatrist and sent the bills to me because she says the reason her daughter is depressed is because of my relationship with her father. In truth, my fiancé and the girl's mother have been separated for seven years, and my fiancé's daughter and I are really close. Furthermore, his ex has accused me of trying to steal her child (probably because her daughter likes me and has a very hard time with her mom).

This lovely daughter is with us every weekend, and it is during these visits that she tells me the barrage of insults about me and her dad that her mom has used in front of her. Hearing these things is painful, but hearing it from an eight year old is devastating. The ex and my future mother-in-law have disliked each other for many years, and have suddenly become allies for one reason: to stop our wedding. I have tried really hard to be nice to them, going out of my way when they ask me to do favors for them. I have even invited them to lunch to talk things out, but they always decline with rude comments like "some of us have to work." The reason I bother with these two poisonous women is because they are always going to be involved in our life, but I don't want it to continue like this. Is there any way I can appease these two, or should I just give up?

This situation, although difficult and infuriating, is not unusual. Frequently, when one parent of a shared child is about to remarry, the remaining parent can behave remarkably—remarkably good *or* remarkably bad. This is for any number of reasons, among them jealousy, fear, disappointment, and anger, to name a few. Your fiancé's daughter is in the middle of a long-standing tug-of-war, played out by people who seem to have no sense of what is appropriate to share with a child. With you in the picture, the daughter is also in the untenable position of hearing terrible things about you and her dad.

When your fiancé's daughter tells you these things, you need to reassure her that you are deeply sorry she is in the middle of this, and regret that she has to hear these terrible things—that it is not right. Reassure her, too, that it is OK for her to tell you what she hears (so that she does not have to hold it inside herself), and tell her that you are doing your best to find a way to stop her mom and grandma from saying such awful things about you. You must take the high road and try to protect the girl. Assuring her that you are there for her, offering her a welcome and safe place without caustic and hateful remarks, is the best gift you can give her. She needs to see that she can handle the words and the feelings and that you will help her.

Regarding your future mother-in-law's attendance at the wedding: If his mother will not give you her blessing, and is against the union, it is better that she not attend. If she does attend, you can alert other guests (friends and family whom you trust) to the potential that there might be a disagreement or an objection at the time of the ceremony. It is up to your fiancé to meet with his mother and explain to her that you are his choice for a bride, and that if she can agree to behave in an appropriate way, then she is welcome to see him get married. If, for any reason, she cannot agree, then he needs to tell her that any disruption will not be tolerated and that she will be asked to leave should one erupt. He can even tell her that she will be thrown out of the wedding if she misbehaves, so she understands how serious you are about her behavior and its consequences, and that his warning (or threat) is real and will be followed by action.

Finally, your fiancé can reassure his mother that he hopes she will get to know you and love you as he has, but that if she cannot or will not, then that is her problem. As for the ex-girlfriend—make sure she is nowhere near this wedding!

MADDENING MOTHER-IN-LAW

Dear Dr. Dale,

When I recently told my mother-in-law-to-be that her son and I were going to get married, she blurted out, "Thank God it's not soon because I couldn't take it." I have since asked her for help, with no support in return. So I decided to take charge and make decisions on my own, because I did not want to wait until she was ready to help me plan. She has since criticized all of the decisions I have made, to the point where she has offended the event manager at the resort I chose. To add insult to injury, she has now told the whole family that I am telling her to stay out of it when I did not.

Because of all the drama of her playing the victim, I was seriously thinking about calling off the whole wedding ceremony and suggesting that we elope—but I have always dreamt of a real wedding and don't want her awful behavior to cause me to change my lifelong plans. I'm under so much pressure that I have been to a therapist to help me with coping skills, but she said my feelings are normal and I'm going to have to work them out myself. Other than the "Serenity Prayer," which is not helping, I don't know what to do. How much control do I give her, and is it disrespectful to ask her to keep her caustic comments to herself?

There are several issues here. First, where is your fiancé and why are you alone in dealing with his mother throughout this process? The "Serenity Prayer" is useful and can help you to feel calmer and at peace with yourself, but it does not take the place of true conversations with those around you. You need to explain to your fiancé that he needs to support you during this time, and ideally have a stern conversation with his mother about how she is behaving. Second, if you have consistently asked your mother-in-law for help and have not received any, then 1) stop asking; and 2) get used to the idea that she does not appear to be supportive.

What you need more than prayer, at this point, is to learn some assertive ways of talking with your future mother-in-law, techniques that will prevent you from being put down while respectfully handling her hurtful comments. When you are insulted you can calmly state that you do not appreciate that kind of comment and will not hear it, that no one should be treated in this hurtful manner, that you would never speak to her in this way and expect the same respect from her. When she disagrees with you and won't let you state your opinions, gently but firmly explain that this is your wedding, and while you respect her point of view, it is your and your fiancé's decisions that will ultimately stand. In short, your fiancé's mother can be a part of the wedding, but she can't belittle it or you.

You can also ask her to treat the people you have hired with respect, but frankly, anyone who mistreats employees or others to their faces is not going to change their behavior just because you point it out. You may be on your own on this one—so just warn those professionals involved in your wedding planning process that your future mother-in-law can be difficult, and you would appreciate their tolerance. Believe me, this is not the first time they will have heard this!

MAMA'S BOY

Dear Dr. Dale,

I am excited to be engaged to a wonderful man and could not ask for a better support system from my family. There is one exception, however. My soon-to-be mother-in-law is absolutely ruining this special time for us. On the day we became engaged, she cried like a child for two hours and completely embarrassed us. From that moment on, she has made me feel like a complete outsider (my soon-to-be father-in-law, by the way, is happy and looking forward to our special day). She looks at me with daggers in her eyes, and if someone approaches me while I am in her presence, she makes horrible faces and completely embarrasses me. She actually made the cutting and thoughtless statement that she would love to return her "gift"—meaning me, her future daughter-in-law! She constantly has us on a guilt trip about how we don't include her in our life, how she feels like she has lost her son, how she wishes she could turn back the clock to before the engagement. We have been dating for almost one year, and I have not yet been invited to her home for dinner.

I don't know why she thinks being so negative and unwelcoming is going to make me go away—it won't, and my fiancé has made that clear to her. Maybe I could understand if I was some terrible person who was pushing her son into some destructive lifestyle, but I am not. I am a successful businesswoman, no children, never been married, and I come from a good family. I have been nothing but nice, polite, and have never even called her on her behavior. However, I have had enough. I don't know what else to do but let her have it.

Your future mother-in-law has already told you exactly what the problem is—she is having a terrible time dealing with the reality of her son's impending marriage. It likely has nothing to do with you. And this is why your fiancé must stop it. She needs *to hear from her son* that her behavior displeases and disappoints him and that he hopes she will be more welcoming of his bride-to-be. He needs to convey that he understands how difficult this time is for her, and that he sees how frightened she is, but that taking it out on you is inappropriate. For your part, when she says she feels that she is losing her son, accept it and tell her that it must be a difficult and scary thing to have happen. It is, actually. And by letting her know that you understand it must be difficult for her, you may be able to ease her fear and pain.

The next time she complains that you do not include her, ask her how she would like to be included, and then assess with your fiancé whether what she is looking for is reasonable or practical. Have you asked her about her own wedding? Have you looked through her wedding album with her? Have you asked her about what it was like when she married your future father-in-law and what it was like for her with his family? Try to engage her—positively—if you can.

If she really persists in badgering you, you can continue to rise above her treatment while still being honest about your feelings. Tell her that you feel her comments and faces of disgust are hurtful and disrespectful to both you and her son, and that if she has a problem with you, she should tell you what it is and the two of you can try to find a way to get along.

Now, having said all this, sometimes changing a person's attitude is just not possible. If you and your fiancé go the extra mile and the situation does not improve, then you will just have to limit your time with her. You can even warn her that if she doesn't change her behavior, this will be the consequence, and while it is not your choice not to spend time with her, this kind of treatment will naturally result in more separate lives, and that instead of gaining a daughter, she may lose time with both of you.

As far as handling your own feelings, do not internalize your anger. Focus on your relationship with your fiancé and the others in your life who are celebrating with you. But we are betting that you will be able to resolve this—because, in our experience, even angry mothers-in-law-to-be want to keep their sons, and when confronted with understanding, may be quite happy to change.

MOTHER-IN-LAW WITH RICH TASTES

Dear Dr. Dale,

My fiancé's mother has been a nightmare. The latest squabble is over the invitation list. My mother is a widow and on a limited budget, and since my fiancé's parents' family (who happen to be quite wealthy) have chosen not to contribute to the wedding reception at all, we have decided on a guest list of 150 people. My fiancé's mother is put out by this number (although when asked if she would like to pay for any extra guests, she has refused) and continues to whine about it. She is pushing me to a point where I am very afraid I am going to lose my temper and cause a rift before the wedding. How do I calm down and deal with her?

Clearly, every mother has a vision of what her child's wedding will be like. It is expected that each parent wants to share the joyful event with family and friends. However, the final decision lies with the bride and groom and, as in your case, the bride's family. Your fiancé's mother does not have to like your decision, but she does need to respect it. And since she has refused to make up the extra cost to invite people she wants, she really does not have any say in the arrangements.

You may wish to enlist your fiancé to help you discuss the situation face-to-face. You can express to her that you understand that she would like to have a larger number, but that it is not possible, given your mother's financial situation. You both need to let her know that what you need from her is her support. Try to take the high road and refrain from losing your temper. If she brings up the invitation list, acknowledge her disappointment: "I know you are disappointed and feel stifled that we are limited to the number we have chosen. But I'm afraid this is the reality of the situation, and it would be better for all of us if we can get beyond it and move forward so that our wedding can be a celebration of joy."

If this doesn't work, kindly mention to her that her consistent reference to the invitation list is not helping the two of you to build a close mother-in-law–daughter-in-law relationship, and that that is something that you really want to do.

NOBODY CHALLENGES MY
MOTHER-IN-LAW

Dear Dr. Dale,

When we told my fiancé's mother we were getting married, she was very happy. If only I had known what she was really thinking! I know she loves me and cares a tremendous amount about me, but I cannot deal with the way she handles situations. I was raised differently, in that if something bothered me or I didn't like the way something was being done, I could voice my opinion or concern. Well, in my fiancé's family, no one ever questions his mother. It's like they are all afraid to speak up and tell her how they really feel. Instead, they just blow it off and let it all go.

So, during the entire wedding planning process, in just about everything, she has had a "suggestion," which is really her way of saying "this is the way it should be done, and if it's not, then it is wrong." She makes me feel like nothing we have done from the beginning has been right, at least according to her.

To make it worse, I feel like I have no support from my fiancé. I feel that he is afraid of her, and instead of talking to her or letting her know she is getting too involved, it is easier for him to just argue with me about it to avoid the situation with his mother. What am I supposed to do?

This is a real problem, not so much because your mother-in-law is who she is (you will not change her), but because your fiancé is choosing to argue with you instead of dealing directly with her. It seems like he does not want to assert his adult status with his mother. Of course, he should not be disrespectful to her. He does, however, need to listen to you, support you, and if necessary, stand up for you. You need to talk with him about this. Tell him you understand that his mother is a powerful woman who seems to have gotten her way in most things in the family. (You do not need to say this critically, but rather just as an observation.) You can let him know you realize how difficult it is for him to stand up to his mother, particularly when it relates to you and your upcoming marriage. Remind him that you are marrying one another to build your life together, the life you want, and that only as adults can you do this. You need to be able to rely on his being an adult to make this happen.

The bottom line is that whoever is primarily responsible for planning the wedding—i.e., you and your fiancé—is who makes the final decisions. That means that everyone else may or may not like the choice, but they have to live with it. It is highly unlikely that everyone involved will like all of your choices, but they are *your* choices. Certainly, compromise is always useful, but being bullied or made to feel that your ideas are worthless is not. Your fiancé needs to talk with his mother about his need to have her respect his (and your) decisions about the wedding. He can remind her that she planned her wedding, and it is now his turn to plan his wedding, and to have the wedding you and he want. He can tell his mother he appreciates her concern and her suggestions, but that you and he are the final decision makers.

As to the issue of being raised in a different environment from your fiancé and, particularly, his mother, where you and your family directly express your true feelings, well, that is great—*for you and your family*. But now you are dealing with people who have different styles and different expectations. Although you need to be respectful to your mother-in-law and to your new in-law family, you can always talk with her, alone and directly, about what you see as the problem. And explain that you need her help in solving it. You can tell her that you appreciate her input, respect her opinion, and that if she has suggestions you are happy to hear them.

However, you need to be very clear about one essential point—that there is more than one way to do anything, and that her way is only *one way*. Your choices, although not hers, are not wrong. You can tell her, kindly, that when she offers her suggestion you feel as if 1) you will be hurting her feelings if you do not comply; 2) you would like to have support for your choices even if they are not *her* choices; and 3) you would like her to appreciate that your tastes are not the same and that that is OK. The wedding may not be "her" taste, but it is yours. You will incorporate her ideas into the wedding whenever you can, but this will not be possible 100 percent of the time. And remember, with this kind of "negotiation" it is important to always and consistently emphasize that you are both in agreement about one thing: that you both love her son!

THEY LOVE—AND CALL HIM!—
TOO MUCH

Dear Dr. Dale,

Both of my parents adore my fiancé and have ever since the first time they met. We met at college, so I am not at home as much as they would like, but they understand that. They call me every day and I talk to them if I have time, and if not I call them back the next day.

My fiancé's parents, on the other hand, call five to ten times a day and if he doesn't call them back they throw a fit. They always want him to come home, and when he does, he brings me with him. But when I am there, his dad just takes him out and leaves me at home. His mom likes me, but his dad hardly says one word to me. He was never like this until we announced our engagement. I don't know what to do to open him up. It isn't a fun trip when the only companion I have is the family dog. What do I do?

You need to talk with your fiancé about the relationship you have with him, both with his parents, and when you are alone. He does not seem to appreciate the importance of "integrating" you into his family and making sure that you are comfortable before going off with his dad. Sometimes parents react adversely when their children become engaged, and this may be the case with your future in-laws. But it is up to your fiancé to lay the groundwork for how he expects his parents to treat you, and it is up to him to assert himself as a man and not as a boy.

As for his parents calling several times a day, you may wish to discuss the frequency with him and suggest that they speak at a specific time during the day, so that you and he have some privacy. But be careful—you may end up being the "bad guy" in this situation, because if he suggests to his parents that it was your idea, and that it is your wish that they stop calling him as frequently as they are used to, the blame will be put on you. Discuss this danger with your fiancé, and agree on exactly what is to be said so you avoid an uglier situation. Ideally, he will assume responsibility and let his parents think that it was his idea.

WHERE IS OUR TIME TOGETHER?

Dear Dr. Dale,

Am I wrong for not wanting to hang out with my in-laws all the time? My fiancé likes to hang out with his fifteen- and sixteen-year-old cousins (he's twenty-five) all the time, and I just can't seem to do it, which makes me look bad. And if I don't want to join them, he runs off with them. I never keep him from being with his cousins, but he never just wants to stay with me. Other people, particularly his brother and his fiancée, have a history of interfering in our relationship. What do I do? How do I make him understand that we should have a life of our own, too? Am I wrong?

You are not wrong. When couples are about to get married, they usually want to spend time together. At the same time, though, they do wonder how their lives will change, and may end up making a concerted effort to continue the same habits (hanging around with their friends or, in this case, cousins) in order to help convince themselves that their lives will not change that much. Our hunch is that your fiancé may take for granted the fact that you are always around and available, so that if he wants to be with you, you are there, and if he doesn't, that's OK, too.

A primary reason to marry someone is because you enjoy doing things together, spending time together, and discovering life with each other. By doing this, you get to know yourself and the other person better. If there are always others around, it is much more difficult to become a couple and develop what is unique to the two of you. That said, in all relationships, there needs to be sensitivity toward what the other person wants and expects regarding time spent together as well as with other people. So explore what your time together is like, and why he would want to spend so much time with his cousins. Look at what happens when you are together. How do you talk to each other? How do you show interest in one another's lives? How good a listener are you? In what ways do you demonstrate your caring for each other? Join him on an outing with his cousins and try to understand what it is that he enjoys so much.

You may find that the time he spends with them is just play time that he needs, for whatever reason, and you will then have to decide how important it is to you that he spend more time with you. Maybe he is a "guy's guy," in which case it will be difficult if he is inflexible. But that does not mean you do not have the conversation. Talk to him and try to understand his needs, what is behind them, and whether he is willing to change them. You may also want to explore what kinds of things you *both* like to do and see if a change of activity will make quality time with you seem more inviting. I suggest you begin the conversation in a neutral place. Go to a place where you are not likely to be interrupted. Begin with "I have something I need to discuss with you that is very important to me. Please listen with an open heart because I have given it a lot of thought, and I would like you to know how I feel, and I want to understand how you feel about it. I have a hard time thinking about marriage without being able to picture or imagine our having a life of our own."

HOLDING ON TO AN ONLY CHILD

Dear Dr. Dale,

I am engaged to an only child who is also the only grand-child on his mother's side. My fiancé's dad is disabled and cannot make many decisions, so his mother is in charge of the household. That said, she has been largely absent from our lives and our wedding. Any friendly conversation or contact I have tried to establish with my future mother-in-law has failed. When I first expressed concerns to my fiancé about his mother's lack of interest in our relationship or the upcoming wedding, he reassured me that her silence was a good thing. He says that she doesn't like many people. How-ever, I have heard through the grapevine that she has lately expressed to people that she believes that this relationship is just an infatuation for her son and hopefully he will be over it soon. My fiancé and I have already begun planning the wedding, which is in six months. How should I deal with such a situation, or should I, too, just let things take their course and hope she comes around and not create a disaster instead of a wonderful wedding day?

For some "only children" the relationship they have with their parents is especially close. In your fiancé's case, in part because of his father's disability, your future mother-in-law may have fears about losing her son and the close relationship they have had for so many years, and she may be in denial. Your fiancé needs to talk with his mom and explain to her that he is very serious, that you are not an infatuation who will go away, and that he needs and wants her support for what is the most important decision in his life. This conversation is not for you to have with his mother, and the sooner he has it the better it will be for all of you. His mother does not have to like you, but he can help her come to terms with the fact that she will soon have a daughter-in-law. Waiting for things to "take their course" may in fact cause a shipwreck; some courses need to be managed, and your fiancé had better take over the wheel.

AM I MARRYING A MAN OR AN ENTIRE FAMILY?

Dear Dr. Dale,

I am sure this is a question often asked, but I am at a loss as to what to do here. My fiancé and I have been dating for five years and are getting married in six months. He gets along well with my family—they have seen him as part of the family for a long time now. The problem is with his immediate family—his sister and parents. It seems they have never gotten past the first stage of acquaintance. I feel as distant from them as when we first met. Add to this that they are somewhat dysfunctional. His sister is a nightmare—very controlling, self-destructive, lying, and manipulative. I know that she has spread a lot of malicious lies about me to his parents, and I feel this may be why there is a lack of closeness between us. I also get the sense that his mother is struggling with her only son's impending marriage. Needless to say, I feel uncomfortable around these people, so we avoid spending time at his house.

I don't know what to do about them. They are not the

type who can look truth in the eye, and instead like to pretend that things aren't wrong. I am worried about what to do when we get married and/or when we start a family. And sometimes I get scared—am I marrying my wonderful fiancé or his family? Can you help me? I am totally confused and feel bad about it all, especially for my fiancé (who has actually dealt with this quite calmly, figuring he is doing what he has to do).

You said his family likes to pretend things are not wrong. Perhaps what you see as "wrong" they see as justified or normal. It is probable that they have a different set of standards of what is right or wrong and that what bothers you may not affect them at all. The way to deal with people such as those you describe is to have absolutely no expectations that they will change their behavior. So, your decision to stay away from all these people, since your interactions lately have been so unpleasant, is a good short-term solution to your problem. Having said that, it is imperative that you treat them with the same respect that you hope, someday, to receive from them. If you descend to their level, you will not only be playing into their dysfunction, you will disappoint yourself by becoming someone you don't like.

The larger issue here is your fiancé's role in the face of family members who, after five years of dating their son, are not welcoming you into their world. He does have a responsibility to challenge his sister's lies and to intervene on your behalf. If you know of specific rumors, he should address them directly. As for marrying your fiancé's family, this is in many ways part and parcel of any marriage. But when you start a family, you will be able to determine the kind of life you want for yourselves, and you can control when and how you see your in-laws.

NO PRIVACY

Dear Dr. Dale,

In the six months that I've been engaged I have been having a hard time with the fact that my fiancé, the love of my life, talks to his brother, who is his best friend, every single day about every single thing in our private life. While I understand that they are best friends, I feel that as an engaged (and soon to be married) couple, we should have our privacy, and I don't feel comfortable with my future brother-in-law knowing so much about us—and about me. I feel betrayed, and I resent the exposure. What should I do?

Your fiancé and his brother have been whispering to each other since they were kids; they've shared everything about life and growing up. This is a good thing, since most men don't have those kinds of relationships, and they bring a healthy component to your fiancé's life. It's likely that he has no idea that he's betraying you—he is simply spending time with a cherished friend and sharing the details of his relationship with another love of his life. He might even be shocked to learn that you feel upset.

That said, you have every right to want your personal life to remain private and your confidences respected. You need to talk with your fiancé right away about issues of privacy. Your new relationship will demand many changes of you and your fiancé, and this is just the beginning of dealing with change.

Be specific about those things you are not comfortable with your fiancé sharing with anyone: specific situations, stories, areas of your life, and things about your relationship that you want to keep between the two of you. Assure him that you always honor his privacy, but that you are now sometimes reluctant to share your feelings for fear they will be shared with his brother.

Setting these new parameters, and giving your fiancé a chance to change his longtime relationship, is fair, but it will take time. Be patient but vigilant. Gently point out specific instances when you feel your fiancé reveals too much, if they happen, and it should work out just fine.

TEN

Friends and Exes

BE PREPARED: With marriage, friendships change. Yes, this is your special time to plan your wedding and come to terms with the changes in your life and your identity, but what about your friends? What position do they play in your life? As a soon-to-be bride, you need to pay attention to the subtle and not so subtle relationship changes that happen all around you, particularly with the friends who have filled your life over the years.

Too often, women plan their weddings, marry, and subsequently leave their friendships behind. This often starts during the wedding process: The friends of the bride will complain that they no longer feel important and valued. Too many brides-to-be put their friendships not only in second place but, more often than not, way down the list of what's important. We often hear from brides that they don't have time for their friends, or that they feel certain friends don't understand what is involved in planning a wedding. But even in married life, women need one another for support, guidance, acceptance, and balance. Friendships require time and nurturing and caring—just like marriage. Even though your days and nights are likely filled with thought of caterers and dresses, it is important that you make the time to maintain your friendships in ways that will be satisfying and gratifying to your friends as well as to you.

Yes, friendships do change, but they can still continue. They may even provide a welcome outlet and mainstay during these hectic months. Numerous studies, as well as the experience of every generation of mothers, grandmothers, and aunts, emphasize the value of women's friendships as the *best* support system to help you get through life. And there is nothing to match the stress-busting ability of a great laugh or cry with your girlfriends.

It is also essential to recognize that your friends will experience their own adjustments and reactions to your impending marriage. Their emotions may range from joy to sadness to fear to anxiety to jealousy to disappointment to relief. And though these emotions can be powerful, they may not have a forum for expression. You may wonder why your dearest friend and roommate of ten years is suddenly picky and uncooperative in her role as maid of honor. In reality, she may be having a tough time adjusting to the reality of her changing status in your world. She may feel distressed to be losing her position as primary confidant, and lonely knowing that she won't be able to rely on you like she once could for "girls night out" or your tradition of a yearly spa weekend. Or, you may be puzzled by another friend's sudden withdrawal from daily phone contact, not realizing that she worries that you don't have time anymore to chat because of all that's going on. And *you* may wonder how *your* impending role as a wife will affect your role as a friend, and are struggling with that adjustment on your end as well. You may find yourself sharing only limited parts of yourself, and of the plans for your wedding, because you wonder whether you are being disloyal to your fiancé if you discuss areas of doubt or concern. Or, you may feel excluded from the single-girl outings you used to participate in.

The stress of shifting friendships can be wearing, and rightly so. There may be tension. You may have arguments that you "just don't need at this time." And when this happens, you can feel betrayed, let down, and shocked at the changed behavior of women you thought you knew so well. These situations can be further complicated if there are issues between your friends and your fiancé. Perhaps you sense that some of your friends aren't exactly fans of your fiancé and vice versa.

So why does this happen? Sometimes it is difficult to know. But here are some things you can do to minimize any friction that occurs:

- Have a talk with your friends about the fact that your own life is changing, that you are trying to do your best, and that this is a time when you really need their support. Let them know the friendship channels between you remain intact—and that they are more important to you now than ever, even if your day-to-day interactions are changing.

- Reassure your friends about the nature of change— yes, things change, but they can also change for the better.

- Have a conversation with your friends about *what you expect* and *what they may expect* during the wedding planning process, especially when it comes to available time together.

- Remind yourself that each of your friends is going through her own experiences with regard to your wedding. You are getting married, and they are not; you are understandably caught up in your own marital plans, and they may feel a sense of abandonment; they may simply miss you and not feel comfortable sharing these feelings, knowing all that you have on your plate; and they may be worried about what happens after you are married: Will you and your new husband still see your single friends? Will your best friend be left out of your new life?

- Make sure that any conflicts between your friends and fiancé don't affect who you value and include in your life. Your fiancé does not have to like your friends (nor you his) and he is free to choose not to share time with them, but the ultimate decision about who you like and who you chose to spend time with is yours.

Perhaps the trickiest aspect of maintaining friendships once you're married involves relationships with your exes. Even if you know your relationship with an ex-boyfriend has transformed into a true friendship without the slightest romantic tension, your fiancé may still feel uncomfortable. What to do? Sneak around? Lie? Not a great way to begin your life as an almost married person. "But," you say, "this person played such an important part in my life and I would not be the person I am today without him. Why is my fiancé concerned? I chose my fiancé and not my ex." This all sounds very reasonable and rational, but the heart is not the head. The larger issue of your friendship with your ex may take some time to work out, but if having your ex at your wedding makes your fiancé uncomfortable, don't do it. Your fiancé's feelings are at stake, and overlooking these feelings on your wedding day is not the ideal way to start a marriage.

As you can tell, it is complicated. But don't despair! To keep your relationships with all your friends intact, talk frankly about what is ahead. Share with each of them what you would like and see if your expectations meet theirs. Above all, remember why they are important to you—and work hard to minimize the opportunities for disappointment and maximize the opportunities for continued meaningful time together.

MY FRIENDS WANT TO MAKE OVER MY FIANCÉ

Dear Dr. Dale,

My fiancé has a beard, and I want him to shave it for our wedding. My friends don't think it's classy for him to have a beard at the wedding, and I am inclined to agree. He, however, is very attached to it. He thinks that my friends and I are asking too much of him. Are we?

For years wedding specialists and mothers have advised brides not to change their hairdos for their weddings. This advice is based on the belief that we all have looks with which we are comfortable, and too drastic a change will make you decidedly uncomfortable on your wedding day—the last day when you need such stress.

Grooms should also feel and look their best on their wedding day. Assuming that you love your fiancé the way he is, why would you want to change his appearance for your wedding? And why would you prioritize your friends' wishes over your fiancé's? If your fiancé feels that his beard is part of who he is, he is entitled to keep it. And your friends' opinions should come second in matters of personal choice and taste such as this.

I DON'T LIKE MY FRIEND'S DATE

Dear Dr. Dale,

One of my best friends, who is also a groomsman, wants to bring a date to my wedding. I know the woman he is dating, and unfortunately do not like her at all. Also, she has gone out with nearly everyone who is going to be at the wedding, and I think it will be very uncomfortable. Do I have the right to invite our friend and ask him to bring someone other than this woman?

This is a tough situation. In truth, each of the groomsmen should be free to bring whomever they choose to the rehearsal dinner and wedding. If you are indeed close to your friend, then talk with him honestly. Be careful that you do not disparage his girlfriend or talk about her unkindly. If you feel you must, inform him that you have something important but potentially hurtful to discuss with him. Gently tell him how you feel and explain that you would feel more relaxed and comfortable on your wedding day and night of the rehearsal dinner if this woman was not present at the events. But in the end, leave the decision up to him.

If she attends after all, take the high road. Be gracious and respectful. You do not have to go out of your way for her, but she is the date of your dear friend, and out of respect for him, you will need to welcome her to your wedding.

I DON'T TRUST MY FIANCÉ'S FRIENDS

Dear Dr. Dale,

I'm about to get married, and my biggest fear is not the wedding, but the day before—the bachelor party. I know and trust my fiancé to not do something totally nuts, but his friends are insisting on taking him to Las Vegas for the party, and I don't trust *them*! I'm afraid that once my fiancé is under their influence, something might happen. Every time I try to talk to him about this, he gets very offended and hurt. What should I do?

Nothing.

Trust is the basis for all good relationships. Fear and trust are two things that are difficult, if not impossible, to reconcile. Although your fiancé's friends may have planned a wild Las Vegas bachelor party, your fiancé is a person in his own right who will need to make whatever decisions he can live with. You are not— nor should you be—your future husband's conscience when he is in what might be a potentially compromising situation.

If trust is important to you as a couple, then each of you must make decisions that will honor each other, your partnership, your love, and your commitment to each other. As for what you should do during that bachelor party: get together with a few of your own friends and have a ball. And let him be.

MY FRIEND'S DATE MAY DISRUPT MY WEDDING

Dear Dr. Dale,

My fiancé and I have a close female friend who has a roommate, and neither of us cares much for this guy. This roommate is gay, but that isn't the issue. (My personal attendant is gay, and he is one of my closest friends.) What bugs us is that he focuses on being gay and openly stares at men, including my fiancé. He's also one of those people who seems to need all attention focused on him.

The problem? We want our friend to come, but we don't want to encourage her to invite a guest because we know she will bring him. It's a delicate situation because the two of them are rather dependent on each other, and he assumes that he is invited. He's just so annoying! What can we do?

None of us can control the behavior of anyone who may attend our weddings, whether they are straight or gay. There is often someone on the wedding list who tells bawdy jokes, drinks too much, flirts, or behaves rudely. If you truly feel strongly, you can tell your friend of your reservations about her roommate's previous behavior and your discomfort, but if you expect her to approve of your reasoning, you will likely be disappointed. You have the right to invite whomever you choose to your wedding. Just remember that with this situation, you run the risk of hurting both your friend and her roommate. The cost may be worth it for you so that you can feel more at ease with the "tone" of your wedding, but do not disregard the fallout that may occur—in the end it may be easier to live with his presence and simply do your best to put him out of your mind on the actual day.

MY FRIEND IS ACTING ALOOF

Dear Dr. Dale,

One of my closest friends has been acting weird since I recently got engaged. We have spent most of our lives being the best of friends; everything we did, we did it together. Now she seems to be pulling away and making excuses whenever I suggest we get together. She never even asks about the wedding plans, even though she has agreed to be my maid of honor. I suspect that there may be some jealousy over my engagement, or fear that things won't be the same anymore. I understand that things can't stay exactly the same, and that she will find new single friends, but I am really worried that I am going to lose her friendship. How do I deal with this?

Friendships change. That is all there is to it. It takes getting used to on everyone's part. Be sure to read our introduction to this chapter, which explains that a few bumps in this transition are natural—that friends often fear the changes that come when one gets married.

You have a history of memories that will always be a part of your friendship. Your friendship will most likely continue, but it will be different, and both of you need to understand this. The reality is that as single friends there is an ease of sharing that changes when one person is married and the other is not, as well as a shift in how available you are to each other. Your friend will likely seek more frequent company from other friends who can relate to her single-girl status and have more free and easy schedules. This doesn't mean, however, that you can't remain close and important to each other's lives.

Now is the time to bend over backward to let your friend know how much she means to you. Start by inviting her to lunch or dinner—just the two of you—and gently bring up the changes you are seeing. Begin by telling her how important a friend she is to you and how much you value her and the experiences you have shared (use specific examples like the first time you traveled to the city together, how she was there for you when your heart was broken at sixteen, waiting for college admissions letters, spending hours on the phone after school, etc.). Reinforce how you could never imagine life without her and that you know things will change but that you are committed to making sure your friendship remains strong and intact. Ask her what she thinks will happen after you are married and share with her what you think

might happen that will make it difficult for the two of you to remain close. Talk about how the two of you can keep each other in
check. The major point is for you to reassure your friend that even
though you have a lot to do now for the wedding, and will be married soon, you need her in your life. By telling her this you are
helping her so she does not feel neglected.

MAINTAINING FRIENDSHIPS
AFTER THE WEDDING

Dear Dr. Dale,

My fiancé has a group of close male friends who have been
his "brothers" since school days, when they got together to
watch and play sports. Throughout the process of planning
our wedding, my sweet fiancé has spent so much time talking with me about parties and showers, the wedding and the
honeymoon, that he hasn't been able to spend time with his
male friends, and I think he feels bad about this. I want him
to know that he can see his friends after our marriage—and
not be afraid that this won't happen.

Life definitely changes once you're married, and one of the
most common complaints from newlyweds is that they can no
longer do the things that were once so easy to fit into their schedules. While this news may seem bleak, it is entirely possible to
have both a happy marriage and strong outside friendships. The
key is to make a concerted effort, with good communication and
planning. You will spend a great deal of time (happily, we might
add) with your new husband, but you both will have to set aside
time for other people. You will need to decide which nights are
guy nights and which are girl nights, and if you are open with

each other about what you want and need, this is easily done. As for the moment, talk with you fiancé and let him know that you support his friendships. Let him know that even though the planning process has been taking up a lot of time, your friends and his friends will always be an important part of your lives—both individually and together. Remember, your friendships are part of what make you who you are as a couple.

SHOULD I KEEP MY EX-HUSBAND'S LAST NAME?

Dear Dr. Dale

I was married once before, and I've kept my ex's last name, since everyone at my work and in my life now knows me by that name. My fiancé cannot wait for me to change my last name to his, but in the meantime he wants my name on the invitation to be my maiden name. I am worried that if I put my maiden name on my invitation, no one will know who I am! My ex's name has been mine for over ten years, and not only is it my legal name, it is the name I am known by. In fact, I'm not sure I want to take my new husband's last name at all! What should I do?

This is a very sticky issue. Your name is *your* name. You became who you are today by traveling along your life's path, and the man from whom you are divorced was part of that path. Along the way, you took his name and made it your own. It's a tough decision, because although you are no longer attached to him, it is understandable that your fiancé feels, at the worst, a bit threatened, and at the least, somewhat uncomfortable about your keeping the name of your former husband.

Start by trying to truly understand the meaning it carries for your fiancé. That said, be sure your fiancé understands that you cannot erase your past, that you are the woman you are today because of all of the people you have encountered along the way— including your ex-husband, and that your desire to keep your old name is *not* out of any devotion to your ex, but rather because you have a history of being known by that name. Your identity is formed at this time and it is continuing to form. Right now, however, you are who you are, with your current name. We suggest you put your name on the invitation, and if you want to change it when you marry, go ahead. Many women change their names and take on the name of their partners. They do it for many reasons, one of which is to make a statement that they are leaving their family and becoming part of another family. Since your present name is not the name of your family but of your last husband, you may wish to change your name as a sign that you are becoming part of another family.

It seems your fiancé is uncomfortable with you keeping your ex-husband's name because he may view this as a way to keep your former husband in your life. With you having his name, it is a constant reminder that you are still attached in some way to your ex-husband. Although the practice is not common, there are couples who hyphenate both names. He takes on her name and she takes on his, and they have two names. If you don't want to take his name at all, be specific about the reasons and be sure you are not putting him down but rather keeping your name as a sign of your own link to your past or to the person you are professionally. Keep your name if you like it, but be aware that your new husband will need time to get used to it.

EXES: CORDIALLY UNINVITED

Dear Dr. Dale,

My fiancé is very much against my continuing a friendship with anyone with whom I've had a past relationship. Although my fiancé and I haven't set a date yet for our wedding, we have begun to compile a guest list. The problem is that I'm now good friends with the current fiancée of an ex. She doesn't know of the past relationship, it was a long time ago, but my fiancé does, and he is against my inviting them to the wedding. How can I not invite them? I've tried to get my fiancé to understand, but he won't budge.

Past relationships are often best kept in the past. Since your friend doesn't know about your past relationship with her fiancé, it would be very difficult (and imprudent) to tell her now, especially without her fiancé's knowledge. You claim that your fiancé won't budge on the issue, but how have you tried to move him, and what have you said? More important, what specific issue disturbs him the most with having this couple at the wedding? Explain to him you are no longer interested in this man, that he is part of your distant past, and you are very good friends with the woman. As you move ahead in your life you want to cultivate the relationship with her and hope he (your fiancé) will support that.

Additionally, explain to your fiancé that you are who you are because of all of the relationships and experiences you have had, and you are not comfortable being in a position to have to either apologize for or expunge anything from your past. Remind him you are here now, with him. Reiterate how you chose him as the man to spend the rest of your life with and you need him to realize your total commitment to him.

HOW DO I INVITE MY FIANCÉ'S KIDS—
BUT NOT HIS EX?

Dear Dr. Dale,

I am marrying a wonderful man who has two children, ages eight and eleven, from a previous marriage. My fiancé and I live together and the children come over every other weekend. I'll have known the children for three years by the time we are married and I have a good relationship with them. I want to make sure they know that they are an important part of our family, even though they don't live with us, so I have asked them to be in the wedding. They are very excited to participate, but we still haven't addressed it with their mother. Even though my fiancé has been divorced for nearly five years, it is apparent that she still has feelings for him. She knows we are planning to get married and is obviously agitated about it.

I have no plans to invite her to the wedding because, in addition to the problem above, she also has a very negative history with his family. But I also don't want the children to feel like they have to hide anything from their mother. Should we discuss this with her and, if so, how should we frame the discussion?

You are not obliged to invite your husband's first wife. Since it appears that she still has strong feelings for him, it would be inappropriate. The children, however, are another story. Ideally, it would have been a good idea to discuss the situation with their mom before telling them, just in case she puts any obstacles in the way. Hopefully, though, she will not. As for the discussion itself, we suggest that you have the conversation, just the three of you, in person. Explain that you want the children to be a part of the ceremony, both as a way to help them with the transition and to feel secure that they will always have an important place in your new home and family. This is a good opportunity to express your caring for her children and your desire to reassure her of your hope that everyone will get along and do things that are in the children's best interest. We assume you are having the wedding at a time when you would normally have the children with you.

If she objects to your having told the children before telling her (she has a point), apologize for not speaking with her first, and then get back on the track of having the kids in the wedding and why. If she pitches a fit and says no, you can gently say you are telling her this and not asking her permission, but rather informing her so she can be aware of what is going on in the children's lives. You are doing this in the interest of full disclosure. Reiterate that since this is such a big step for you as a family, you wanted to be respectful of her role in the children's lives by telling her.

Whatever you decide, stay clear of having the children decide what they want to do. It will put them in the untenable position of choosing their mother over their father (or vice versa), and when they do that, they come out the losers. If she still says no, you must decide whether it is worth a fight. Again, since you have already told the children, they will likely be disappointed and angry at their mother, and may put pressure on her to give in. This puts them in the position of taking sides. Again, not a good way to begin your stepfamily life together. If she refuses to have them participate or makes it intolerable for the children, you may need to reconsider. In this situation the children's emotional well-being must come first.

MY FIANCÉ'S FORMER FIANCÉE

Dear Dr. Dale,

My wedding is only a couple of months away, and I am marrying a great man. We've talked about all the important issues, and we agree on pretty much everything. There is one thing, however, that we haven't resolved, and that's a very close relationship that he maintains with a former fiancée. I know that I trust this man, but why does this friendship have to be such an important part of his life? Should I be concerned?

You have shown admirable restraint and sensitivity in this matter, which bodes well for your future marriage. One question does arise: Has your fiancé asked you to meet this woman? Many times, having the opportunity to meet the person and develop an understanding of their past relationship can help you to see why her presence in his life (which now means your life) is so important to him. It may also help to reassure you that the dynamic and interaction between them remains casual and friendly and nothing more.

However, if you feel threatened by this relationship, or if you have feelings of jealousy, talk to him calmly and openly about your feelings. Ask him what aspects of the past relationship are important to him. The qualities he will mention are not necessarily things he feels you are lacking, but simply facets he craves in his life. Keep in mind that you are the woman your fiancé has chosen to spend his life with, and he clearly sees you as a strong, secure woman, or he would never have been so open about his admiration for this woman in his past.

ELEVEN

Fighting with Your Fiancé

I N THIS BOOK, most of the attention is focused on you, the bride-to-be. This book is, in fact, *for* you. But you would not be considering *any* of these issues if it were not for the groom! Ah yes, that wonderful person you share your dreams with, and plan to build a life with and grow old with. He also wonders about the modifications in his life, the responsibilities he will have, whether he will be a good husband and father and son-in-law. Just like you, he is concerned with how your dreams and goals will affect him and vice versa.

The time before marriage, particularly the months involved in planning a wedding, are filled with conflicting emotions. Don't for a minute think that you are the only one going through this! Few people deal with these emotions head-on, and they are more often experienced as impatience, disrespectful behavior, pickiness, flared tempers, and a fair (or unfair) amount of arguments. Some of these arguments are about really important issues and others aren't. In fact, stop a soon-to-be-married couple in the middle of an argument and ask what they are arguing about and they will likely say "the flowers" or "the seating" or "the menu." But let's be realistic—there's usually much more to it than that.

One of the major catalysts for conflict is the entire planning process itself. Making all of these decisions regarding the wedding is not only time consuming but often confusing, and it may not warrant the same level of importance for each of you. What makes matters worse is that many brides jump to the erroneous conclusion that this kind of conflict arises because the groom does not want to get married. But in truth, this is rarely the case. Sometimes it's because they feel incompetent doing the things they are asked to do and they don't want to do poorly. If you see his eyes glaze over when you discuss the menu options for the wedding after a long day at work, stop right there. Instead, sit down on a weekend morning and talk about how difficult it is for you to shoulder the burden of responsibility of making such important decisions. Create a list of what needs to be done and say, "These are the tasks that need to get done before the wedding. Which ones do you feel you can do?" If he balks, you'll need to explain how you feel when he resists participating: "When I ask you to do something and you give me that response, I feel as if you are not interested or excited about our marriage. It makes me feel as if I am doing this for me and not for us. I would appreciate you participating in ways you are comfortable with and being there for me to discuss some of the decisions that affect us both." For example, suggest setting up an appointment with the caterer to discuss the options and arrange to have a tasting together.

It may be that you come to an understanding that he prefers that you do all the planning. Some grooms are just not into wedding particulars. If you can, accept this, and give up the fantasy of having your fiancé "plan" the wedding with you. Call your mom or best friend and have fun doing this stuff with them. Acceptance is part of the deal when you agree to marry someone.

If you find yourselves fighting frequently or feeling angry with each other more than normal, step back and examine the root causes. What could be causing these feelings other than the immediate situation? Disappointment about losing your "old" lives? Fear about entering a relationship that you are committed to for life? Frustration because you are stressed out and don't feel you have the help you need or because you're not seeing eye-to-eye financially? If you find you are hanging onto anger and the arguments are occurring more than is comfortable for either of you, you owe it to yourself and to your fiancé to figure out what is behind it and deal with it honestly. Whatever the catalyst, step back and don't lose sight of the big picture: that you love each other, and though marriage is an adjustment, the flip side of that adjustment is the wonderful life you will have together.

One last bit of food for thought: If you find yourself arguing a lot, remember that one of the most important things you can do for yourself and your fiancé is to develop caring and empathy for yourself and for him. Enlist your soon-to-be life partner to help you through it rather than alienate him. If you begin to trust him as your ally and friend in this process, you can help him learn how to feel better about the difficulties you both may be experiencing—rather than push each other away.

WOMEN WON'T STOP HITTING
ON MY FIANCÉ

Dear Dr. Dale,

My fiancé is very good looking and regularly attracts the attention of other women. I have been cheerful about it, but it is beginning to upset me. We have a wonderful relationship, and he reassures me that he loves me and is singularly attracted (as well as devoted) to me, but for as long as I can remember, this has happened and I do not want it to become an issue between us.

It's natural for attractive men and women to be admired by members of the opposite sex. And you can't really ask your fiancé to go out of his way to be unattractive so that the admiring glances stop. That said, the person who is the object of the attention needs to give the appropriate response—the message "I am not interested" is easy to read. Is there something in your fiancé's reaction that disturbs you? Or are you concerned deep down that you are not "good enough" for him? Once you decide what you think the problem is for you, sit quietly with your fiancé and tell him of your feelings. Whether you feel inadequate or jealous when other women are coming on to him, or just tired of having this interfere with your ability to have fun together, he needs to know. You may want him to say or do something that will reassure you whenever another woman enters "your space." Maybe you want him to reach for your hand, put his arm around you, introduce you, but whatever he does, the core issue is for you to feel secure in his love and be reassured that he does love you, and it is you he has chosen.

I FEEL LIKE I'M PLANNING OUR WEDDING ALONE!

Dear Dr. Dale,

My fiancé and I are supposedly sharing the expenses for our upcoming wedding, but whenever I attempt to discuss any plans or ideas, he becomes irritable and stressed out. As a result, I have stopped talking with him about things, and have assumed all the planning myself. He never asks how things are progressing, never asks if I need help with expenses, and never asks if I'm happy with the way things are going. However, when I ask for his share of the expenses, he accuses me of not carrying my load, or of needing things that are unnecessary.

My fiancé and I live in different states, so there is no way he can know how much time and expense I've put into the plans so far. But now, because of his attitude, my own stress and anger have gotten the better of me, and I finally told him to just forget about helping with the wedding expenses at all. Now I'm stuck paying the rest of the costs, and I feel like he hasn't put any effort into this all-important occasion. Why is he acting like this?

There may be any number of reasons why your fiancé is behaving in this fashion: Perhaps he is uncomfortable with the idea of the wedding itself; or perhaps the cost frightens him, or is beyond his means. It may well have been that you each had different expectations from the beginning, and that is why there is such dissension now. But one thing we know for certain: It is impossible to plan a wedding with someone—or for that matter, to truly know a person—when there appears to be so little calm, reasoned discussion. Nothing will be able to proceed in a productive fashion until you and your fiancé have a full and measured discussion about your expectations and how you intend to handle things going forward. Begin a dialogue with your fiancé and explain your building frustration and feeling of isolation in planning this wedding. Explain further your disappointment with his lack of involvement and apparent lack of interest.

You said you were both supposedly sharing the expenses. Who supposed what? What was this based on? Did you have a conversation in which each of you discussed who would be financially responsible for what? If this is what happened, remind him that you both accepted the responsibility of sharing expenses, and you saw this as part of the partnership you were building. Tell him it was out of sheer frustration that you threw up your hands and said, "Fine, forget it, I will pay for everything." Sometimes people say things they don't mean because it appears to be the easier road at the time. By taking responsibility for speaking from anger and frustration you are now thinking clearly and can go back to your original agreement (if in fact it was an agreement) to share expenses. He needs to know you are unprepared and unable to foot the whole bill. From now on, call, e-mail, or write each other with all of the plans and remain calm, and differentiate between financial and emotional decisions.

FIGHTING OVER HIS MOTHER

Dear Dr. Dale,

To keep the guest list (and cost!) to a certain number and to be able to include all of our adult family and friends to our reception, my fiancé and I, along with our families, decided early in our planning stages that we would hold an adult reception. We did make an exception for close relatives who are in high school because there are only three in total. When

I received the "revised" guest list from my future mother-in-law, she had added children from her family as well as from her neighbors: all below high school age. She also added an "and guest" to the invitation for a sixteen-year-old cousin. This caused much grief between my fiancé and me because he was unwilling to talk to her about it. I took it into my own hands, and it ended with a battle between his mother and me. Eventually, but with much resistance, she told my fiancé that she would take them off of the list, and we never talked about it again.

Until now. Invitations will be going out in a couple of weeks, and my fiancé told me, "I know that you are going to be mad, but my sixteen-year-old cousin is bringing her boyfriend to the wedding." I did blow up because I was so angry, and from what he had told me weeks ago, everything regarding the list had been settled. I am not only angry with my future mother-in-law for pressing this issue (and I could go on and on about other things that she's tried to control, thereby causing conflict between all parties, including my parents, in planning this wedding), but I am so angry and hurt that he agreed to this without even discussing it with me. He is stating all of the reasons that his mother told me the first time. This is not the first time something like this has happened.

My fiancé and I get along great, and it seems like most of our battles deal with conflict between his mom and me. I've come to accept that I will have to put up with a controlling and uncompromising mother-in-law, but I'm afraid that my fiancé's behavior in this matter is a trend. Am I being unreasonable?

Your fiancé's decision to disregard and override your preference is, indeed, upsetting. It is less the fact that his mother intervened, but more that he redecided something that affects both of you and that had already been settled. Change is inevitable, especially regarding wedding plans, but this kind of scenario does not bode well for the future of your communication. Sit with your fiancé quietly so that you have his full attention (not in front of the TV). Tell him there is something bothering you and you want to discuss it with him. Ask him if he will listen and talk about this with you. Once he says that he will, tell him that the incident with his sixteen-year-old cousin and her boyfriend is what brought this matter to the fore, but it is not just about the cousin and the boyfriend. Tell him you are concerned about how he handled it.

The problem for you is that he made a decision about something problematic and sensitive and acted on it behind your back. Explain that as you begin your life together you need to know you can rely on him to be honest and trustworthy, and that if and when he has a problem with you that you can trust he will work it out with you. Let him know you are concerned about the influence of his mother and will need his help in learning how to keep acceptable boundaries around your new life together. Tell him you know that the transition into being a husband will be difficult for him, and together you need to learn how to build your lives separate from his parents.

MY FIANCÉ SAYS HE'S TOO STRESSED OUT TO HELP

Dear Dr. Dale,

My fiancé and I are very much in love, but right now he is under a lot of stress from work as well as from the costs of the wedding. As a result, he has not been helping me plan any part of the wedding. Initially, he helped me decide on the location, but now he can't be bothered with anything, saying he has enough stress. I can handle the details, and let him handle the bills, but it would be nice to have his support and feedback during this special time. Should I continue to try to involve him or just let it be?

There is no doubt that it would be better to have your fiancé's involvement and feedback, because then you would feel that you were truly sharing the experience. However, one of the most important and sometimes difficult challenges of becoming a couple is learning how to listen and to respond lovingly to your partner's needs and wishes. It is important that you both determine what he is able to be a part of—will it be the actual planning, or will he only able to offer support and interest in your efforts? Once you decide what your roles and expectations are, try to minimize the surprises or changes to those roles. Both of you should always make time to discuss the wedding—you don't want to make some of the larger financial decisions without him—but be sure that you are sensitive to one another's busy schedules.

SQUABBLING OVER DETAILS

Dear Dr. Dale,

Ever since my fiancé and I began planning our wedding, we have gotten incredibly testy with each other. We fight over the smallest details, none of which are of any great importance, as we both admit once we make up. Even though we're not married yet, we sound like an old married couple, harping all the time! (Sad to say, we sound like my parents.) What happened?

Often couples argue and become testy with each other prior to their wedding. The reality of becoming man and wife is a big adjustment that is sometimes difficult to take. Rather than deal with the subtle discomforts of how dramatically our lives are changing, we become irritable and quarrelsome with the person we most adore.

This dynamic can be heightened during the wedding process because "getting married" becomes *very real* when you get into the nitty-gritty of wedding planning. You may or may not have realized the significance of this major step, and now that you are planning to share your life (and decisions) with someone, it hits rather suddenly. For starters, why not take that list of things that need to be done and split it up into three columns. You take one column, and whatever is on your column you have free reign in the decision department. Same with his column of things to take care of. And then in the third column, you either do these things together or split them up, but the final decision is to be shared. This way, you are each taking responsibility for much of the nitty-gritty wedding planning work and can appreciate one another.

It is important to recognize and express your appreciation for each other as you go through the process of planning the wedding. Too often, couples don't pay attention to the things they do for each other or the qualities they have, and these appear to go unnoticed. Make sure you not only notice and pay attention to your fiancé's wonderful aspects, but tell each other in ways you both believe. You say you sound like "an old married couple." Guess what? There are many "old married couples" who really like and respect each other and who do *not* fight over the smallest details, but rather recognize what is really important and worth making a big deal about.

So, find a different way to talk to each other. You will both need to be calm, to give a little. Clearly your parents were your model, but not a very good one in the communication department. Appreciate that there are myriad changes going on with you and your fiancé and that what you need from each other are ways to be allies, not adversaries. Take time to do things that are unrelated to the wedding planning so that you can enjoy being engaged. Remember, the wedding planning process is not supposed to take over your life. Engagement is about spending time together to plan the life you want to have together. The wedding is not going to be your whole life.

I WANT, HE WANTS

Dear Dr. Dale,

I would like to have an intimate ceremony in our brand-new house. My fiancé wants a big ceremony in a reception hall. I'm not keen on the reception hall idea, and since we cannot afford the kind of place I'd ideally like to be married in, I'd rather have the simplest and the least expensive—like getting married during our honeymoon (a two-week cruise in Europe).

I am trying to communicate to him that all I need is "us," but he wants to make sure all of his relatives are with us. What do I do? How do we compromise?

This is a good test of the ability to compromise for both of you, to understand what is important to each of you, and to find a solution in which you will each feel at least some of your needs will be addressed. If you are concerned about the financial aspects and do not want to get married in a place where you will not feel comfortable (a reception hall), is that worth preventing your fiancé from having the wedding he would like, which would include his friends and relatives? You are trying to communicate to him that all you need is "us" and he is trying to communicate to you that he wants "more than us" at the wedding. For him, the wedding is a time to profess his love for you in front of witnesses—those relatives who are meaningful to him. Like it or not, you are going to have to compromise.

P.S. Some cruise ships will have a wedding ceremony on the ship prior to sailing, so that if your relatives are able to come, they can see you get married on the ship, have a small reception, and then wave from the gangplank as you sail off into the sunset.

PASSIVE-AGGRESSIVE GROOM

Dear Dr. Dale,

From the beginning of our engagement, my fiancé has said, "Just tell me where and when to show up. I've done my part." Now it's a year before the wedding. I've started thinking about different aspects of the wedding, since I've assumed from Day One that I would be the primary person putting this together. My fiancé keeps saying that this will be my day and that I should plan it the way I want. But when I tell him about the different things that I want, he tells me that he doesn't like them or makes a face. I'm starting to feel very stressed-out because I'm only getting negative feedback. When I approach him about it, he says that he's giving me good feedback, and he won't discuss it further because he's staying out of it. Help! I think it's bad luck to kill the groom before the wedding! Vegas is looking better and better!

Your fiancé's definition of "staying out of it" is unusual. When people stay out of it, they are not involved. They do not offer opinions and are not a part of the decision-making process. Your fiancé is clearly a part of the planning and decision making because you have invited him in, sought his counsel, and incorporated him and his opinions into the process. You need only ask yourself *why* you are doing this—after all, he has given you full freedom to plan the wedding any way you want. Why not take him at his word? If he is not willing to be helpful and constructive, then you need to refrain from continuously asking his opinions and plan the wedding in such a way that you can enjoy it.

NOTHING IS GOOD ENOUGH FOR MY FIANCÉ

Dear Dr. Dale,

My fiancé and I just got engaged in April, and we're planning to be married in September. The main problem is that every single place that I find that's affordable and nice, he refuses. It's either too "far away" (a thirty-minute drive from where we live, but near the church my mother attends) or "too inconvenient." He feels that no one will want to come to our wedding or reception if we don't make it easy to get to. I want to have a nice—and affordable—wedding, and the only way this seems to be possible is to go further from the place where his parents and family live than he'd like to go. How do I deal with this? I don't want to have our reception in some dingy, dirty, small place! We're supposed to be doing this 50-50—but it's as though I'm doing 90 percent of the work, and nothing I do or look at or decide on is good enough. How do I discuss this with him without hurting his feelings?

Before you go running all over town, sit down with your fiancé and have a serious talk. Find out from him the kind of "feeling" he envisions for the wedding and then tell him what you have in mind. If the two of you share a vision of the kind of wedding you want, you will know whether you should be looking at the local VFW hall, a country club, the historic mansion on the hill, the private room at the local pub, or the ballroom at a classy hotel. If you don't, and you don't discuss things and find a way to compromise, you will continue to be in this ridiculous no-win situation. Search for common ground, and understand that when you hold different visions, you need to respect your partner, and he needs to respect you. Your tastes and preferences are part of each of your separate visions.

The way to compromise is to find something you can both relate to or agree on. It may not be exactly what you or he wants, but it can be something you both can live with—such as finding a lovely hall but having to drive an extra thirty minutes to get there. There will be some aspects to your wedding that you do not want to give up. Think of what they are, write them down, and ask him to do the same. Then come together and discuss which items are the most important to you and which you are willing to be flexible about. Take one at a time, and you will find a workable balance together.

Keep in mind that if you make all your decisions based on what you think your guests will want, as opposed to what you want, you may end up having a wedding for everyone else except you. If going a bit out of town will give you the venue you desire, then tell him that asking your guests to drive for one half hour is a small inconvenience if you will be pleased with your wedding. Most wedding guests expect to cater to the bride and groom's wishes, and they do so gladly, out of love for the couple and a desire to be with them on their special day.

WE CAN'T AGREE ON *ANYTHING!*

Dear Dr. Dale,
 My fiancé and I can't agree on a single thing to do with our upcoming wedding. This should be a happy, exciting time,

but it is absolutely dreadful—in fact, I'm almost ready to call it off. When I found a place for our reception that was only available at lunchtime, he demanded an evening event. But now that *he's* found a place that is only available at lunch, it is perfectly OK. When I want flower arrangements for the tables, he says we have to watch expenses, and yet he refuses to reconsider his guest list of one hundred and twenty people and a five-hour open bar. If he's like this now, how will he be after the wedding?

Planning a wedding can certainly bring out the extremes in people. Both couples and their family members can get under each other's skins during this time—and often over not-so-important decisions. You are right to consider whether or not your fiancé is a person capable of compromise, but try to recall the tone of the wedding planning from the beginning. Is it possible that your fiancé only wanted more of a say in the decision making early on, and that is why he is so obtrusive?

You might want to sit down and calmly discuss the things you both hope to stand firm on and the things you are both willing to compromise about. Keep in mind that you might need to compromise on everything. You also need to let him know that you are hurt when, after making plans, he turns them down or alters them drastically. Tell him that when he shoots down your ideas you feel hurt, because you feel that he is not valuing your input, and it makes you question whether anything you offer is good enough. Explain to him your unwillingness to move forward when each decision you make is met with a negative response. It is terrible to feel as though your input is not valued, and since your fiancé has exhibited this attitude toward you, you might want to make an extra effort to be sure you're not sending him the same message. Get everything out in the open and examine it together, and try to map out a plan for moving peacefully ahead.

SHOULD WE POSTPONE IF WE ARE
FIGHTING ALL THE TIME?

Dear Dr. Dale,

What happens if one of us is having second thoughts four weeks before our wedding? I believe this is a direct result of a lot of petty arguments, not communicating well, and our having different agendas for the wedding, which surely result from our having a heavy case of the nerves. I feel like everyone I know who got married never had a doubt beforehand, and I wonder why I am questioning so much. Do you advise us to postpone the wedding?

Many brides and grooms have second thoughts before their weddings. Often these second thoughts have to do with being preoccupied with the wedding details and not focused on one another. Now is the time to put all the planning chaos aside and think about what it is that you really love about each other and why you wanted to be together in the first place. You may need to sit down, shut out the world, and discuss what you want out of this relationship, and from one another. You also may wish to talk with a counselor or member of the clergy to understand the other's point of view. Either way, try to discuss with your mate why you have different wedding agendas and try to understand why each of your visions is so important to you. You do not have to agree with your mate, but you do have to listen to what is important to him and try to understand why—and then you may both need to make compromises. Making sacrifices for the happiness of the other person is an important part of any marriage. If you can do this, you will very likely get past this rocky patch and have a long and happy life together.

HE WANTS TO CALL OFF THE WEDDING

Dear Dr. Dale,

My fiancé is threatening to call off our wedding. He says that he is not ready. When I talk with him he says that he has been pressured and that I am looking for a way to trap him. He has also made comments about his manhood being taken away. I don't understand all these statements, and I don't think he understands them either. I feel like he's experiencing "cold feet" clichés! I am thirty-one and he is twenty-eight. I just don't know what to do. Can you help?

Your fiancé is afraid of losing his freedom and his individuality. We wonder what his models of marriage have been like. Have you tried talking with him with a counselor or clergy person? Often people get "cold feet" before a wedding, and he is not the first man to raise these complaints and fears. That said, we are surprised that you have not heard this kind of talk from him before, since this kind of language is often indicative of a person's underlying beliefs and attitudes about marriage. If he has not had the healthiest models of marriage in the past, he may be making these statements because he doesn't truly understand what a healthy, lasting marriage is about. You may have different visions for what your married life will be like—and that's a problem. Try talking with him with a counselor or member of the clergy. Find out *why* he feels he has been trapped and *why* he feels marriage will make him less manly. If he's merely experiencing jitters, they will likely pass. But if he really holds these beliefs, you need to ask yourself whether this man is someone who can give you the kind of marriage you want.

TWELVE

Sticking Up for Yourself

"WHY IS EVERYTHING A BATTLE?" "Doesn't anyone listen to me?" "Whose wedding is this anyway?" "If I am the bride, why is my mom making all of the decisions without consulting me?" "If we already agreed on a lavender color scheme, why is my mother-in-law looking at green dresses?" "Should I say something? I mean, is it that important?" "Why does everybody have an opinion about what I should do?" "Why aren't people behaving the way I expected?" "And by the way, why do I have to invite kids to my wedding if I don't want to?"

No two ways about it. There can be some *major* contention when you are faced with the issue of whether or not to stick up for yourself when you are planning a wedding. Why? Because you end up dealing with your entire relationship with your parents and new in-law family! It is not only about what you and your fiancé want, but also what others who have guided you throughout your life want for you (and for them). Too often the bride winds up sticking up not only for herself but also for her family—either her soon-to-be in-laws or the family that raised her. But you may also find that you have to stick up for yourself when various assorted relatives threaten that they won't "sit next to *her,*" or that they must bring their children because they "cannot get a sitter," or even when the wedding planner refuses to send you frequent updates so you can feel comfortable that she is as on top of things as she claims.

At what point, and in what way, you may ask, does this entire fiasco stop, or at least come under control? Depending on the relationship you have, the personalities of the players, how strongly you feel about the issue at hand, who has to prove what to whom, and whose dream is about to be realized, it may never come under control, but it can be managed. Keep your vision in your mind, and that will help make it happen.

Even when you remain strong when confronted with well-meaning assaults on your decisions, it is still often difficult to deal with these forceful and often inappropriate opinions. Perhaps you don't want to rock the boat (especially if it is the new "love boat" of your fiancé's family), and you may therefore be hesitant to give your opinions about issues that are really important to you. You may be so grateful to your parents for giving you the wedding, that you may not feel you have the right to suggest something different from what they have their hearts set on. Or, without realizing it, you may be making a fuss over every detail without paying attention to what is really important, thus developing a reputation as someone who is impossible to deal with, unwilling to compromise, and unable to work out difficult situations.

The first step in taking charge when you feel your wedding is running amok is to take a deep breath and face reality. And your—and every other brides'—reality is that *everyone has an opinion!* Announce your engagement, and before you know it you will be on the receiving end of any number of ideas that are *perfect* for you and your wedding. And, as if that isn't enough, all of these folks believe it is fine and dandy to express that opinion, either privately or in front of the entire family at Sunday dinner, opening up for discussion what you thought was a private conversation about color choices, meal selections, or whether cousin Willie's five kids are going to be invited. If you want to be treated respectfully, treat these opinion givers accordingly. Even if they do not respond kindly, you are still better off because you will have begun to change the way you deal with your parents. You will feel better about yourself.

It's important to stand up for yourself in an adult manner, because as a person about to be married, you are accepting the responsibility of becoming an adult. An adult is a person who treats others respectfully and understands what is important, what is worth "going to the mat" for, what is negotiable, and where to draw the line. As you face your parents and others as an adult and stick up for yourself, you're saying, "I'm a person with my own tastes, wishes, desires. I'd like to discuss them with you, adult to adult." As you stand your ground as an adult, remember: Your goal is to be respectful in the process. Be careful not to go into this situation with an "I'll show you" or "I'll punish you" attitude. If your feelings are hurt or not being considered, don't be childish and stoop to a low level. Take a high road and respectfully assert your choices and the reasons for those choices.

Remember, this is about a process, not about winning. Sticking up for yourself is about expressing who you are and what's important to you; appreciate that someone else's point of view may be as valuable to them as yours is to you. Listen empathetically, understand what they're saying, why they feel the way they do or want what they want, consider it, and if you are still sure of *your* position, assert it with respect and kindness. It is up to you to understand that each person involved in planning your wedding has an agenda (or a dream, or an expectation) for what it should or could be. Even in the face of everyone else's agendas, there are many ways to achieve the wedding *you* would most like to have.

So, here's our first word of advice: If the opinion givers are not crucial to the decision-making process, try not to get insulted or angry. Simply say, "I'll think about it," as you don that beatific smile and thank them for their interest. Just keep in mind: You will not stop people from giving their opinions, but you can manage your own reactions when they offer them.

Our second piece of advice is to pick your battles. As an adult you can decide what is and is not really important. Sit quietly and think seriously about what is truly significant to you. We are reminded of the young woman who was dedicated to her college and wanted an intimate wedding in the university's chapel, followed by a casual outdoor lunch in the faculty center garden with her closest friends and relatives. Somehow, she fell down the rabbit hole and eight months later was the center of a five-hundred-person wedding gala in an extravagant hotel ballroom. Why did this happen? Because after two months of parent-child combat, she and her fiancé decided it wasn't worth fighting over any longer, and as long as they had the "elements" that were important to them, she could "live with" the gala. But she needed to get to the place where she not only could live with the gala, but also enjoy the experience. In this case she could, and she did. Some might say (and some did) that she gave in, folded under pressure, and sold her bridal soul. Perhaps she did, but she decided, as an adult, what was important to her.

It sometimes takes time for people to come onboard in the way you would like them to, and you need to understand that some people will never behave the way you had hoped. That doesn't necessarily mean they are unsupportive or unhappy about the wedding. Know who you are dealing with and learn how to ask for what you want in an adult way. Try to temper your expectations so that you don't set yourself up for disappointments. But always remember, it is your wedding, so go get married in the way that will make you happy.

THE WEDDING OF (WHOSE?) LIFETIME

Dear Dr. Dale,

My mother and father are determined to give my fiancé and me a large, "over-the-top" wedding, despite the fact that we want a small, intimate one. There is no winning this battle with my parents, since they feel as if it is their wedding, and I don't want to go through the planning process full of resentment. And they are wonderful parents—they are generous, they adore my fiancé, they do not demand control of the details—they just want us to have a grand wedding. How can we argue with that without seeming ungrateful? I know that it is supposed to be our wedding, organized and designed the way we want, but to tell you the truth, it is hard to argue when your parents just want to give you everything they can. Any thoughts?

This *is* a tough ticket to ride! First and foremost, brides and grooms are much happier, and things go much more smoothly, when they prepare and experience the wedding of "their" dreams. The wedding is, after all, *your* day. But of course you know that; it would appear, however, that this is *not that clear* to your parents. If a lavish wedding is really a done deal, and you don't feel you can attempt to change your parents' minds, sit down and decide with your fiancé which aspects of the wedding can be designed and implemented to your specifications, such as the vows or the music. Then stick firmly to those requests and specific elements that will create the intimate wedding you desire and deserve. Other, less important items, can be handed over to your parents, a parent of your fiancé, or a good friend. This will allow your parents to still feel involved and connected to the wedding *they* want. Everybody wins.

CAN WE BREACH TRADITION?

Dear Dr. Dale,

My fiancé and I are both Armenian, and we are having a bit of a problem regarding the post of maid of honor. Armenian tradition places the groom's sister in this position, but my fiancé and I are not really interested in adhering to this tradition and, as a result, I would like to place my sister as maid of honor. However, my fiancé's father, mother, and sister are up in arms, seriously objecting to this breach of tradition, and they are demanding that his sister take this role. We've tried to explain to them that we are also Americans, and American tradition allows the bride to select whomever she wants to stand by her side. My fiancé firmly believes they should respect our right to select whomever we want. What do you think?

Few things drive families crazier than tampering with tradition and rituals that have been practiced for generations. We assure you that you are not the first couple to walk through this particular familial fire, and you will not be the last. However, with that in mind, you cannot expect your fiancé's family to be supportive of your decision if it goes against what they believe is traditionally appropriate. After all, their belief in their traditions has helped to make their families strong, and have led to you being married to a wonderful man who seems very sensitive to your needs.

Of course you have the right to select whomever you want to stand as your maid of honor, but you must realize, as you already have, that this decision is not without consequences and emotional cost within the family. Explaining to his parents and sister that you are not practicing what tradition requires is clearly not enough to help them feel OK about your choice. The challenge for you and your fiancé is to be sure that you understand the impact of your decision and to appreciate that the consequences may send a ripple (or a tidal wave) through the family. The best you can do is make it clear to your families that you are not rejecting tradition as a judgment against them, and try to keep them involved in every other aspect of your wedding. Reassure them that your decision is not about moving away from the principles and values that you share, and that you intend to remain true to your cultural heritage going forward.

COLD RECEPTION

Dear Dr. Dale,

My fiancé and I are planning a wedding that will be just for us. We are having our ceremony at a resort, and after our honeymoon, we'll have a large reception for family and friends. My mother is furious with our plans, because she thinks I'm taking my wedding day away from her, and as a result she won't help with any of the planning, and we can't talk at all without fighting. She has, however, agreed to help financially. But there is still a problem: We had hoped to have the reception at the restaurant she owns, which would have been a real money saver. However, she refuses to allow this to happen since I am not getting married her way. How can I salvage my relationship with my mother and still be happy on my wedding day?

You cannot have it both ways: The wedding *you* want and family financial support for a wedding your mother doesn't want. It is your mother's prerogative to want to see her daughter get married, and you and your fiancé have chosen to have a ceremony that prevents that. That, too, is your prerogative, but there are consequences. We assume you've told your mother why you have chosen the ceremony you have, and that you've expressed how much you need her help. She doesn't have to approve, but she will at least be aware of how you feel. Beyond that, since your mother has been generous in financially supporting your wedding, you should find another venue for your reception that is affordable and acceptable to you, then ask your mother to be an honored guest.

EVERYONE IS MAKING DECISIONS BUT ME

Dear Dr. Dale,

Everyone wants to have a say in the planning of my wedding. I want black bridesmaids' dresses, my grandmother wants lilac, and my mother-in-law wants blue. I love both of these women, but I'm not sure if I am obligated to do what they want—even if my mother-in-law is paying for the wedding. Is it still my wedding? My fiancé thinks I should pick what I like. I'm ready to just call it all off. Sounds drastic, I know—but I so would like to feel that I have something to say about my own wedding!

It sounds like you are deeply frustrated and ready to call off the wedding. We really understand! So many brides feel similarly. It seems as if everyone feels it is their right to offer up their opinions when, in fact, few people remember to ask the bride and groom, "What would you like?" "What kind of wedding do you envision?" "What would make you really happy?" Sometimes they don't ask because they don't care, and sometimes they don't ask because they lose sight of who the wedding is for (and often it is for the parents, or at least they think so!).

As far as your in-laws paying for the wedding: We don't know what kinds of strings came attached with their offer to pay. Did they say "We will pay for the wedding but we want it done our way?" If not, please talk with your grandmother and mother-in-law and tell them that you appreciate their preferences, but that you really want a wedding where the bridesmaids wear black, and you would appreciate their honoring and supporting your choice. Just as a question: Do you care if your mother-in-law wears blue and your grandmother wears lilac? If you don't, you can offer to have them choose their own dresses in blue and lilac.

WE'RE BEING ACCUSED OF BEING SNOBBY!

Dear Dr. Dale,

Help! My fiancé and I want to have place cards. We think it's polite and helpful to our guests. My mom insists she's never been to a wedding where people are assigned seats and insinuates we are trying to be "snobby" or outdo other family weddings. We're not! I am afraid that our guests on my side of the family will probably think the same. Our family weddings have generally been on a smaller scale (balloons and VFW halls). Does wanting something more make me snobby?

Your desire to have people seated in a manner you find helpful and polite is entirely up to you. You have an image of the type of wedding you want and you are able to make it happen. Some family members may feel challenged and threatened by something different or new and ascribe a pejorative meaning (like "snobby") to it, but that is not your problem. This can be hurtful, but ultimately the choice is yours. Enjoy your wedding and the fact that you will know exactly where everyone is seated!

LOCATION, LOCATION

Dear Dr. Dale,

I grew up in Connecticut but moved to the San Francisco Bay Area six months ago. My fiancé lives here as well. We want to have our wedding here in California, since it's my dream to have an outdoor wedding (which I can do in the Bay Area), but my parents are against it. My fiancé and I are planning and paying for everything here. My parents have said that they aren't coming and want me to foot the bill for an additional Connecticut reception. Help! What do I do? I can't afford to do a reception there and have a full wedding here. I can't make my parents come. How do I avoid a total breakdown in our relationship? Please advise!

Parents have dreams for their children's weddings, too. Your parents want to celebrate your marriage on their own turf, presumably so they can share the celebration with local family and friends. Can you blame them? You are correct in that you cannot make your parents come to your wedding, but you can explain what their absence will mean to you and your fiancé and that you would like to have them with you on this special occasion. If that cannot happen, try to explore ways in which you can still have the wedding you desire but also participate in a separate party with your parents. Does it have to be a full-blown reception? Is it at all possible for you to have a small reception (perhaps a cocktail open house) to accommodate your parents' desires? If the point is to have the Connecticut contingent celebrate with you and your family, it can be done in a number of ways and it does not have to be expensive. Perhaps they would be willing to share some of the cost, or perhaps there is someone's home you could use to host an informal gathering.

WE CHOOSE NO BOOZE

Dear Dr. Dale,

My husband and I eloped last year, but we are now planning a church ceremony, and this church discourages drinking and dancing. However, my husband and I don't want to impose our choices on our friends and family, some of whom will be flying in from great distances to be with us and might well be shocked by what they may think is a lack of typical celebration activities. How do we maintain our own core beliefs and practices without offending others, and what can we have instead of a cocktail hour after the ceremony?

You and your husband have the right to any kind of reception you choose. Simply tell your guests beforehand that this will be a liquor-free event but nonetheless a celebration. Your party after the wedding can have an assortment of drinks that are all liquor-free, including fruit punch, assorted flavors of sparkling water, sparkling apple cider, and nonalcoholic beer.

You may be surprised to know that there are many people who are happy to celebrate a joyous event without liquor! As for any disappointment people may feel at your nonbibulous event (no matter how far they've traveled), these are people who love and care for you and your husband, and hopefully their refreshments are decidedly less important.

WON'T SOMEBODY LISTEN TO ME?

Dear Dr. Dale,

I am about to get married and I am having a difficult time getting people to take me seriously. I feel as if everyone around me "yeses" me, and then goes and does whatever *they* want. Frankly, this is how my family has treated me my whole life and I am tired of it. For example, my fiancé and I want a small wedding outside in the country, but my parents want a more formal affair at their country club. I do not want a bridal party, but my mother says that I must have all of my cousins as bridesmaids and ushers. My fiancé and I want to get married in the summer so we can take a long honeymoon (we are both teachers), but my mother thinks it will be too hot and wants a winter wedding. We also want to have a grownup wedding, but my parents think people should be able to bring their kids if they want. How can I deal with their dismissive attitudes and behavior toward me and my wishes?

Take a deep breath. You are about to go through the wedding planning portal labeled "What is really important to me?" Your letter reminds us of someone we knew whose wedding was the wedding of her parents' dream. It was in a large hotel ballroom with several hundred people in gowns and tuxedos, with only two tables, in the back, for her friends. There was a dance band but nobody danced much. She and her new husband spent the night walking around with her parents being introduced to all of the guests who were, for the most part, her father's business associates, who she had never met before. She hated her own wedding! Not until their fifteenth wedding anniversary, with their three children in attendance, when a friend threw her a surprise anniversary party, did she feel they finally had the kind of wedding she had always wanted. It was an outdoor, spring garden party with her closest friends, a great band, and a selection of her favorite foods and loads of delicious desserts.

Sometimes a major life passage such as a wedding can be a watershed event used to redefine the parent/child relationship. This is the time for you to finally stand up for yourself and, as an adult, discuss what you are willing and not willing to agree to for the wedding. You are getting derailed and the train hasn't even left the station! You do need to sit down with your fiancé and decide right now which issues are vital and which aren't, and which are negotiable and which aren't. Keep in mind that you are going to have to compromise on some things—and use those compromises as money in the bank with which to bargain for what really matters most. Then call a family meeting.

Sit down with your parents and describe the wedding you want and why you want it. Talk with them calmly and respectfully about what is both desirable and practical for all of you. Find areas of agreement. When your parents dismiss you or speak disrespectfully, or give you the impression that they will do whatever they want despite your desires, call them on it. Remember: Your relationship will never change if you allow this dismissive treatment.

You may not be able to turn around a lifetime habit of disregarding you and your choices, but you certainly can begin to think of yourself as a woman who deserves to be heard and taken seriously. Do not give in. Remain strong, with your fiancé by your side. Our guess is that everyone around you will respect you and follow your new signals of strength.

THIRTEEN

Money

I N THE MAD RUSH toward marriage, many couples over-look—or choose to deny—the issue and the importance of money. Marriage is more than an emotional partnership: It is a financial one as well. Most of us have issues with money, and if they're not out on the table when the wedding process begins, they will be before it's over.

By the time most people marry they have been managing their finances independently and, whether they know it or not, have likely developed some habits that may be annoying or startling to each other. The attitudes we develop about money are frequently based on the relationship our parents had with money—and each other. Now is the time to try to separate yourself from those attitudes and decide which are truly your own. Start by sitting down with your fiancé and asking yourselves some questions that you may not have considered before. As you do so listen closely to the answers you hear in your head and heart as well as the ones you hear across the table.

- How do you feel about sharing expenses? Making a budget?

- Do you think that because you make more money than your mate that you should have a greater say in financial matters?

- Can you share in all financial decisions, or are there some that one or the other of you finds frightening, alien, or overwhelming?

- Do you find the concept of owing money nerve-racking? Can you fathom putting the entire cost of your wedding on credit, then paying off the sum in the first year or two of your marriage?

- How do you feel about accepting money from your or your fiancé's parents?

Eventually, any finance-related conversations will likely involve your future in-laws and your parents. This can prove tricky. For instance, you may discover that your fiancé is generally inclined to follow his father's advice regarding money, even if it means following a budget that doesn't necessarily fit with the wedding you both envision. If your parents are contributing financially, be sure you're clear up front. Do you understand the conditions both stated and unstated that come along with accepting money from parents? Are you aware of the strings that are attached when you accept money from either of your parents? Are you willing to discuss these strings when deciding whether to accept the money and conditions?

If there are conditions (you have to live nearby; your wedding will have to be of a certain type, whether you like that type or not; you will have to wear Grandma's wedding dress at the ceremony; they will pay for your honeymoon but you have to go to Uncle Phil's condo in a place you have no desire to visit), then at least you know what you are committing yourself to. If the stakes are too high or the strings too tight, graciously decline and get married at the town hall with a party on your friend's porch. You will be happier because you will be free and on your own. If you are willing to risk not having the money, you may be in a better place to accept it when it is offered without strings. It's your call.

In addition to understanding the impact of the parental tie and your own views on money and power, here is a vital checklist that you should keep in mind:

- Are you and your fiancé on the same page as to what is reasonable to pay for a wedding?

- Are you and your fiancé in agreement about whether you are willing to go into debt for this wedding, and if so, how much, on whose credit card it will be charged, and how do you intend to pay it off?

- Are there certain "splurge" areas you can agree on—i.e., your dress, the band, the food?

- Are you hiding or lying about the true costs of certain items for fear of your fiancé's reaction?

- If one family is contributing more, are you and your fiancé OK with that?

- Are you keeping score about who is paying for what, and is anyone feeling cheated?

- Do you or your fiancé feel your parents "owe" you a wedding that is beyond their financial means or different from the one they are willing to give you?

- As you have begun planning this wedding, have you seen aspects of your fiancé's spending or saving or investing habits that make you uncomfortable? Have you approached him to talk openly, honestly, and often about these frustrations, insecurities, disappointments?

- Are you satisfied with the way you and your fiancé adjust to changes in financial commitments related to the wedding (i.e., added costs and how to cover them)?

- Have any of your friends or relatives commented to you about your fiancé's bank account or ability to make or save money? If so, do you share those concerns and have you shared these comments or concerns with him?

- As you plan the wedding, are you discussing with your partner what you will do (spend, invest) with the money you will receive as wedding presents?

- Are you and your fiancé in agreement over how your money will be handled after you are married? Have you discussed joint or separate bank accounts, who contributes and how much to daily living expenses, vacations, big-ticket items, savings, charity, education, and so on?

Above all, remember, as with love, so with money: balance and fairness. You and your fiancé are from two different backgrounds.

Your attitudes, feelings, thoughts, beliefs about money were formed by each of your personal histories and experiences. As you come together to plan this wedding, make every effort to understand your own as well as your fiancé's points of view related to what money (in particular, financing the wedding) means to each of you and how open you are to discussing and sharing financial decisions.

BREAKING THE BRIDAL BANK

Dear Dr. Dale,

My sister got married earlier this year, and because she is thrifty and her tastes are simple, her dress only cost three hundred dollars. The dress I want is nearly two thousand dollars. My dad is in shock and wants me to buy a dress that is more like my sister's. But I am not my sister, and I don't want to give up the dress I want, even though my father can't afford it. Any ideas?

You and your sister are different, so you will want and need different dresses, but even after you consider the fact that someone may not want to spend two thousand dollars on a wedding dress, perhaps your parents are afraid of spending a significantly greater amount of money on you than on your sister. Parents often fear showing favoritism, both with gifts and emotional involvement. It also sounds as though your father has real financial constraints, and unfortunately, you are going to have to walk within those limits. That doesn't mean, however, that you need to mirror your sister's budget exactly. Talk to your father about the range of dresses and their costs, and then discuss paring down other costs to allow for the dress of your dreams. Perhaps if you tighten the budget in other areas you can still have a dress that you want without breaking the bank.

CAN BRIDESMAIDS' DRESSES COUNT AS GIFTS?

Dear Dr. Dale,

My fiancé and I are paying for our wedding ourselves, but being the money-conscious person that I am, I knew that having my sisters in my wedding would be a financial strain on them. But I cannot imagine my sisters not being with me. So to help them I chose to purchase all the materials myself and make my bridesmaids' dresses, including those for my two bridesmaids who are not family. The only thing I asked each of them to purchase is their shoes. I am even providing accommodations for my whole family, as I live in another state. So here's my question: Should I still buy them thank-you gifts, as is typical with bridesmaids, or can the dresses be considered gifts?

Your generosity in making all of the dresses is certainly worth a lot. You do not have to buy a gift, but you might consider doing something equally creative that would serve as a token of remembrance. Would it be possible, while you are making the dresses, to make a small lingerie bag or drawstring travel pouch out of the same fabric to serve as a gift? You could put some potpourri or sachet inside, or a small bottle of perfume. The fabric itself will always serve as a reminder of your gratitude for your friends' and sisters' participation in this special day, and of their importance as part of the fabric of your life.

MY PARENTS SUDDENLY CAN'T PAY!

Dear Dr. Dale,

We had planned (after discussions with my family many months ago) that they would pay for the wedding, as most brides' families do. However, it now seems that my family may not be in a position to financially help with the wedding—or at least not in the amount we had originally planned. I understand that they are not under any obligation to pay, but now, with the church, hall, catering, and band booked, the bills are adding up to thousands and thousands of dollars. My in-laws and fiancé want a huge, fancy wedding and are willing to pay for it. And my in-laws are not complaining, but my fiancé is very angry with my parents. I don't mind if we have a small wedding, a wedding that we can afford, but he is set on a big wedding. Help!

As adults, you have the right to sit down with your parents and explain to them that you are at the point of needing to know if they can help you pay for some of the wedding and, if so, what they are able to afford. They can give you a specific budget, and then you can either stay within that budget or add to it from your own monies or those of your in-laws.

Before accepting money from your in-laws, you need to make sure that your parents are OK with this. They may feel strongly about giving you a wedding within their means and *not* accepting help from anyone else. Alternatively, they may be grateful to have help. If this is the case, you can either accept their offer of a smaller wedding or not, but if you decline, or insist on allowing your fiancé's parents to contribute, be prepared to have to finesse the situation. As for your fiancé, he will simply have to let go of his anger toward your parents. They are under no obligation to give you the wedding that *he* wants or expected, especially if they can no longer afford to do so.

FINANCIAL BACKTRACKING

Dear Dr. Dale,

My fiancé and I have planned our wedding for later this year, and we have made many financial plans and inquiries regarding that day. Last month we were notified that we qualified for a home, and so we have chosen to buy, using money we had previously allocated for our reception. The problem? We already paid for one hundred invitations and one hundred reception cards, at a cost of four hundred dollars, not to mention wedding favors that cost six hundred dollars, a cake at four hundred and seventy-five dollars, my wedding dress at eight hundred dollars, the site and the pastor at five hundred dollars, and photographer at nearly two thousand dollars. Other costs include my fiancé's suit, bridesmaids and ushers outfits, flowers, and a disc jockey. Many of our guests are coming from out-of-state. The invitations have not yet been mailed, but all but approximately three hundred dollars of our expenses are nonrefundable. What should we do? My mother thinks it's rude to invite guests only to a ceremony, and equally inappropriate to have a mere cake and punch reception. Given that our ceremony is rather late in the afternoon, my mother feels the guests will expect, and are entitled to, dinner. Please help!

You cannot pay for what you cannot afford, but being honest with your guests can solve your dilemma, complicated as it seems. You can send out the invitations with an amendment, which will explain what has transpired. You can then tell your guests that you want them to come to the ceremony, as well as a cake and punch reception, or you can enlist some friends to help you arrange a potluck dinner for those who have come from a distance. This dinner could be held in the common room of your church (if you have chosen one) or in a home of a friend or your parents. If you want the people you've invited to be with you, you can find a way to have a different wedding from the one you had planned—perhaps an informal one with everyone contributing something. And don't worry about your mom—any of these choices are perfectly acceptable from an etiquette perspective.

The other option is to forgo the ceremony as well and be married by the pastor in the church study with only your immediate family present.

MONEY TENSIONS WITH MY FIANCÉ

Dear Dr. Dale,

The circumstances of my engagement are unusual because I am working on a project in Singapore and my fiancé is working on a project in London. We plan to marry in Jakarta. I will join him in London the following year. Because I am close to Jakarta, I began to work on the planning. It is hectic finding the church, the priest, the choir, and so on.

Suddenly my fiancé told me that his parents cut the wedding budget because they wanted to spend the money to go to Bali after the wedding. I was hurt and upset by this last-minute change. It's not about the money but the fact that they'd rather spend it on a trip to Bali than on our wedding. It seems this was a misunderstanding on his part, and he spoke to his parents and things seem to be fine again. However, afterward, he accused me of being superficial, implying that I was talking only about preparing the reception of the century and not focusing on the spirit of the wedding itself. He is afraid that I am not ready to marry him and that I will end up leaving him if he cannot support my lifestyle.

My family is wealthier than his, and I realize that his profession will not guarantee him a lot of money, but I believed he knew me and had the faith in me to know that I made up my mind and that I am committed to him. But these money issues seem to be tearing us apart!

Distance sometimes makes the heart grow fonder, but it can also exaggerate communication difficulties. Planning a wedding when the bride and groom are continents apart is far from easy. Your issues, however, have less to do with booking the church and the choir than with each of you feeling secure in your choice of the other. And, by the way, the fact that his parents budgeted a specific amount of money for the wedding is their prerogative. If they change the amount and want to go to Bali, that is also their prerogative. You and your fiancé need to know that you are ready to live your lives together because of the people you are, not whether he has enough money.

He seems to be concerned that your distress about his parents' change in plans reflects a concern that you may not be able to live a less grand lifestyle. If your family is wealthier than his, and you want to, perhaps you can offer to share in the expenses of your life together to maintain a style to which you have become accustomed and hope to keep. If not, you will need to reassure your fiancé that being disappointed about what you understood to be one amount to work with turning into something less does not mean you are unable to accommodate your lifestyle should that be required. His insecurity is based on his own fear that he will lose you if he cannot support you in a grand style. You need to make every effort to reassure him that money is not going to determine whether you and he have a solid relationship. You can only do this by actively engaging him in discussions that reinforce for him the reasons you are marrying him, why you are attracted to him, and why you chose him to be your life partner. Money comes and goes. Each of you need to feel secure that you can trust the other to be there for the good as well as the difficult times, when they come.

MOM AND HER GUILT TRIP

Dear Dr. Dale,

My mother has "budgeted" five thousand dollars for my wedding, and is still being stingy about it. She does not co-operate with my organization; she is not even interested in the wedding notebook I made for her. I know that without her money I can't have a wedding, but she says that if she does not have a say, I do not have her money. Furthermore, she persists in making me feel guilty about getting married because she did not prepare for it financially. I'm trying my best to have as small a wedding as possible, but all she can do is talk about money, money, and money. We have not even picked anything out yet! Please tell me how I can have a wedding without her guilt trips.

You don't really have much choice except to accept this five thousand dollars as a gift and include her in your decision-making process for certain aspects of the wedding. Start by asking her which specific parts of the planning she would like to contribute to. Perhaps she only feels that her input is relevant to particular issues. If she wants to have a hand in everything, you will need to try another approach. Tell her that you are very grateful for her gift but that an equally special gift to *you* would be to let you and your fiancé make the choices that are best for you. Once you have established some boundaries and rules of engagement, you can fully utilize her desire to be involved and include her.

And, as far as her making you feel guilty, she really cannot do that without your full cooperation. What do you have to feel guilty about? That she did not put money away for the day when her daughter would marry? Remember, you and your spouse can always offer to chip in to cover some of the costs, or enlist your friends to help in ways that would defray expenses.

MY HONEY HAS NO MONEY

Dear Dr. Dale,

My fiancé and I have been engaged for approximately nine months (eight more months till the wedding). The reason that we're having a long engagement is because we are supposed to be paying for the whole wedding ourselves. The problem is that I've been paying for all of the expenses up to this point (deposits for reservations, etc.). He's starting a new business and doesn't seem to be able to help out with the costs. But at this point I'm starting to feel resentful. I've even been thinking about canceling the wedding, since he does not seem to show a sincere desire to share. This experience makes me wonder if I will be paying for everything in the future, such as a house, children, etc., while he struggles to fund his dreams. Am I just a meal ticket? I know that a lot of these are questions that I have to ask myself. I do love him with all of my heart, as he's a wonderful man (or I wouldn't have said yes). I've tried to talk to him, but he says he's doing the best that he can. And I am very concerned about the future.

If assuming full responsibility for the wedding expenses had been your original understanding, or if you subsequently agreed to assume the expenses, at least temporarily, that would be different. But in this situation, it is important to understand that the issue is not whether you provide financial support for your soon-to-be husband, and whether you pay for future expenses such as a house and children, but rather whether you feel you have a partner who wants to and is willing to make sacrifices to share financial obligations. Saying he is doing the best he can may not be good enough. Tell him you are feeling overburdened and that you did not expect nor are you comfortable with financing the entire wedding. Explain to him that you support him in making his career dreams become a reality, but that in the meantime he needs to become financially responsible and share in the expenses.

Many women are the breadwinners for their families. That is not the point. You are experiencing something different. Your fear about whether you will be supporting your future family seems rooted in a strong feeling that he is not going to be able to hold up his end of the bargain. Try to discuss working within a financial plan that can satisfy both of you. If he is a person who does not appreciate his role in financially contributing to your life together, you may have to reconsider this relationship.

PAYING TO BE IN CONTROL

Dear Dr. Dale,

I'm a first-time bride, and I'm over forty. The groom and I are hosting our wedding, and recently my mother offered to pay for the reception. However, she would like to invite some of her friends and a few relatives who I do not respect and do not want present on my wedding day. I have made my desires known. Is that wrong—especially since she's being so generous?

It is not wrong to make your own desires known, but it can certainly be grist for the family mill! You need to talk to your mother and clear up whether her offer to pay for the reception is conditional upon her being able to invite the guests she chooses, including those you do not respect. If this is the case, you can always choose to pay for the reception yourself in order to not feel obligated. But if she is insistent, and you can't afford to foot the bill yourself, you may have to resign yourself to having these people present. That said, it is possible that upon hearing your case your mother may have a change of heart—especially if you broach the subject in a calm, respectful manner that acknowledges her generous financial contributions, and explain your desire to have a perfect, peaceful day that you can remember your whole life.

WE CAN'T PAY FOR THE WEDDING WE WANT

Dear Dr. Dale,

My fiancé and I agreed to a small wedding that we could both afford, for which I'm grateful, as I am a college student with a lot of loans and debts, and I don't have a steady job because of my class schedule. My fiancé has a full-time job, but it doesn't pay well. We wanted to get married in May, but the way things are going, I think we're going to have to postpone the date. Even with a small guest list, the money goes so quickly. My fiancé and I have already signed a contract with vendors for photography, videography, and flowers, which I now think was a mistake. I am trying to think of different ways to save money, but it is not working, and every time I try to talk about setting some fiscal ground rules with my fiancé, he always says we have to wait and see. I have already shortened the guest list, but I feel like I am not getting anywhere. Can you please help me before I lose my mind?

Sit with your fiancé and decide how much money you will actually need to have the wedding you both want. After you have established this budget (the ground rules, as you called them), work within it scrupulously—and together. You may find that you can live—and happily—with a simple potluck wedding reception in the church social hall or at a friend's home, rather than a catered affair. You can save money, but that is not the main issue. Instead, you need to talk with your fiancé about the expectations you both have. It is entirely possible to get married simply and elegantly without paying a fortune. If you absolutely cannot sacrifice some of the details you have in mind, such as food and music, then you may have to wait a long time, and who knows if you will ever have the money? If you don't want to wait, draw up a budget and then become creative about how you make it work.

STRANDED AT THE ALTAR—
BY BROKE PARENTS

Dear Dr. Dale,

I recently became engaged, and now I'm faced with planning a wedding that no one has the money for. My parents, who spent at least ten thousand dollars on my younger brother's rehearsal dinner, now have no money to pay for any sort of wedding for me. They are recently divorced, and they both try and make me feel better by saying they'll work something out. I am not going to delude myself and wait for that to happen, however, since I could be waiting for a long time. But when I tell them I don't want to wait, they get irritated and angry. Since my fiancé and I are faced with paying for a wedding all by ourselves, it looks as if there won't be much of one, since we don't want to go into debt for it and would like to put our funds toward our honeymoon trip. Part of me wants to just elope and be done with it, since we've been together for two years and have no reason to put things off. I am torn, however, since I would like for friends and family to be there, and I find myself worrying about everyone's feelings being hurt if they aren't included. I know that my friends will understand, but my parents may not. Should I just do what I need/want to do or make myself crazy trying to please my noncontributing family?

One of the most important things to remember when planning your wedding is just that—it's *your* wedding! If you and your fiancé are ready to marry and are fine with the idea of eloping, or going to the town clerk or the office of the religious leader you respect, then you can do that. You are under no obligation to anyone to host a wedding you cannot afford. Afterward, you might also host a lovely dinner at your favorite restaurant or your home, and invite your parents and your closest friends. Instead of thinking about what your wedding will not be, think of what it can be. Remember, "modest" does not imply one without feeling. And then you can have the money you need for a wonderful honeymoon together.

THEY PROMISED MONEY BUT CANNOT DELIVER

Dear Dr. Dale,

My fiancé and I have been living together for over two years, and we are ready to get married. Both of us decided

that we would have a small, perhaps modest, wedding because it would be more intimate and mean more to our families and to us. My father and mother have been promising
me that they will help financially, and now, nearly at the last
minute, they have told me that they cannot help us pay for
anything. So now we are paying for the whole wedding ourselves—we were counting on about half the cost being
footed by my parents. His parents are already paying for our
honeymoon, as well as the cost of the rental of the hall. I am
at a point where I might have to call off the wedding! Help!

If your parents have suffered an unforeseen financial setback,
they likely feel as upset and disappointed as you, so confronting
them won't help matters. Instead, try to engage their practical, if
not financial, help and ask them to help you figure out how to
have a lovely wedding at half the cost. If for some reason you feel
that a genuine financial setback is not at the root of the change
(maybe they just want the money to buy a fancy car), then you
need to tell them, calmly yet directly, that you have been planning
the wedding based on what they promised you and you are asking
them to reconsider their decision since you would like to move
forward as planned. If they say this is not possible, then perhaps
you can also discuss with your fiancé's family the possibility of a
less expensive honeymoon and use some of those funds toward
your ceremony. Since you already have the use of the hall, perhaps
your mother can help you put together a group of your family
friends to prepare some of the food for a buffet. Or, instead of having a dinner, have a dessert, champagne, and coffee wedding, asking if friends can prepare an assortment of desserts. People get
married—happily—in all kinds of ways. Later, when you and your
fiancé are stronger financially, you can throw yourselves a grand
anniversary party.

IS IT OK TO ASK FOR FINANCIAL HELP?

Dear Dr. Dale,

My wedding is only four months away, and neither my fiancé nor I have the money we need to pay for the reception. By the date of the wedding, we should have half of what we need, but it is clear that we will need to get the remaining money from somewhere else. We were trying to do this mostly on our own, and my fiancé is hesitant to ask anyone for more money. My fiancé's grandparents have hinted that they may be able to contribute, but have not actually made an offer. Do you feel it would be appropriate if we asked them to make a contribution? And should we ask them for help now or wait until we know exactly how much we will need?

Planning a wedding is precisely that—*planning*! You and your fiancé are learning a great life lesson for your future together, even though right now it may feel scary or humiliating. It sounds as if you have not planned your finances well enough to pay for the wedding you want to have. The desire on your part to pay for the wedding independently is only noble and practical if you can actually afford the wedding you are paying for. The life lesson here is this: You cannot plan a wedding—or anything else for that matter—and assume that others will step in to foot the bill. The first thing you need to do is sit down and make a budget that includes both where you are now and where you hope to be. Then you essentially have three choices: 1) You can have the wedding you can afford; 2) You can go into debt paying off the bills for a wedding you cannot afford (if the vendors will allow you to do that); 3) You can depend on others to foot the bill.

If you do eventually decide to ask your grandparents for financial help, do so earlier rather than later, so that you can make the appropriate arrangements for your reception as well as any money-saving adjustments. You and your fiancé should sit down with your grandparents and ask if their offer to help with the costs of the wedding or reception was serious. Tell them where you are with your planning and expected expenditures, present them with your budget, and discuss what funds might be possible on their part. Keep in mind that they may offer to pay only for the photographer, or the flowers, or the music, and you must respect what they feel is reasonable and within their limits. You might also suggest that if they help to pay for large portions of the wedding or the reception that will be their wedding gift to you.

If they cannot help you out, you will have to look for creative ways to minimize costs.

TIMES AND MONEY HAVE CHANGED

Dear Dr. Dale,

I am engaged to be married. Three years ago, my sister was given thirteen thousand dollars by my divorced parents (ten thousand from dad and three thousand from mom) to put toward her wedding. Last month, when I announced my engagement, my father indicated that he and his wife were willing to give us four thousand dollars, and my mother advised me that she could not contribute at all unless we waited until next year, citing the stock market as the reason. My dad's reason was that "things have changed" for them since my sister married, even though he bought my stepmother a Mercedes last fall. What do I do?

Sometimes life just doesn't seem fair. And coping with the unexpected by being adaptable is part of being an adult and a skill that will stand you and your fiancé in good stead. There has been a tremendous change in the economy over the last few years, and people's personal finances do fluctuate with the times. Your father and mother are willing to be as flexible as they can to help pay for your wedding, but you must be flexible too.

You can choose to have a more modest wedding, or you and your fiancé can contribute more than you had expected and have the kind of wedding you had envisioned.

Remember, it is never essential that parents give their children a wedding, so be grateful for their gift—no matter what the size. And take this as an opportunity to be creative, and make your wedding unique for its significance and sentiment rather than splendor.

MY FIANCÉ WANTS TO WAIT

Dear Dr. Dale,

My fiancé and I have been planning for our wedding, which is a month from now. I got my dress, made the arrangements, and my aunts are all chipping in. One is paying for the reception, another will bake the wedding cake, and a third will sew the dresses for the flower girls.

My fiancé just told me that he wants to wait at least a year, until he has more money so that we can have a nice honeymoon. I really don't care about the honeymoon and told him that I just want to marry him. I want very much to make this wedding work and still get married as we planned! Is there a hidden message in his change of heart?

It is not a good idea to plan a wedding if one of you wants to wait. You need to consider why the original date seems more important than marrying your fiancé when you are *both* ready. Having enough money for the honeymoon may not be reason enough for you to postpone the wedding, but he seems to think it is. The larger question: Is he using that as an excuse to postpone because he is not ready to get married? You need to talk with him about his true feelings and, if he feels you are rushing or pressuring him, think about whether that is the way you want to begin your life together. It may be that he truly feels rushed, and if this is the case, select a date that he can commit to and talk about his financial plan for saving for the honeymoon. This may be his way of biding his time or it may be his way of moving at a pace that is more tolerable for him. Many brides and grooms feel hesitant somewhere along the way as they get closer to the wedding date and everything seems to be more real. If he is feeling hesitant, talk together with your member of the clergy or a relationship counselor so you can understand what is bothering him.

WHO GETS TO REHEARSE AND WHO GETS TO EAT?

Dear Dr. Dale,

My future mother-in-law has specified a certain number of guests to be allowed at the rehearsal dinner. I would like to include my family from out of town, but that exceeds the number allotted. She said that if we can't stay within the number she's allotted then she will have the dinner at home on the deck on paper plates. This is not what I envision or want with the very formal motif of our wedding. What should I do?

Your mother-in-law has the right to limit the number or determine the "style" of the rehearsal dinner if it goes beyond her financial limit. If you are set on having a formal dinner to go with the feeling of your wedding, then give your out-of-town guests the name of a good restaurant (you can buy their dinner if you wish) and tell them you look forward to meeting them later for a cocktail or dessert. Another option is to explain the limitations and ask them to contribute to the extra costs of expanding the guest list so you can have the kind of dinner you would like. Be careful, though, that your future mother-in-law is not insulted by this idea.

MY IN-LAWS WON'T SHARE EXPENSES

Dear Dr. Dale,

I am very lucky that my parents have offered to pay the full amount for my entire wedding. However, I feel that it is unfair to put this huge twenty-thousand-dollar burden solely on them. I know that it is traditional for the future in-laws to pay for the rehearsal dinner and some flowers, so I e-mailed them the cost for the flowers. Well, now they are very angry at the suggestion that they help out. They make twice the money my parents do and live half the lifestyle. I don't think that they dislike me, as my fiancé and I have been together for six years (since high school), and they have always been very kind and warm. All of a sudden, though, they seem angry about every little thing, from our decision to have no children at the wedding to the fact that their estranged family members are not to wear denim to the affair. I don't even know how to talk with them anymore. Any advice?

If you could rewind the tape of this interaction, you might want to stop at the spot where you decided that your parents should not pay for the entire event and then assumed that your fiancé's parents should pay for the flowers and the rehearsal dinner. Whether it is traditional or not, it is *always* better to discuss these decisions and expectations *up front* so that nobody feels they are either taken for granted or unappreciated. Perhaps your future in-laws assumed that your parents would pay for everything. Whether or not they did, it was you who assumed too much by e-mailing them the floral costs without first asking them whether they would be willing to participate financially. It is irrelevant that they make twice the money that your parents do and that they live, according to you, half the lifestyle: This is a judgment we suggest you stay away from, because it really has no bearing on the issue at hand.

Since you said that you have known these people to be warm and kind, it seems to us that you may be dealing with hurt feelings. Rather than being told what they are to do, financially and otherwise, they would probably like to be asked. Nobody likes to be taken for granted. You need to reach out and talk with them. Begin by saying, "I am sorry if my e-mail offended you. I would like to begin again and talk about the wedding." Perhaps you can meet them for lunch—with your fiancé there as well—to explain the situation and graciously ask if they would be willing to contribute. Your fiancé does not have to condone your previous e-mail, but you and he should be in agreement about broaching the topic with his parents and how you would like to enlist their help. If they do not wish to contribute, then you have your answer and can proceed accordingly to plan the wedding within the budget that you and your fiancé and your parents can afford.

I DON'T WANT A THIRD-RATE WEDDING!

Dear Dr. Dale,

My wedding is taking place in less than five weeks, and I am out of time and money. I have no cake, no wedding rings, no decorations for the reception, no flowers, no limo, and I also can't afford a photographer. On top of everything else, I'm so stressed out that I don't know how to think or what to do to help myself. My fiancé and I have already bought the invitations, and our friends have already purchased plane tickets to attend our wedding. Our honeymoon tickets are reserved, as is our hotel, so the wedding can't be postponed. To make matters worse, I need to have my wisdom teeth removed, and my parents are drowning in debt and can't help with either my oral surgery or my wedding debts. On top of it all, several bridesmaids have backed out, and the dresses all had to be redone at great expense. I'm tired of doing everything by myself, and I don't want a cheap, third-rate wedding, but I don't know what to do. I wanted this day to be beautiful and spectacular. But what kind of wedding can poor people have, anyway?

The first thing you can do is to quickly gather your wits about you. It is clear that you are feeling overwhelmed. Many brides-to-be have dreams of a wedding that is beyond their financial means, and the concern is not whether the poor can have a beautiful wedding, but rather why you think you should begin a marriage and life with another person with an expensive wedding neither of you can afford. Rather than rearrange the finances of your fiancé and your family and friends and jeopardize your own financial future by racking up debt, you might want to rearrange your priorities. The wedding is but for a few hours; a marriage is for a lifetime. However, it seems as if you are equating your worth with your wedding, and since you feel you have to settle in some way, that makes you and your relationship with your fiancé seem less than first-rate. This is a self-esteem issue, not one of party planning or organization. You still have five weeks, so get creative, and this time focus on what's really important. If you can, change your mind and have a charming wedding in your home with home-cooked food and the love and support of your closest family and friends. That will be the beautiful wedding you want and deserve.

MY SISTER HAD A LAVISH WEDDING—WHAT ABOUT ME?

Dear Dr. Dale,

Several years ago, when my sister got married, she was given twenty thousand dollars by my parents to put toward her wedding. But when my fiancé and I recently announced our engagement, my father indicated that he and his wife were unwilling or unable to participate in our wedding with any money at all.

I am crushed. My sister had a fairy-tale wedding, but at this rate, even with us shelling out several thousand dollars, we will not be able to do much of what we wanted to.

My fiancé says I just need to let it go and that we will deal with these new circumstances. I know life isn't fair, but is there anything at all I can to do point out the obvious injustice here and how I am feeling like they care less about me? This wedding is no surprise—my fiancé and I have been together for almost two years! Please help me, as I can't help my feelings.

The "injustice," as you call it, is really a disappointment because your expectations of a fantasy wedding have been dashed. You had expected to have the same treatment as your sister but, alas, it is not to be. However, you are making an enormous (and possibly wrong) leap when you say your parents' inability or unwillingness to give you the money means that they care less about you. The fact that less or no funds are available does not mean that you are less important. Your family, along with the rest of the country, may have suffered financial setbacks in recent years and may not have the resources they once did. This is the reality, and sharing your views on this "injustice" with your parents will likely not do any good at all—in fact, it may only serve to cause further tension and disappointment.

Your fiancé's advice is wise—let it go and the two of you will deal with it and handle it together. Yes, it is disappointing, but there is nothing you can do about the fact that sometimes life is not fair and there are always going to be things that happen along the way that surprise us. You and your fiancé need to take this as a challenge to become creative and discover how you are going to put together the wedding that will suit you.

Remember, there are many kinds of weddings, and you now have the chance to design a wedding that, in truth, will not be the one you dreamed of, but may turn out to be much better.

FOURTEEN

ALL YOUR LIFE, whenever you imagined the moment you would take your wedding vows, the image that filled your heart and soul was of you, your groom, and your clergy in front of the altar, together in a celebration of love and spirituality. But in our multicultural twenty-first-century world, the reality is often more complex. And the truth is, that as much as your religion will likely take on great importance during this deeply significant moment in your life, it can also bring up conflicts and challenges. Religion is a highly sensitive issue, and questions of religion in your ceremony and in your lives together are linked to family traditions, familiar rituals, and beliefs that are very important to you and to your fiancé. Unless you share the same religious views, this aspect of your wedding will need to be tackled very thoughtfully and carefully, with the utmost respect for each other's beliefs.

How you plan your wedding ceremony, and what place religious ritual will have in it, really totally depend on how open you are to religious differences and how flexible you are to someone else's view of God, even if it is very different from yours. This is a fundamental question, and hopefully you have already begun addressing these issues if you are planning on spending your lives together.

There are two kinds of marriages where religious differences take on greater importance. One is interfaith ceremonies (Catholic and Jewish, Muslim and Protestant, etc.), and the other is intrafaith (Baptist and Lutheran, Reform Jew and Orthodox Jew, etc.). You may think that intrafaith is easier to deal with—wrong! Our experience is that any differences are always an issue, as people tend to focus on those rather than on the things they share. Additionally, marrying within a religion may or may not mean you are marrying within a similar culture with similar sensibilities and expectations.

Most couples prefer to marry in a house of worship or with a member of the clergy overseeing their union, and for many, deciding who will marry them is the first hurdle. Some people of the cloth will not oversee an interfaith or intrafaith union, so the priest, minister, or rabbi who saw you through all of your life transitions may not officiate at the wedding because you are marrying someone "out of the faith" or who is not "religious enough." (Remember, sometimes, the clergy who will not be able to officiate can attend as a guest and still offer a blessing.)

Sometimes during courtship differences on major issues, such as religion, are swept aside by the romantic rush of feelings. But the differences will reemerge, and may even cause resentments. If you find yourself in a major argument with your fiancé about issues involving your beliefs or the way you worship, or you cannot agree on having some meaningful symbols or rituals at the ceremony (that may be offensive to either your fiancé or his family), the first thing you need to do is, trite but true, take some time and step away from it all. Then come back slowly, calmly, and open to compromise. If you want your fiancé to become a compassionate listener about such an important issue, find a time when you can quietly discuss what is important to you. You may feel that because God or the essence of your faith is involved, the stakes are higher than when you have an argument about other, more mundane issues. This may be true. You may not have even realized how "committed" you were to having a specific ritual included until you were facing its exclusion. But remember this: You cannot expect your partner to understand your personal commitment to God or ritual just because he loves you.

Faith and religious practice or connection is personal—and many people do not know how to articulate it even to their partners. If you are entering into an interfaith union, there are many questions that need to be addressed. For too many couples there is an unspoken agreement to minimize their connection to their religious heritages in order to avoid facing their differences. The problem with this approach is that differences often show up around life-cycle rituals, such as religious holidays, the birth of children, illnesses, or death.

As you are planning your wedding and dealing with the part religion will play in your ceremony, ask yourselves the following more general questions, which should help you in the process. Remember, the goal is not that you and your partner agree on everything, but that each partner feels valued, heard, understood, and appreciated.

- Are there issues in your religious life that you are not willing to compromise on? What are they?

- Which aspects of your religious heritage and upbringing have you kept? In what ways do you want to participate in a religious life that is similar or different from the one in which you were raised?

- How do your parents' views on religion affect you? What expectations might your parents have of you and your fiancé?

- How do you want to celebrate religious holidays? Is attending services important to you? Is gathering with family important to you?

- Do you want to go to your house of worship regularly, just on holidays, or is attending a house of worship not important to you? Is it important to you that you attend with your fiancé?

- How large of a role for religion would be comfortable for you in our home and marriage? For example, would you want to participate in daily prayer, or have religious objects in the house?

- Is it important to you that you learn more about each other's religions?

- Would you be embarrassed to tell people that you had another belief system?

- Are your parents or your friends upset about your religious differences? How do you think their reactions would affect you?

- How would you feel if you chose to donate money to or volunteer at another house of worship or religious organization?

- Would you want your fiancé to convert to your religion? Would you want to convert to his religion?

The best way to treat and resolve religious issues is to deal with them as you would other challenges in your wedding—as if you were tackling problems with your caterer or bridesmaids. Use your best negotiation tactics, listen to everyone's points of view, and then remember that this is your wedding, and you and your fiancé should make decisions based on what you and he want. What if your future mother-in-law insists on you having a Catholic Mass ("it will be disrespectful to the Catholics at the wedding not to have one") even though no one in your family is Catholic? What if the Orthodox branch of your Jewish family will not attend your ceremony unless the men and women are seated separately? What if even you and your fiancé can't agree—you'd love a choir, but he hates the idea? To help you get through this decision-making process, here are some strategies:

- As in other wedding-related issues, the key word is compromise. Choose your battles, and compromise and be flexible about things that are less important to you.

- Educate yourself about religious similarities or differences. Talk about what is important to include and what you can live without. Discuss it with your parents. Families differ regarding what is acceptable and unacceptable, appropriate or inappropriate.

- In some religions there is little room for creativity, but in many there is much opportunity to have the ceremony reflect the religious convictions you hold dear. Understand which aspects of your religion you want to emphasize as part of your ceremony and determine beforehand what your soon-to-be husband's feelings are about this.

- Many couples who join in an interfaith union try hard not to offend and go for the "lowest common denominator." Afterward, they may or may not feel they really did have a wedding that reflected either of their backgrounds or faiths. Not only should you try not to offend, but you should try to incorporate what is important and meaningful to both of you as you begin your life together.

You may choose to have a more religious ceremony out of respect for your relatives who would be offended if you did not. You may choose to "tone down" the religious references for the same reason. You may create your own rituals to reflect the joining of your two religions. Whatever you decide, be sure you are creating the kind of ceremony you both will feel comfortable with. You are two unique individuals, from two different backgrounds, about to bring your lives together. As you plan your wedding, be bold in celebrating the parts of your heritages that have helped to make you who you are.

MASS OR NO MASS AT A WEDDING

Dear Dr. Dale,

My fiancé is Catholic, and I am Methodist. We have decided to have our wedding ceremony in his Catholic church, since I am not practicing my faith. His mother is very upset because both of us have decided against having a mass at our service. According to her, this is not fair to all of the Catholic people who will be at the wedding, since they will have to go to their own churches the next day, and this would be considered inconsiderate of us. There is a mass at the church at four o'clock, and our wedding is at five-thirty, so Catholic guests could attend a service before our wedding. The bishop at the church has told me that this is perfectly acceptable. What do you suggest we do?

You are experiencing one of the major issues that most interfaith couples face when they get married. Even when the couple makes a decision that is appropriate for them, it is inevitable that someone in one of the families is offended. It appears that you are trying to plan a wedding that will suit the spiritual needs of both you and your fiancé, and while your future mother-in-law may think you're being inconsiderate, there is nothing you can do about her perception. You are free to design your ceremony as you wish. Why not insert a slip of paper in the invitation informing those who plan to attend that your wedding is at five-thirty and a mass is scheduled for four? This way, you will have inconvenienced no one. If those guests attending wish to celebrate mass on their own, either before the ceremony or on their own the next day, they are free to do so, and they even have the blessing of a bishop. Remember, you cannot make everyone happy, and it is not your job to take care of others' spiritual needs.

WHO WILL OFFICIATE AT OUR INTERFAITH MARRIAGE?

Dear Dr. Dale,

I am Jewish and my fiancé is Christian. I have been attending the same synagogue since I was born, and I have a close relationship with my rabbi. I am very upset, because he has informed me that he refuses to officiate or coofficiate at an interfaith wedding. I want my faith to be represented, but by someone who represents *my* faith. I have no idea how to make my ceremony complete in this way.

This is no doubt very hurtful, especially since you've probably imagined a wedding with your spiritual adviser present who has officiated for much of your life. As difficult as this may sound, try to respect your rabbi's position, which is obviously based on spiritual philosophies that are important to him. It's certainly not personal. If you can't have your lifelong rabbi present, try to find another who is comfortable coofficiating.

Once you find such a rabbi, have him or her meet with the other clergy so that family traditions and religious preferences and differences can be dealt with. This is not a time to offend, nor is it a time to defer. You don't want to lose a Jewish wedding any more than your fiancé wants to lose a Christian one. You *can* have both, but the key is flexibility among all of you. You may not have the exact ceremony you dreamed of and planned on, but you will certainly have many of the elements you want and deserve.

It may comfort you to know that we hear this problem all the time. Many, many clergy of all faiths are not comfortable officiating at ceremonies that involve more than one clergy person. That is why it is quite difficult to find clergy who are willing to participate in such a joint ceremony. But they do exist, and you will find one. Just remain flexible so the main goals and dreams of your ceremony will happen.

HOW CAN I INCLUDE MY DISAPPROVING PARENTS?

Dear Dr. Dale,

My parents are Orthodox Jewish, and I neither follow nor believe in their faith. I am getting married in my fiancé's church, where his entire family has celebrated their weddings. My parents are choosing not to attend the ceremony, as they don't feel comfortable coming into a church. They are, however, coming to the reception. The larger questions have not come up about the wedding ceremony, as my parents won't be there. But as they will be at the reception, I am concerned about the "father-daughter" dance.

My father and I do not get along, and the thought of enduring a "father-daughter" dance makes me very uncomfortable. My fiancé is very close to his mother, so I could never eliminate the "mother-son" dance. See my problem? My parents have deliberately decided not to be at my wedding to give me away and witness the most special day in my life, so I don't feel right honoring them with a dance at the reception. I just can't figure out how to solve this.

Your parents clearly are having a difficult time with the reality of your marrying outside of their faith, and your decision to marry in the church of your fiancé makes a very bold statement. It might be that if you and your fiancé had chosen to marry in a "neutral" space (a home, a meeting hall, a hotel ballroom), your parents would be able to happily attend and participate in this special day in your life.

Since you have decided to marry in a place that is religiously unacceptable to them, you have no choice but to accept that they will not be in attendance at the ceremony. But your parents *have* agreed to attend your reception (they could have refused to come at all—we have encountered this more painful circumstance many times). This shows effort on their part.

You have been firm about getting married in your fiancé's church; perhaps you could be less firm about this dance. You may not get along with your father, but you could honor your parents, regardless of their not attending the ceremony, with this dance. Of course you are free to either dance or not dance with whomever you choose, but consider the true meaning of such a dance: It is a simple way of making sure that your parents are included in this day.

If you choose not to dance with your father at all, and your husband dances with his mother, it may add to the awkwardness of the situation and emphasize the difficulty your parents are experiencing with your marriage. It will surely stand out that you and your father have not danced. Do you really want to send such a message to your guests, your fiancé's family, and your own family? Here's one option for the problem: Why not begin the dance with your father, then break out of the dance to continue with your husband? Perhaps your father can then dance with your mother, or your fiancé's mother. This could be a way to include them, and to extend your hope that they will be a part of this newly merged family.

IS GOD EVERYWHERE, OR ONLY IN CHURCH?

Dear Dr. Dale,

Ever since I was a little girl I've always wanted to have my wedding reception in a historic mansion. I'm not very religious, although I do believe in God, and I think it's somewhat hypocritical to go to a church just to get married when I don't even go to church on Christmas, Easter, or any other day of the year (unless I'm going to someone's funeral or wedding).

The point is that my fiancé's mother is horrified and cannot understand why we don't want to get married "in the house of and under the eyes of God." My belief is that God is everywhere. What difference does it make where you are? I really don't want a church wedding, but now I think my fiancé might be caving into his mother's wishes, as he has recently mentioned searching for the church just in case we can't find a "suitable" place for a ceremony. As a compromise my parents even offered to have my fiancé's old minister from his hometown officiate at the ceremony—paying for his travel and hotel costs just to pacify his mother. In this way, we could make sure that the ceremony would have both religious and personal touches. My fiancé really appreciates this, but his mother has not reacted at all. I'm also worried about complicating things for our guests by having them have to go to two different places for our wedding—the church for the ceremony and the mansion for the reception. It adds frustration, expense, and just a general feeling of hassle, and that's just not how I envision our wedding. Help!

You have strong opinions about God and religion and how people can and should worship, and you are entitled to those opinions, based on your beliefs. You question, however, your fiancé's and his family's equally strong opinions and beliefs as to whether they are applicable and suitable for your wedding. Whether or not the wedding ceremony is in the church makes a tremendous difference to his family. Perhaps, as many people feel, a ceremony in a civic hall, even if it is beautiful, is not the same as a "house of God."

It is unlikely that arguing will change their minds. The fact that you believe God is everywhere is not the issue. His family, for their own reasons and comfort level, feel that a sacrament such as marriage should be held in a church. They are not alone, by the way, in their belief.

So what should you do? Try to work with your parents' offer to have your fiancé's family minister officiate at a ceremony in a civil setting. Perhaps your future in-laws may feel a bit more comfortable with this prospect, and that the space where he stands to of-

ficiate will be "sacred" space. You and your fiancé need to decide
what you are going to give up so the families will be at ease. If you
do not have a church wedding and his family boycotts and decides
not to attend, will it be worth it?

Only you and your fiancé can decide whether it is worth it to
you to have a wedding in a place where his family will be so uncomfortable. One could, of course, argue that you will be more uncomfortable in the church, so why should you get married in a
place where you are uncomfortable? It is not a simple question,
and only you and your fiancé can find the answer. Whatever you
do, you need to enlist your fiancé. First, however, find out what he
wants. If he is willing to stand up to his family and push for getting married in a nonchurch space, then you need to be sure he
will not resent you. If you are totally alone and it becomes a cause
célèbre between the two of you, you may have to give in and have
your ceremony in the church.

Whatever you do, remember that you are marrying someone
whose upbringing and past are part of him and have helped to
make him who he is today.

MY FIANCÉ WON'T HONOR MY RELIGION

Dear Dr. Dale,

My fiancé and I are having a problem with planning our
wedding ceremony. We are from two different religions and
I have agreed to be married in his church and to raise our
kids in his religion. The only thing that I ask is that we use
my mother's choir, as it was a gift to us from my mother. But
my fiancé won't have it. I keep getting the refrain "I am the
groom, and because you're the bride you have been in charge
of everything, and since your family is paying I have had

nothing to say about our day." I feel that if he can't see that this is something important to me and make a small sacrifice for me, then we are in big trouble.

It is certainly difficult that your fiancé will not accept this "gift" from your mother as a way to acknowledge and include your religious background and form of worship. As far as it being "your" day or "his" day, a wedding is about the joining of two people and two lives. Each of you comes from your own traditions and histories. You are about to pledge a life of sharing and choosing what will work for each of you and both of you. Hopefully, it also means taking the best of what each of you has to offer, and the best is what works best for you *as a couple*. You may wish to examine this with your fiancé to understand what specifically is so objectionable and why he seems to feel threatened by having your mother's choir at the service.

Compromise is everything. It does seem that you have been doing most of the compromising. Sometimes it is a religious question that brings out other feelings of insecurity and stress. Try to find out why he feels so adamantly about this, and then discuss the importance of compromising on both your parts. In a way, you are right—you may be in trouble if such a request, important to you and not crucial to the wedding, cannot be understood by your fiancé. So—talk, talk, talk. Be sure he is not reacting to your mother's gift because he sees it as a way to have your religion represented at the ceremony. If this is the reason, talk with him and the member of your clergy, and try to understand what he is afraid of. You have agreed to marry in his church and to raise your children in accordance with his faith. It is possible he sees this "gift" as an intrusion of another religion. His objection may be a red flag to caution you that he is rejecting not just the idea of having your mother's choir in attendance but also part of you—your religion. If this is the case, you will have to discuss with him your stand regarding your religion, your family involvement, and what you need to feel so that you and your family are full participants in this wedding ceremony.

CHOOSING BETWEEN A FATHER'S WISHES AND OUR OWN

Dear Dr. Dale,

My fiancé's father is a pastor, and we had planned all along for him to marry us. However, both of us want to have wine and dancing at our reception, and my fiancé's father disapproves of both. We haven't asked him yet, but if we make him a part of our ceremony, don't we have to agree with his wishes for our reception? We don't want to make a sticky situation out of this. My family would think we were crazy if we didn't dance at our reception, and we are beginning to think it would be better to find a different minister to marry us. That would mean hurting my future father-in-law. So now we feel we are caught in a vicious circle. What should we do?

Honoring your fiancé's father by having him marry you is certainly a lovely gesture. However, you and your fiancé need to feel that your wedding will reflect the kinds of beliefs and feeling you both want. You actually don't have a problem yet, because you are assuming that because your future father-in-law does not approve of wine and dancing that he will not officiate. Why not talk with him and let him decide for himself? You can let him know that you would appreciate his blessing and officiating at the ceremony, and that, in addition, you hope he will attend and participate in the reception of your design. Inform him that there will be music and dancing and wine at the reception, a choice you and your fiancé have made. The decision of whether or not to attend will then be his. Alternatively, you can offer to have another minister, but make it clear that you still hope that, in this case, your father-in-law will still attend the ceremony and reception.

You may also wish to ask yourselves: Which is the more important consideration for your wedding—having your future father-in-law preside over the ceremony, or having the kind of reception you want? You may indeed be forced to choose, but if you and your fiancé can agree on this issue, it will guide you in making the decision that's best for you.

HOW CAN WE COMPROMISE
ON LOCATION?

Dear Dr. Dale,

I no longer belong to any church and am not particularly interested in joining a new one. My fiancé doesn't attend church either, but if we did, he would be Baptist and I would be Catholic. My mother and her family want our wedding to be Catholic, or at least to have a Catholic priest performing the ceremony. All our families have agreed that they are OK with a two-officiate wedding.

The problem is the Catholic priest. He won't do the wedding outside; he has informed us that the ceremony must be held inside the church. But we have already paid for our dream location! We love it, and I do not want to lose it over a religion I'm not really interested in. Help!

This is tricky, because the Catholic Church does have a policy against weddings being performed outside of the church, and that is probably not negotiable. If you and your fiancé are intent on getting married in this particular place, and it seems that you are, that appears to be a stronger desire than getting married by a priest. That means that you believe that the place where you are married has more importance than who will marry you. If this is the case, then that is fine. Bear in mind, however, that either choice makes a statement about the life you are about to embark on with your fiancé, and speaks to the values and beliefs you will perpetuate in your new household.

You and your fiancé need to determine how you can best accomplish the "feel" you want both for the day of the wedding as well as the rest of your marriage. For example, at a Catholic wedding, the couple promises to raise their children Catholic. Have you and your fiancé discussed this? Also at a Catholic wedding, communion is served, but only to regularly practicing Catholics, and you would need to qualify to receive communion. Therefore, your fiancé and none of his family would be allowed to take communion. This may be off-putting to some of your guests, who may come from a community where any who believe in Christ are invited to participate, regardless of denomination or regular church attendance.

Does all of this seem worth the potential tension if you do not feel strongly about being Catholic? It is not a decision to be undertaken lightly to appease members of your extended family—rather, it should mean something to both of you.

TWO RELIGIONS AND STUBBORN PARENTS

Dear Dr. Dale,

My fiancé and I are having problems with both of our families. His family has disowned him because I am not Jewish, and my family isn't thrilled about our union either. They really do not want me to marry someone outside of our faith, which is Catholic. My mother has not been supportive, and she constantly questions me about why I need to get married at all. My sister, on the other hand, has been told that all of her wedding expenses will be paid in full, even though she is not even engaged and has no plans for marriage, simply because she has promised to marry a Catholic.

The tension among all of us has gotten so bad that my fiancé and I have considered eloping to avoid all of this craziness. I love my parents, and I want them at my wedding, but not if they continue to act in the way they are right now. Help!

First, understand that you are not alone in this painful dilemma. Many couples who face interfaith marriages find that this commitment comes with unbelievably complicated and hurtful challenges. People who have strong faiths are most often reluctant to let go of their beliefs, whether for themselves or their children, and this results in what can seem like stubborn, inflexible behavior that damages everyone.

So we expect, and understand, that it is difficult for you and your fiancé to try to convince your families to understand and support your upcoming wedding and marriage. This also makes it difficult for the two of you to face marriage and all of the changes it brings without the family support you desire and need. But while this will be difficult, it is not impossible. Sometimes, parental disapproval can help to unite a couple as they join together against what they feel are adversaries. As strange as it seems, at a time when a young couple usually needs and relies on their parents, the absence of a supportive family forces the couple to discuss many issues they would not have discussed because they would have been taking them for granted. These could include where and how to celebrate holidays; discovering ways to honor each of your spiritual lives in ways that are meaningful to both of you; discovering ways to communicate openly as you keep your own relationship strong despite the disapproval from your parents; and finding meaningful ways to reassure one another, validate your love and commitment for one another, and remind yourselves what it is about each other that you cherish.

Consider very carefully the decision to elope, because although it appears to be an attractive alternative that choice may ultimately alienate you even further from your families. Is this a risk you are willing to take? If it is, then you are perfectly within your rights to marry and begin your new life however you choose. Before making that final decision, however, arrange to sit with your parents and explain to them that you want them to share this special day with you and that you hope, in time, they will come to know and appreciate your fiancé. Tell them why you feel he is such a good partner for you, and why you think marriage is the right choice for the two of you. They should be told that you are seriously going to take such a step as elopement if they do not fully support the love you have for each other, and get involved in a positive way as you plan your wedding.

Regarding your fiancé's family, if they have disowned your fiancé, it is unlikely they will move from their position. But what does that mean? Are they not going to see him or communicate with him? It is likely that unless he decides not to marry you, he will not be able to have access to his family. Although he can attempt to speak to a rabbi (perhaps their rabbi), it is unlikely they will alter their attitude and decision. If they are observant it is unlikely they will be open to an interfaith ceremony, but it may be worth an inquiry. If your fiancé is willing to reach out to his family, he can write them a letter acknowledging their disappointment and asking for an opportunity to talk with them about his life choice. Sometimes this can open the door to a dialogue. Sometimes not. It may be that you and your fiancé will have a relationship with his parents in the future, but you both need to come to terms with how much reaching out you are willing to do before you give up.

MY FIANCÉ IS UNCOMFORTABLE WITH MY RELIGIOUS TRADITIONS

Dear Dr. Dale,

My mother is insistent that my fiancé and I stand with our parents beneath a gazebo during our wedding ceremony, as this is the manner in which traditional Jewish marriages occur. My fiancé is not Jewish, and he feels very uncomfortable about having our parents up there. I have no opinion on this matter, but I would like very much to meet my mother's wishes, since she hardly asks me for anything. How do I make this decision without choosing between my fiancé's wishes and my mother's?

Becoming an interfaith couple requires a great deal of understanding and a willingness to appreciate and accept certain faith traditions—some of which are prescribed for the wedding ritual itself. If you explain your desire to have your mother with you during the ceremony as part of a tradition that *you* would like to continue, your fiancé might have an easier time accepting it. (It is actually not an unusual thing to do—to have parents up at the "altar" with the bride and groom, so it is puzzling as to why your fiancé would object to this.) Try not to make the choice into a "my mother or my fiancé" situation because, in fact, you need to decide what works for you and your fiancé—this wedding is about the two of you, after all. But to have your mother up there with you at this important moment seems like a simple enough request, and given that it is a part of your heritage and who you are, should be important to your fiancé as well.

Acknowledgments

We thank our literary agent, Janis Donnaud, a wonderful, always available supportive partner, whose helpful ideas and insights "rock," and who was and continues to be an active part of this project.

We thank Ann Campbell, our creative and totally on-target editor at Broadway Books, along with her assistant, Ursula Cary. Both kindly assisted us, made this process of publishing easier, and worked very hard to help us get it done.

We'd like to acknowledge the many people who shared their wedding-related stories and questions—our beloved friends and the hundreds of people whom we met in person and online through WeddingChannel.com. Rosanna McCullough of WeddingChannel.com offered her support and confidence from the very beginning. And a big thank you to Jim Grissom, Kate Perri, Rachel Griffiths, and Maia Harrari, whose friendship, humor, assistance, and wonderful editing skills saved our sanity on a regular basis.

Dale dedicates this book to her husband, Rob Rosen, the love of her life, and their wonderful sons, Jono and Josh, and their wives, Tracy and Yael. How convenient that both of her sons got married during the writing of this book! And to Daryl, her sister, who introduced her to Rob. And a special thank you from the bottom of her heart to her mother, Sylvia, who gave up her dream of a large, spectacular wedding for Dale—and instead gave her an unforgettable intimate ceremony, under difficult circumstances, in her own home.

Annie thanks her mother, who totally planned Annie's spectacular wedding (that's some trick for the mother of a control freak) and managed to deal with in-laws and wayward florists and relatives in questionable dress without batting an eye; and her husband, Gary, who smiled through wedding dramas and tears and has been smiling through the thirty-year marriage ever since.